Marx and History

Marx and History

From Primitive Society
to the Communist Future

By D. Ross Gandy

University of Texas Press, Austin & London

To My Father
D. Truett Gandy, M.D.

Library of Congress Cataloging in Publication Data

Gandy, Daniel Ross, 1935–
  Marx and history.
  Bibliography: p.
  1. Marx, Karl, 1818–1883. 2. Engels, Friedrich,
1820–1895. 3. Communism—History. I. Title.
HX39.5.G34   335.4'092'4   78-23945
ISBN 0-292-74302-5

Contents

Prefatory Note

Everyone who wants to understand the twentieth century must examine the ideas of Karl Marx. Those ideas have gained worldwide influence: they penetrate intellectual life in Paris, Mexico City, Rome, and Tokyo; they inspire revolutionary struggles in Asia, Africa, and Latin America; they shape official political ideology on one-third of the earth. This book, based on a study of the forty-volume *Marx-Engels Werke*, explains the Marxist theory of history.

Karl Marx and Friedrich Engels carried on one of the great intellectual collaborations in the history of scientific research. On 22 November 1860 in a letter to Bertalan Szemere, Marx says that Engels must be considered his "*alter ego*." Paul Lafargue, who knew both men, writes in his "Reminiscences" about Marx: "I have seen him read whole volumes over and over to find the fact he needed to change Engels' opinion on some secondary point that I do not remember concerning the political and religious wars of the Albigenses." This shows how close the collaboration was. "Engels once told me," writes Eduard Bernstein in *My Years of Exile*, "that the only questions over which he and Marx had ever seriously quarreled were mathematical questions."

Marx and Engels were not Siamese twins; there were occasional differences between them. Some scholars claim that there was a divergence between the two men on philosophical matters. But in historical and social theory the differences between them were minor, and the study of such discrepancies belongs in learned journals. Although in this book we often note the specific contributions made by either Marx or Engels to historical sociology, it is convenient to treat them as joint creators of a theory of history and society. In the text all numbered references are to their works.

Acknowledgments

Under A. James Gregor I wrote a Ph.D. dissertation on Marx at the University of Texas in 1967. Gregor convinced me that serious study of Marx must be based on research in the *Marx-Engels Werke*, an idea that really made this book. James Cockcroft, a sociologist in Livingston College at Rutgers, for years urged me to write this work and supplied helpful criticism. Bill Lucas and Michael Pincus, two friends of mine from the old days on the New Left, did a lot of hard work on the drafts. Professor Donald Hodges of Florida State University, who combines the study of history, sociology, economics, and philosophy in the best Marxist tradition, saved me from several mistakes in interpretation. And Instituto Fenix in Cuernavaca, where I teach history, generously supported my research.

Marx and History

I. The New Marxism

From the Renaissance to the present, science has followed the only path rising toward knowledge. The path wound through mountains of data, along conceptual precipices, and over barriers of fact. Now and then it gained a summit, and the valleys spread out below. These peaks were theoretical breakthroughs for science; they opened new horizons of knowledge. Which peaks were the most important? Scientists argue about this question, but Marxists claim that four theoretical achievements rise above others:

> The earth goes around the sun. – Copernicus
> All objects attract one another. – Newton
> Man belongs to the animal kingdom. – Darwin
> Economic change is the motor of history. – Marx

These are watersheds of human thought, say Marxists, for before each discovery humanity's thinking moved in one direction; afterwards it flowed in another.

No one doubts that in astronomy, physics, and biology these names mark turning points: Copernicus, Newton, Darwin. In social science scholars divide over Marx. Social science differs from physics, and Marx knew one reason why: the study of society arouses those "passions of the human breast, the Furies of private interest."[1] But historical research has often risen above those passions, perhaps because historians study the remote past. Historians at least agree that Marx's work caused fundamental changes in the study of history. Even his critics have borrowed concepts from him.

In 1859 Marx summed up his ideas on history in a famous preface to his book *A Contribution to the Critique of Political Economy*. His summary ends with the observation that "in broad outlines Asiatic, ancient, feudal, and modern bourgeois modes of production can be designated as progressive epochs in the economic formation of society."[2] For a century Marx's interpreters have speculated about the meaning of this concise remark in his preface.

Official Marxism

One reading of the preface has gained worldwide infuence. Official Marxism, the ideology of Russia and China, interprets the preface as a philosophy of universal history. In this interpretation, history develops in a straight line from lower to higher social forms. Productive forces, the key factor in social change, drive historical evolution up through a series of class systems: slavery, feudalism, capitalism. The productive forces—tools, techniques, machines—expand steadily, pushing humanity up the staircase of economic development.

In the Soviet textbook *Fundamentals of Marxism-Leninism* Otto Kuusinen puts it as follows: "All peoples travel what is basically the same path. . . . The development of society proceeds through the consecutive replacement, according to definite laws, of one socioeconomic formation by another. . . . Mankind as a whole has passed through four formations—primitive communal, slave, feudal, and capitalist—and is now living in the epoch of transition to the next formation, the first phase of which is called socialism" (pp. 153–54). Most societies pass through these five modes of production. Here and there a stage is skipped, but not often, for each mode contains the elements of the next.

In climbing this single ladder of development, humanity moves through the stages at about the same time. The slave mode of production, for example, covered the whole planet. Everyone knows that slavery filled the Roman Empire, but in *A Short History of Precapitalist Society* the Soviet historian Y. Zubritsky says that "slave-owning despotic states . . . were the most typical state formations of the slave-owning period of history, and were widespread in Asia, Africa, and America" (p. 45). He finds the slave system in Egypt, Mesopotamia, Sumeria, Babylon, India, China, Assyria, Arabia, Persia, Greece, Rome, and in various parts of Africa and Central and South America—slavery was universal. Everywhere one human being wore out another, as a peasant sweats a donkey.

In 1928 the Chinese Communists adopted this view of history at their Sixth Party Congress. The Party decided that China had passed through three of the five modes of production: primitive communism, slavery, and feudalism. In the twentieth century it entered a transition period between feudalism and capitalism. In chapter 1 of *The Chinese Revolution and the Chinese Communist Party*, Mao Tse-Tung describes China's historical development as follows: "Up to now approximately 4,000 years have passed since the collapse of the primitive communes and the transition to class society, first slave society and then feudalism. . . . Chinese feudal society lasted for about 3,000 years. . . . As China's feudal society developed its commodity economy and so carried within itself the embryo of capitalism, China would of herself have developed slowly into a capitalist society, even if there had been no influence of foreign capitalism." The revolution enabled China to jump through the capitalist stage and move toward communism.

Official Marxism in Russia and China lays down an iron schema for world history. The leap from each stage to the next is a social revolution: one civilization perishes and another is born. Each birth is violent, marked by blood and death—force is the midwife of every old society pregnant with a new one.

A powerful nation has spread official Marxism across the planet. Almost every country has bookshops carrying the works of Kuusinen, Afanasyev, and Chesnokov in cheap editions. These books teach a historical theory both simple and complete that satisfies the craving of the mind for generality, austerity, and clarity. For over forty years communist parties have spread this theory among the workers and students of the world.

The theory has influenced economists, sociologists, historians, and philosophers. In our century it is the most widely accepted philosophy of history; it even shows up in the arts. Diego Rivera, the best painter of our hemisphere, covered the government buildings of his country with a Mexican version of the theory. Rivera begins with scenes from an idyllic Aztec age of primitive communism; he paints on to the enslavement of the Indians by the *conquistadores*, traverses the age of feudalism under Spanish colonial rule, ushers in capitalism through the Mexican Revolution, and sketches the future communist society.

Official Marxism has produced a large literature on its theory of history. For two generations Soviet scholars have documented it, turning out libraries of historical research. This is philosophical history in the grand style: the river of history flows away toward a goal, bearing hundreds of societies, cultures, and civilizations, each classified and explained. Marx, so we are told, first mapped the river. He charted the currents and pools and rapids of world history. In the theoretical schema of the *Communist Manifesto* he provided a universal formula for human progress: tribalism—slavery—feudalism—capitalism—communism.

Like Hegel he was a spectator of all time and existence.

The New Marxism

During the 1960s a new Marxism rose against the official theory of history. In the West some Marxists challenged the standard interpretation of the preface of 1859. They argued that Marx meant something else, and their view has gained wide influence. Even a few Soviet scholars have adopted it. This book, among other things, develops and documents the new interpretation of Karl Marx.

Marx and Engels did not see history as straight-line progress through world class systems; their conception of history was multilinear. Some lines of development led into agelong stagnation. Others progressed rapidly, then ran into a dead end. Some stalled and collapsed, or went into reverse, returning to an earlier stage. One line spiraled up through higher and higher levels into capitalism, but this took place in a corner of the globe. This corner soon drew the world into capitalism.

Humanity has not passed through a series of universal social forms. A worldwide system could hardly emerge, for the disruptive elements of history—wars, invasions, conquests, migrations, crusades—have continually thrown whole peoples off their developmental track. "Mere chances such as invasions of barbaric peoples, even ordinary wars," write Marx and Engels, "are sufficient to cause a country with advanced productive forces and needs to have to start right over again from the beginning."[3]

Marx and Engels see conquest as the main disruptive force in economic evolution. A conquest may cause a new mode of production to arise on the conquered territory. "A conquering people," says Marx, "divides the land among the conquerors establishing thereby a division and form of landed property and determining the character of production; or it turns the conquered people into slaves and thus makes slave labor the basis of production."[4] Sometimes the conquerors finish off an old society and leave a new page for history to write upon. When the Germans conquered the Roman Empire, for example, they swept away the old civilization, and feudalism grew up in its place.[5]

Sometimes the conquerors bring their mode of production with them.[6] Consider the Normans: they captured England and Naples, then forced upon these areas the most perfect form of feudal organization.[7] The British conquest of India provides another example, for the English broke up the old methods of production and brought new ones.[8]

Sometimes the conquerors allow productive forces to go to ruin because they don't know how to use them. The Christians did that with the irrigation works of the great Moorish civilization in Spain.[9] Or conquest may disrupt a nation's economy, so that it slowly runs down and stops. This happened in Phoenicia after Alexander's conquest, and its productive forces disappeared from history.[10] Or a barbarian conqueror carries out brutal destruction, leaving only ruin behind.[11]

Throughout history barbarians have circled around civilizations, ready to attack any weakness. Nomadism is a powerful historical force. For a thousand

years a series of horse-riding nomads flowed back and forth over the Eur-
asian steppe, striking down into China, India, Persia, Mesopotamia, and
Europe. The Scythians, the Huns, and the Mongols invaded the civilizations
of the world.

Another region of nomadism was the Arabian peninsula. Bedouins often
poured into the surrounding civilizations to plunder.[12] From Palmyra to the Ye-
men, from Egypt to Persia, the area is strewn with the wreckage of peoples
who met this fate. Their irrigation works can be smashed, points out Marx,
and this "explains how a single war of devastation has been able to depopu-
late a country for centuries and to strip it of all its civilization."[13]

Europe continually fought off barbarians. They came from Asia through the
broad interval between the Ural mountains and the Caspian, riding across the
open spaces of southern Russia, and struck home in the heart of the European
peninsula. These invasions met resistance, and the struggles shaped the his-
troy of the great peoples all around–the Russians, the Germans, the French,
the Italians, and the Byzantine Greeks. Engels thinks that invasions might
compress the provinces of a feudal land into a nation-state, and mentions
Russia's struggle against the Mongols as one example.[14]

Invasions and migrations have played such an important role in history that
before Marx historians saw war as the key to the historical process. "Up till
now," say Marx and Engels in their first important work, "violence, war, pil-
lage, murder, and robbery have been accepted as the driving force of history."[15] Historians wrote about kings, battles, treaties–and no more.

Marx and Engels criticize this political and military history as extremist.
While admitting the importance of wars and migrations, they call them elements
of discontinuity in history, not the essence of history itself. The economic
evolution of the nations, not their wars, is the core of the historical process.
War might disrupt this evolution and even wipe it out, but development usually
begins anew. And many times a conquest is no more than an interruption.

Marx and Engels know that the conqueror may maintain the mode of production of the land captured.[16] Where the conquest is permanent, the barbarians often adjust themselves to the productive forces of the civilization they
take over; they are assimilated by the vanquished and adopt their language.[17]

A conquering nation can pass on to new adventures, leaving everything
as it was and an agent to collect tribute.[18] Sometimes a conqueror moves the
captured mode of production to a new land. Athens succumbed to Macedonia,
and Philip fell before the Roman legions: each conquest bailed out the slave
system, which had reached a dead end. Slavery could continue, with the transfer of its economic base to a different nation and a higher level. Again and
again the system evolved into a cul-de-sac and conquest revived it.[19]

To sum up, war and conquest have had varying effects on economic development, but everywhere made it an uneven process: humanity as a whole did not develop through similar stages at about the same time.

Marx and Engels describe several lines of social evolution out of primitive communism. They believe that primitive communism was nearly universal at the dawn of history: people lived in village communities based on the common ownership of land.[20] In Asia these communities evolved into a system of Oriental Despotism. The self-sufficient communities slept through the ages under the sway of the despot, who taxed and ruled and defended them. This society remained at a low level of economic evolution, the Asiatic mode of production.[21]

Around the Mediterranean another line of evolution from primitive communism produced a higher social system: the ancient mode of production. The ancient mode arose out of primitive communism with the fusion of several tribes into a town by agreement or by force.[22] The city-state is the economic unit of the ancient mode, and the history of Rome reveals the basic pattern of development. The city-state went through a thousand-year evolution. Through the centuries its mode of production developed a class system with patricians, plebeians, and slaves.[23] Slavery was the basis of the system. Slave production finally evolved into a dead end: there was no way out or round or through.[24] Barbarians were knocking at the gates, and the ancient mode of production collapsed under the German invasions.

Before the invasions German tribes owned land in common.[25] But the conquest caused their primitive communism to explode in a new line of economic evolution.[26] From the German invasions there arose in Western Europe the feudal mode of production.[27] The feudal mode contained the germs of a higher system: capitalism. This system matured in the womb of the feudal mode, then burst forth as the bourgeois mode of production, which spread out of Western Europe across the earth. "The need of a constantly expanding market for its products chases the bourgeoisie over the whole surface of the globe. It must nestle everywhere, settle everywhere, establish connections everywhere."[28] It draws the world into the capitalist system. Capitalism evolves toward the final revolution.

For Marx primitive communism is the source from which history flows: some modes of production evolved a long way from communism, some not so far, some scarcely at all. In primitive communism each person is a member of the tribe and so fused with the herd as to be hardly aware of being an individual. How can one person's skills and needs be separated from those of companions? "Man is only individualized through the process of history," writes Marx. "He originally appears as a generic being, a tribal being, a herd animal. . . . Exchange itself is a major agent of this individualization."[29] People begin to produce goods for exchange. Trade arouses new needs, differing pleasures, fresh productive powers. Exchange means production for a market; it transforms people and forces them into specialized labor.[30]

The Asiatic mode of production did not develop far from primitive communism. The ancient mode developed further and was therefore more progressive. The feudal mode was more progressive still, for it contained the seeds of higher systems: feudalism gives rise to the bourgeois mode, and the bourgeois mode to the communist. In his preface of 1859 Marx lists in order modes of production further and further removed from primitive communism: Asiatic, ancient, feudal, and bourgeois.[31] The Asiatic mode does not give rise to the ancient mode, nor the ancient mode to the feudal. These modes are different lines of historical evolution out of primitive communism. History is multilinear.

The official view that Marx held a unilinear theory, however, has deep roots in Russia; even before his death, there were Russians crediting him with such a theory. The sociologist Nikolai K. Mikhailovsky claimed that Marx was arguing this: feudal Russia must generate capitalism, pass through that whole economic stage, and finally reach socialism. Marx complains of his Russian interpreter, "He feels he absolutely must metamorphose my historical sketch of the genesis of capitalism in Western Europe into an historico-philosophic theory of the general path every people is fated to tread, whatever the historical circumstances in which it finds itself."[32] England was a feudal nation and had evolved into a capitalist one; Russia was a feudal nation, and a flicker of capitalism had appeared. Would capitalism evolve in Russia? Marx says he is not sure.[33]

Russia had a different history from that of England. Russia had missed the Renaissance. It had missed that bourgeois attack upon Western feudalism, the Reformation.[34] Feudalism slowly fell apart in Western Europe, but in Russia it stiffened,[35] and the peasant communes formed its strange foundation.[36]

Therefore no one should generalize from Western development to Russia. To jump from English to Russian feudalism, argues Marx, is risky. It means building a theory on doubtful historical analogies.

Today many Marxists build theories on just such analogies. They leap from English feudalism to Indian, Nigerian, or Mexican "feudalism." Since England evolved into capitalism, so must these countries: England shows them the image of their own future.

In India most communist theoreticians, whether reformist or revolutionary, argue that their country is feudal, with capitalism growing. Many believe that the capitalist stage must not be skipped. In his book *New Theories of Revolution*, Jack Woddis, a leading communist authority on Africa, sees feudal sectors in northern and western Nigeria and warns against skipping stages in the struggle toward communism (pp. 69, 100). In chapter 10 of *La democracia en*

México, the prestigious Marxist sociologist Pablo González-Casanova argues that Mexico is semifeudal and that Marxists should be allies of the national bourgeoisie as it develops the country toward mature capitalism.

How did this theory taught by official Marxism come into being? Though Lenin attacked the unilinear interpretation of history in *What the "Friends of the People" Are* (1894), near the end of his life he endorsed it in his article on *The State* (1919). Soviet historians, led by Vassili Strouve, gathered volumes of evidence to support it; and in 1938 Stalin stamped his approval on the view worked out by these historians. In chapter 4 of his *History of the Communist Party of the Soviet Union*, Stalin presents their five modes of production as a universal sequence for humanity. Since world communism recognized him as its leading theoretician, this became the view of official Marxism; to this day most scholars in Russia and all historians in China defend it. Official Marxist textbooks, widely distributed, teach it; and communist parties often base strategy on it. In the United States many Marxist organizations embracing Maoist ideology spread this interpretation of Marx.

Marx's views on history are scattered throughout his writings. The present work draws them together in a single presentation. It also provides ammunition against the official distortions.

History and Marx

In the 1840s the young Marx searched for a meaning in past events. History was just becoming an academic subject; digging up the past through professional scholarship had hardly begun. Marx had a handful of the facts we have today.

In the 1840s economic history was an unexplored field of study. Marx's and Engels' knowledge of this field was incomplete, as they later realized.[37] Some progress in the development of this field was made in the second half of the nineteenth century, but at the end of the century Engels complains that "economic history is still in its swaddling clothes."[38] He urges Marx's German disciples to study "economics, the history of economics, the history of trade, of industry, of agriculture, of the formations of society."[39] Up to now, he says, little has been done. But since Marx has shown the importance of the economic basis of society, "all history must be studied afresh."[40]

In the twentieth century history has indeed been studied afresh. Partly because of Marx's work, vast research in economic history has taken place. Armies of archaeologists and historians have explored the social and economic base of the ancient world. Modern Europe has commanded even more attention. A large literature on the rise of capitalism has appeared: economists, sociologists, and historians have studied its development out of feudal society into the industrial world of today.

Since Marx's time, the collection of ancient inscriptions, the discovery of the papyri, and the analysis of old coins have transformed the study of history. The new sciences of anthropology and archaeology have thrown a flood of light on the past: scientists have studied primitive societies and dug up civilizations. They have developed new methods of dating events in remote epochs. They have opened the area of Asian history.

In his preface of 1859 Marx lists the economic systems of history, a list made up before most history was discovered. Some thinkers of the new Marxism discard this list and take another approach. Others consider the list useful and stick to Marx's periodization of history. As we examine Marx's modes of production, every student should ask how the concepts might apply today. Even a Marxist need not hold to the list of economic epochs worked out a century ago. Since Marx wrote, libraries of historical data have appeared, and Marxists are applying their concepts anew.

II. Precapitalist Modes of Production

Primitive Communism

Prehistory

Several million years in the distant past, human beings emerged from the animal kingdom. For ages they wandered over the world before they began to record their doings.

Humanity is like an old man who finally learned to write–and opened a diary in the last months of his life. A few months are of little importance in a human life. Fifty centuries are the same bit of humanity's total past, the fraction set down in writing. Before written history lie those countless epochs when primitive men and women roamed the earth, made tools of stone, and painted the walls of caves. Marx was preparing a book on prehistory when he died. His notes for the book passed on to Engels, who wrote it himself: *The Origin of the Family, Private Property, and the State*. Engels' theory of prehistory reaches back to the birth of the human from the ape.

Engels tells the story of human origins as follows. Perhaps a million years ago, a highly developed race of anthropoid apes lived somewhere in the tropical zone. They were covered with hair, had beards and pointed ears, and lived in bands in the trees. Fruits, nuts, and roots were their food. These animals began to walk upon the ground, their gait became erect, their hands developed the skill for making simple tools. Hundreds of thousands of years passed before the first flint was fashioned into a knife. As humans in the making began to labor, they found that they had something to say to each other. Language appeared. Labor and speech changed the brain of the ape into that of the human.'

Engels' hypothesis about the emergence of humanity from the apes has received confirmation from anthropologists studying ancient remains in Africa. In *Scientific American* (September 1960) Sherwood Washburn shows in his article "Tools and Human Evolution" that some modern anthropologists agree with Engels' basic idea, although today prehistorians date the origin of human beings much earlier than Engels did.

The social form of these earliest people, says Engels, was probably a primal horde. In the horde there was no private property; everyone shared the tools and food in simple communism. There was spontaneous sexual promiscuity: every woman belonged to every man, and every man to every woman. Jealousy, an animal emotion, had disappeared as humanity freed itself from the ape. There could be sexual relations between brothers and sisters, and even between parents and children. Humans knew no family whatsoever.[2]

For ages, says Engels, humanity lived in this Lower Stage of Savagery. Finally humans learned to make fire, a development of their productive forces. They advanced into the Middle Stage of Savagery. In this stage they began to fish, to hunt with the spear, and to make better tools of unpolished stone.[3]

The primal horde evolved into the first form of the family: group marriage. With group marriage the incest taboo appeared; brothers and sisters no longer had sexual relations with one another. The horde divided into kinship groups. Each group contained mothers, brothers, sisters, cousins, aunts, uncles, nephews, nieces. Inside the group sexual relations were taboo. But any woman in one group could have sexual relations with any man in another group–a woman had many husbands. When she had a child, no one knew who the father was, and the child stayed in her group. The group was a circle of blood relatives in the female line. Social and religious customs grew up in each group and separated it from other groups in the tribe. For the group or clan Engels uses the Latin word *gens* (plural, *gentes*). A tribe was made up of matrilineal clans or gentes.[4]

Ages passed, continues Engels, and humanity invented the bow and arrow. This advance in the productive forces brought humans into the Upper Stage of Savagery. The bow made hunting an everyday affair, and wild game became regular food. The bow and arrow was the decisive weapon: a tribe that had it could destroy one that did not. Primitive peoples next invented finger weaving, carved wood into vessels, and fashioned tools of polished stone. They settled in villages. Their main social form was still the tribe made up of matrilineal clans or gentes.[5]

The discovery of pottery making pulled them up into the Lower Stage of Barbarism. In this stage, group marriage evolved into the pairing family. The old kinship groups or gentes continued; everyone had to marry outside the gens. But now a woman only married one man. She knew who the father of her child was, yet the child stayed in her gens. In this pairing family either person could end the marriage at will: there was equality between men and women.[6]

With the taming of animals, humanity arrived at the Middle Stage of Barbarism. Before this, all tribes had been desperately poor: there was little wealth, and food had to be won day by day. Primitive tribespeople worked together to beat off starvation; they were necessarily communists. But now they had herds of cattle, sheep, and goats–and the herds grew. At first they were common property of the gens, but as individuals built up herds, private property struck root in primitive communism. Next came the invention of agriculture, and in the beginning the gens owned and tilled the land in common. House and village communities formed. Slowly individual land tillage appeared, each family working its plot. The community still owned the land and occasionally redistributed it, but when this stopped, private property triumphed.[7]

Private property transformed social organization. Men owned cattle and wanted to pass them on to their children, but the pairing family of the matrilineal gens prevented this. The father had to leave his property to his sister's children; his own children belonged to his wife's gens and inherited from her brother. So the men carried out a revolution: they switched the children to the gens of the father. The gens became patrilineal, and the father passed on property to his sons. The woman lost all her rights. She could no longer end the marriage at will; she must be faithful to the man and obey him in all things. The wife had to serve her husband, while he could seduce other women and visit prostitutes.[8]

Monogamy had arrived.

With the discovery of iron, humanity entered the Upper Stage of Barbarism. Iron axes, spades, ploughs, and swords pushed tribal society up toward civilization. People built wagons, ships, chariots, and walled towns with towers.[9]

Property was gathered in the hands of a few, with the inevitable results: the rise of classes and the invention of writing propelled humanity forward into civilization.

Thus prehistoric humanity, according to Engels, passed through six stages on its way to civilization: Lower Savagery, Middle Savagery, Upper Savagery, Lower Barbarism, Middle Barbarism, and Upper Barbarism. Engels argues that all civilized peoples went through these stages, and that primitive societies around the world are still going through them. The stages are a schema of universal social evolution.

Engels and Marx were following the ideas of the anthropologist Lewis Henry Morgan published in *Ancient Society* in 1877. Like most nineteenth-century anthropologists, Morgan believed in cultural evolution. He held that all cultures evolved according to a single pattern, and thought he could trace this pattern in the history of any society. And since primitive cultures in different regions naturally developed along a single track, Morgan believed that there was no need for cross-cultural contacts: once a society began to evolve, it spontaneously passed through certain stages of social evolution.

How do prehistorians now view these evolutionary assumptions of nine-teenth-century anthropology? Marxist prehistorians sometimes accept them, especially Soviet Marxists. But most prehistorians, explains Glyn Daniel in *The Idea of Prehistory*, have modified the evolutionary outlook. Though many of them believe that primitive cultures evolved independently of one another, they see some contacts between cultures. They hold that from time to time cultures influenced one another and are not convinced of parallel evolution; they doubt that primitive cultures evolved through the same stages. They think that little is known about the evolution of prehistoric culture.

Marx and Engels worked with a method often used in the nineteenth century: they took the comparative study of surviving primitive societies as the key to prehistory. Today's primitives, they assumed, are copies of what our civilizations were long ago. In the savage tribes still living in African jungles, Pacific islands, and American forests, Morgan and Engels saw "social fossils" revealing prehistoric stages of cultural evolution. They compared primitive cultures at hypothetical stages of progress and worked out a general course of development.[10]

Today most prehistorians consider this method conjectural. Unverifiable hypotheses, evolutionary assumptions, gaps filled by guesswork–the method includes all of these. Prehistorians have dropped this method for the safer results of archaeology. Only what archaeologists dig out of burial mounds or find in ancient campsites counts as evidence of prehistoric life.

But archaeology tells us little about the social forms of prehistoric peoples. From their tools and tombs we learn nothing about their economic organization and social life. If archaeology is our only road into prehistory, humanity's remote culture may be forever lost.

By contrast Engels' anthropology gives a colorful description of prehistoric social life. Engels has influenced some Marxists. In the 1930s Soviet anthropologists began to classify prehistory into stages suggested by Engels' work; they spoke of preclan society, clan society, and class society–an evolutionary schema. But most prehistorians view this schema with suspicion. It might be correct, they say, yet how can archaeology confirm it?

Since 1960 Marxist dogmatism in anthropology, as in all intellectual spheres, has steadily diminished in the Soviet Union. Outside the Soviet Union, Engels' anthropology influenced Marxists like Wilhelm Reich, now widely read on the New Left. The admirers of Reich's celebrated work *The Invasion of Compulsory Sex-Morality* should bear in mind that he assumes the correctness of Engels' anthropology.

Many Marxist prehistorians, like V. Gordon Childe in chapter 3 of *Man Makes Himself*, take up a critical attitude toward Engels' theory. Even tougher on Engels is the well-known Marxist anthropologist Kathleen Gough, who writes in

Monthly Review (February 1971) that neither matriarchy nor sexual equality ever existed, as far as we can tell by the evidence (p. 52).

Communism

Marx and Engels argue that the social evolution of humanity starts from a stage of primitive communism. What can we say of this idea in the light of modern research?

Stone age peoples lived by food gathering and hunting for millions of years. A few thousand years ago they invented agriculture and tamed animals, thus preparing for civilization. We can divide the problem of primitive communism into two parts, as Marx does: the hunting stage and the agriculture stage.[11]

During the Pleistocene epoch cave dwellers gathered fruits, nuts, and berries, killed game, and caught fish. What was life like in those primeval forests?

Australian tribes still living at the Stone Age level practice primitive collectivism. In *The Native Tribes of South-East Australia*, Alfred William Howitt gives this report on a typical tribe: "Food, including in that term all game caught by the men and all vegetable food obtained by the women, was shared with others according to well-understood rules. Thus there was a certain community in food, and there was an acknowledged obligation to supply certain persons with it" (p. 756). But though the customs of contemporary tribes suggest prehistoric communism, they cannot prove it. Such tribes, points out Childe in chapter 3 of *Man Makes Himself*, may have evolved in directions not taken in the Pleistocene, or they may have regressed.

A stronger argument for the existence of communism in the Pleistocene is this: scarcity probably forced humans into communism. Life in the primeval forest was hard and dangerous, so people formed groups and stayed together. Food was scarce. When men and women found it they must have shared, for that was the way to survive. Hunting was cooperatively organized. Everyone had to work, and to work for the group. There was no surplus and no hoarding: the struggle for life drove primitives into communism.

With the low level of productive forces in the Pleistocene there may have been hunting and eating in common. One analysis of hunting societies based on recent evidence concludes that prehistoric hunters probably had communist tendencies. This analysis appears in chapter 8 of *The Anatomy of Human Destructiveness* by Erich Fromm, a social scientist working in the Marxist tradition. But some Marxists have attacked the argument that scarcity produced communism in the Pleistocene. Was there really scarcity? Recent studies of labor time in hunting societies, says the Marxist anthropologist Maurice Godelier, show that hunters have a good deal of leisure. And in the Pleistocene, he explains in *Sur les sociétés précapitalistes*, hunting societies occupied fruitful regions of the planet instead of the marginal zones that civilization has pushed them into today (pp. 120–21).

Marx and Engels were convinced that primitive communism existed, and Engels draws an attractive picture of hunting societies. The Iroquois tribes, living in the New Stone Age, provided a model he applies widely. He points out that the Iroquois have none of the machinery of the political state: kings, nobles, governors, soldiers, police, judges, courts, prisons–all are missing. And yet everything runs smoothly, for when a quarrel arises the whole group of those concerned, the gens or the tribe, settles the dispute. Several families run a household in common, and the land is tribal property. Administration of this communist economy is simple and democratic: everyone follows habit and custom, or the people themselves decide what to do. The communist household and the gens take care of the old, the sick, and the disabled–no poor exist. Everyone is free, and men and women live in equality. "This is what mankind and human society were like before class divisions arose."[12]

Engels speaks well of early communism, but he is not guilty of primitivism. He argues that this stage was inferior to civilization. He notes the war between tribes, the cruelty of the warfare, the stunted productive forces, the religious superstition, and the power of nature over people. Primitive communism, he thinks, was better than civilization in only one way: its morality.[13]

A few thousand years ago humanity discovered agriculture. The shift from hunting to agriculture eventually brought a change from tribal property to family property–this much scholars agree upon. But the phases of the transition are a subject for endless argument.

In the nineteenth century historians argued that prehistoric tribes wandered over the earth in search of pasture for their herds. Finally they learned to plant crops, and settled in village communities based on the common ownership of land; these communities were supposed to extend from India to Ireland. Marx and Engels accepted this theory of agrarian communism.[14] But the twentieth century saw the theory attacked, as scholars looked for ways to weaken the growing influence of Marx. They searched for private property in land in remote periods. They found some. To what extent village communism was a phase of social evolution is disputed to this day.

Marx and Engels, like many socialists, held two theses about the agrarian communities: (1) the land was owned in common, and (2) *sometimes* the land was tilled in common. Sometimes people sowed the land together and sang happily through the harvest–a great collective effort. Through the ages, common tillage gave way to individual tillage: the community assigned each family a plot, and from time to time redistributed the land. The family worked its plot, but the community owned the land, and periodic redistribution fostered equality. Redistribution, however, finally stopped: the family became the owner of its plot, and the children inherited it. In this way, reason Marx and Engels, humanity arrived at private property in land.[15]

What does twentieth-century scholarship say about their view? Although there is some evidence for the thesis that there was common ownership of the soil, the thesis of common tillage is doubtful (as the founders of Marxism sensed). Max Weber says in his *General Economic History* that from the beginning there may have been periodic redistribution of communally owned land, but with individual tillage. He concludes that nothing definite can be said in general terms about the economic life of primitive people (p. 36).

How much do Marx and Engels stress the theory of agrarian communism in their writings? Not very much. In the 1840s they worked out their conception of world history before the theory appeared. In the 1850s Georg Ludwig Maurer developed the hypothesis that communism existed in ancient Germany. Analogies from other lands, especially Russia and India, led to the theory of an agrarian communism as the beginning of all economic evolution.[16] Marx and Engels accepted this theory and worked it into their conception of history, but it is not a keystone in the structure of their thought.

Marx calls the breakup of the primitive communities the beginning of progress: "They restrained the human mind within the smallest possible compass, making it the unresisting tool of superstition, enslaving it beneath traditional rules, depriving it of all grandeur and historical energies."[17] He is no admirer of primitive communism.

The Asiatic Mode

In the nineteenth century Europeans viewed Asian societies through a special lens, the concept of *Oriental Despotism*. They saw Asian civilizations as eternal. Despots were supposed to rule over them, kings raised to the level of gods: often people could not gain their presence and had to consult them through messengers. These despots taxed their peoples without pity. Europeans believed that the peoples of Asia lived a simple life in villages, where they produced their tools and food. In a faraway palace the Oriental despot, surrounded by ceremony and mystery, ruled through a pyramid of officials. Oriental countries languished under the Asian sun, like stagnant pools in a backwater of history. This picture of Asia, based on scanty and unreliable sources, fascinated the European mind.

The concept of Oriental Despotism was developed by Montesquieu in the first part of *De l'esprit des lois* (chapter 1 of book 2 and chapter 4 of book 5). Hegel took over the concept and made it famous through his *Vorlesungen über die Philosophie der Geschichte*, especially in sections 1 and 2 of part 1. In his

Principles of Political Economy, John Stuart Mill accepted this concept of the East and analyzed the Asian economy; the "Preliminary Remarks" to this book strongly influenced Marx. Thus French materialism, German philosophy, and English economics built up the nineteenth-century's picture of Asia.

These are the major features in the portrait of Oriental Despotism:

(1) The despotic ruler was all powerful. The only law was the power of the army and the will of the king. He could kill with a word, without trial or reason given, and sometimes he passed this privilege to his mother or chief wife. For a careless remark people found themselves in the snake pit.

(2) There was no privately owned land: the despot (or state) owned it all. The despot allotted land to personal favorites or to village communities, but he was the landlord of the realm.

(3) Thousands of villages, scattered throughout the country, were the basis of the economic system. (Big towns were more like military camps than market centers.)

(4) The villages were selfsufficient. Each village grew its own food and made what it needed. It had a blacksmith, a potter, a schoolteacher, a priest. At home the women spun and wove clothing.

(5) The lands of Asia cried out for water; irrigation was a necessity of life. So the state built and kept up waterworks. Because the despot controlled life-giving water, he had the village communities at his mercy.

(6) The state took the surplus product from the villages; they had nothing left to exchange with one another. So there was little or no trade between them. The trader's caravan was a rare sight.

(7) Because the despot took the surplus from the village communities, he could live in luxury. From dark to dawn he reveled in wine, feasts, and harems. His splendid palaces, filled with slaves, were the envy of Western travelers.

(8) Asian societies had evolved into a cul-de-sac. They were stationary. Social stability was a universal feature of these societies: in them there was no progress, no dynamism, and no change. For thousands of years Asia dreamed under its despots—like an opium addict.

Though Marx first encountered this concept in Montesquieu and Hegel, he learned more from classical economics, for the concept appears in the writings of Richard Jones, James Mill, and John Stuart Mill. Marx several times cites Jones on Asia in chapter 24 of his *Theories of Surplus-Value*. He had certainly read James Mill's *The History of British India*, which was the early nineteenth century's standard work on Indian history. The first book of John Stuart Mill's work on political economy was a formative influence on Marx's conception of Asia, especially section 6 of chapter 7.

Marx and Engels, as men of their age, saw Asia through this conceptual lens; it colored all their thinking about the East. Again and again this vision of

Oriental Despotism appeared in their writings, and they often used the term itself.[18]

This picture of a static Asia puzzled and fascinated Marx. Why was the East immobile? What had stalled its development? Was its paralysis permanent? Throughout his life these questions worried him; and though his main interest was Europe, Marx again and again returned to his Eastern studies. He never fully explained Asian stagnation, and he never stopped trying.

Marx was a disciple of Hegel. Hegel had taught him to expect continual social change, to study what was coming into being and what was passing away. For Hegelian dialectics, clashing opposites develop toward new social forms. Dialectic "includes in its comprehension of the existing state of things the recognition of the negation of that state, of its inevitable breaking up," says Marx. "It regards every historically developed social form as in fluid movement, and therefore takes into account both its transient nature and its momentary existence."[19] Marx expected every social form to develop, grow old, and pass away. Yet India was frozen at one level of development: the country's "social condition [had] remained unaltered since its remotest antiquity."[20] And there was China, "a giant empire, containing almost one-third of the human race, vegetating in the teeth of time."[21] The stagnation of the East was a riddle.

Some students looked for the solution in Buddhist or Hindu religion; in his *General Economic History* Max Weber later saw the solution in the caste system (p. 271). Marx and Engels turned to the economic structure of society for an answer. They formulated the concept of an "Asiatic mode of production," in which there was no economic change. India suggested the model for this economic formation: it had a "stationary character," and no social revolutions had occurred there,[22] in spite of "all the aimless movement on the political surface."[23] In his *Notes on Indian History* Marx traces the chaos on the political surface of Asian society. Here is a typical passage:

> 1225. Shamsuddin conquered Bihar and Malwa, and was–1232–recognized as King throughout Hindustan proper; he died in 1236 at the zenith of his power, and was succeeded–1236–by his son Rukneddin; in the same year he was deposed by his sister! who seized throne. 1236–1239. Sultana Razia, her love affair with an Abyssinian slave at the court outraged court nobles; Altunia, Chief of Bhatinda, revolted, took her prisoner, she fell in love with him and married him; he then led army to Delhi; nobles defeated him, put her to death; she was succeeded by her brother –1239–1241–Muizzuddin Bahram, terrible despot; he was murdered; succeeded by Rukneddin's son–1241–1246–Ala-uddin Mas'ud; assassinated.[24]

But Marx notes "the unchangeableness of Asiatic societies, an unchangeableness in such striking contrast with the constant dissolution and refounding of Asiatic states and the never ceasing changes of dynasty. The structure of the economic elements of society remains untouched by the storm clouds of the political sky."[25] This passive economic basis explains Asian stagnation. The changing despots, turning in circles between pleasure and madness, the waves of barbarians sweeping down on the capital–these revolutions were meaningless. Political winds blew, but the economic structure of society was like granite.

The Asiatic mode of production reached far beyond geographical Asia. For Marx it was a social form embracing many non-European civilizations. It included ancient Mexico and Peru[26] and societies in North Africa,[27] the Middle East,[28] and Central Asia,[29] as well as India[30] and age-old China, that "mummy carefully preserved in a hermetically sealed coffin."[31] Russia, too, was part of the mode, though sometimes Marx and Engels treat tsarist despotism as a form that became semifeudal in the seventeenth century.[32]

The Asiatic mode grew up on a social base of village communities, each owning and tilling its land in common.[33] Primitive communism was "that spontaneously developed form which we find on the threshold of the history of all civilized races."[34] Beyond Europe, especially in the desert running from North Africa through the Middle East to India and Central Asia, climatic conditions forced the primitive communities to develop irrigation. For this the centralizing power of government was needed.[35]

In Asian societies primitive governments emerged to serve the communities. And Engels tells "how he who was originally the servant changed gradually into the lord; how this lord emerged as an Oriental despot. . . . However great the number of despotisms which rose and fell in Persia and India, each was fully aware that above all it was the entrepreneur responsible for the collective maintenance of irrigation throughout the river valleys, without which no agriculture was possible there."[36] To explain the stagnation of this mode of production Marx and Engels worked out two hypotheses.

In the picture received of Oriental Despotism private property in land was missing from Asia: the state (despot) was the "real landlord."[37] The despot allowed his favorites or the village communities to use the land, but he owned it and took the surplus product from those who tilled it. The rise of Oriental Despotism was in striking contrast to European development. In the chain of economic evolution in Western Europe, Marx and Engels traced the following sequence: tribal property, feudal landed property, the property of the guilds, manufacture capital, modern industrial capital.[38] In Asia the shift from tribal property to state-owned land had broken the chain near its beginning. Without private landed property no feudalism, no class struggles, and no social revolutions could arise. There had never been a social revolution in Asia.[39] Marx and Engels formed a hypothesis to explain Asian stagnation: *the absence of private landed property arrested social evolution.*[40] "Private property in land," writes Marx, is "the great *desideratum* of Asiatic society."[41]

Marx never abandoned this hypothesis,[42] but he was not satisfied with it: he wondered if private landed property had *always* been absent in Asia.[43] Contemporary research has further undermined the hypothesis, as we shall see.

In the seventeenth and eighteenth centuries the European belief that private landed property was absent from Asia grew up gradually. In those centuries information about India came from the tales of merchants, missionaries, and ambassadors. François Bernier, associated with the court of Louis XIV, was one of these. He visited India in 1668 and wrote about his travels. He may have misunderstood the agrarian system of the Mughal empire in reporting that there was no private property in land. Bernier's idea eventually became part of the concept of Oriental Despotism, and wound up in Marx's "Asiatic mode of production." Marx himself cited Bernier to document the absence of private landed property in Asia.[44] In *India at the Death of Akbar* (1920) William Harrison Moreland, like many older scholars, argued that Bernier was basically right (pp. 90–94). But now some specialists are saying that he was mistaken.

What about the centuries of Indian history before Bernier appeared on the scene in 1668? In recent years scholars have made an intensive study of the agrarian system of old India. In "Interpretations of Ancient Indian History" Oxford scholar Romila Thapar reports in *History and Theory* (1968) that the study of land grants reconstructed from very old inscriptions indicates that there *was* private property in land and that the rule of property changed over the centuries (p. 333). Thus Marx's doubts about Bernier's thesis have acquired foundation. Because of these doubts Marx worked toward a second hypothesis to explain the inertia of Oriental societies, a hypothesis he struggled with again and again. Let us see how it developed.

The Asiatic mode of production was made up of countless village communities, each village producing what it needed. "One of the material bases of the power of the state over the small disconnected producing organisms in India was the regulation of the water supply."[45] Control of the army and the waterworks made the state all powerful. It could take the surplus from the villages: products not directly consumed went into the storehouse of the despot, who used them to buy luxuries.[46] Despots often dealt harshly with those who could not pay. Consider the Indian ruler Tughlak: "As his treasury was empty," writes Marx, "he imposed most ruinous exactions on the people; taxes were so heavy that the poor fled to the forests; he drew a cordon of troops round these and then had the fugitives slaughtered in a grand hunt in which he took part, riding the men down like game."[47]

Therefore the villages had little left for trade with one another–they produced for their own needs, not for exchange with other communities or the outside world.[48] The villages were thousands of "disconnected atoms" with no roads between them.[49] Each was a little world in itself. The men tilled the fields while the women wove fabrics. Other tasks fell to a dozen people: a judge, a bookkeeper, a priest, an astrologer, a schoolmaster, a washerman, a barber, a carpenter, a potter, a blacksmith, a silversmith, and a water overseer who distributed the water from the common tanks for irrigation.[50] They needed nothing from outside, and life within flowed in the grooves of habit and custom.

Marx was working out this hypothesis: *the Asiatic mode was stable because the self-sufficient villages, robbed of their surplus by the despot, could never undergo social change.*[51] Underlying this hypothesis is the assumption that trade is a key factor in economic evolution. In the Asiatic mode no trade could arise between villages, and this doomed the system to stagnation.

Each village practiced farming and handicraft, but both of these pursuits are conservative. Developments in the productive forces are rare in peasant farming, because a farmer working in the traditional way is sure of producing bread, while new and untried methods may lead to losses.[52] And handicraft in primitive conditions is equally hidebound: in the workshop each artisan continues to operate in the traditional way.[53]

Trade is much less conservative. Trade brings new things from abroad, things that arouse thought. New crops and new ways of making things come into being. Trade breaks up traditional life, creates many needs, fosters the spirit of competition. Private property is latent in all primitive communities; trade draws it to the surface and turns it into commodities.[54]

In the Asiatic mode of production the despot killed trade between villages, and this was the secret of the mode's paralysis. The Asiatic mode arose out of primitive communism, developed a centralized state, and settled into the village system. The villages arrested the mode's evolution; they "transformed a self-developing social state into never changing natural destiny."[55]

The Asiatic mode of production, embracing many Oriental civilizations, is a basic concept in Marx's historical thought. There are discussions of the mode scattered throughout the writings of Marx and Engels; no student of Marxism can miss them. What do Soviet Marxists say about the Asiatic mode?

Official Marxism has sometimes seen the Asiatic mode as a variant of slavery and sometimes as a variant of feudalism. Slavery and feudalism are the only precapitalist modes admitted by official Marxism, so the Asiatic mode must be a form of one or the other. This interpretation is surely wrong, and we can safely dismiss it.

A more interesting question is this: what is the status of Marx's Asiatic mode in the light of modern research? To answer this we must recall that Marx's writings on Asia are a century old. He worked out his theory of an Asiatic mode to explain stagnant Oriental Despotism, a concept that hypnotized the nineteenth century. But scholars now believe that the image of Oriental Despotism gave a false picture of the East. The Orient was not stagnant, though in the nineteenth century little was known about the area and it seemed to have no history.

In Marx's day the lack of data made a serious knowledge of Egypt and the ancient Middle East impossible. Almost nothing was known about the history of Africa, and information on pre-Columbian civilization in the Americas was scanty. The study of Indian and Chinese history was just getting under way. In his concept of an Asiatic mode of production Marx included all these areas. His portrait of the Asiatic mode, based on India, showed a despot exploiting primitive communities; but this picture did not fit all Eastern societies. Did it fit India itself? Not throughout several millennia of Indian history, says the Marxist scholar Maurice Godelier in *Sur les sociétés précapitalistes* (pp. 42–43). But in *Social Origins of Dictatorship and Democracy*, Barrington Moore, Jr., shows that Marx's image of Asia reflected well the stagnation of the Mughal empire (pp. 317–30). Marx's hypotheses can explain why no bourgeoisie emerged to push India toward capitalism in the Mughal empire that preceded the British.

Today Orientalists reject the image of a changeless East. In his article in *History and Theory* Romila Thapar sums up their outlook as follows: "They assume that all societies change and that in a period stretching from 2500 B.C. to A.D. 1000 Indian society and its institutions must have undergone change; it is the work of the historian to study the nature of this change. The idea of a static society is clearly no longer tenable" (pp. 334–35). This view dissolves the problem Marx set out to solve. The picture of an inert Asia made him wonder why the dialectical standpoint had broken down, so he developed an "Asiatic mode of production" to explain it. The problem was a false one, though his solution is of interest, for it suggests the reason why capitalism never emerged in Asian civilizations. The centralized state grabbed surplus wealth for itself and prevented the emergence of a strong bourgeoisie. In his *Marxist Economic Theory*, Ernest Mandel gives a description of this confiscatory policy of Asiatic despotisms and its economic effect (pp. 123–25).

Marxists now take the dialectical view that Asian societies change: they study every nation's history as a process of economic evolution, social development, and cultural transformation. A recent example of Marxist work on the East is Damodar Kosambi's *Ancient India*.

The Ancient Mode

In the nineteenth century the concept of evolution was in the air. Everything—the physical world, the animal world, the world of human culture—was supposed to go through a process of evolution. Evolution meant development from the simple to the complex, from the lower to the higher. Evolution meant progress, although here and there regressions and stagnations might occur. It was the nature of reality to change, grow, develop. "Progress," said nineteenth-century philosophers, "is not an accident, but a necessity. It is a law of nature."

Matter developed from clouds of gas into our sun and planets (cosmic evolution); a single germ evolved into the vast spectacle of plants and animals (biological evolution); and humanity progressed from savagery through barbarism into civilization (cultural evolution). Sir Edward Tylor, the founder of anthropology who preached the schema of savagery, barbarism, and civilization, counted among his friends Spencer, Lyell, Huxley, Wallace, and Darwin.

Marx and Engels, with their Hegelian conception of the world, worked on the basic assumptions of evolutionism from the beginning. They easily absorbed the nineteenth century's growing fascination with evolution: they read Darwin with enthusiasm[56] and studied the evolutionary anthropology of scientists like Tylor and Morgan.[57]

Certain evolutionary assumptions underlie all the thinking of Marx and Engels on prehistory. We have seen that they think of primitive hordes as naturally developing along the same track: once they have begun to evolve they pass through similar stages. Civilizations, too, develop according to general laws. If the historian discovers a pattern of development in one nation of the ancient world, for example, it can probably be generalized to a few others. This boldness in laying down hypotheses gives their work an interest missing from today's history. In their study of the ancient Mediterranean civilizations based on slavery, Marx and Engels take Rome as the model of socioeconomic evolution.[58] They see Rome as the "classic example" in which the development can be studied "in its purest and most clearly marked form."[59] They expect that generalizations from Rome to other and earlier slave cultures, such as Greece, will prove valid.[60] For this reason they take Roman development as the paradigm for "the ancient mode of production."

The ancient mode ran on slave labor. Around the Mediterranean, slavery became the dominant form of production among all peoples who were developing beyond the primitive community.[61] But slavery barred the way to further economic development, and every nation living off slaves finally deteriorated.[62] The slave masses worked for the free, who themselves were divided into rich and poor. Between free rich and free poor raged class struggles, struggles that weakened the state; and these weakened states often went to pieces in the common ruin of the struggling classes.[63] This happened when a stronger nation pounced on a weakened one. Greece was conquered by Macedonia, and Macedonia by Rome. In each case, the slave system, caught in a blind alley, was saved by the conquering nation. The conquerors shifted the center of the system to their own country, and the whole process repeated itself on a higher plane. This continued until the disappearance of the ancient mode in the death of the Roman Empire.[64]

The evolution of Marx's ancient mode goes through four stages: primitive communism, ancient classical production, the ancient mode of production fully developed, and the fall of the Roman Empire. We must trace this movement in detail.

As we have seen, the history of the old Mediterranean world, like that of every other area, began with scattered tribes living in primitive communism. At first glance, these primitive communities looked like those of stagnant Asia, but the Mediterranean area was destined for "a more dynamic historical life."[65] In these communities the engines of change began to hum. Unlike Asian villages settled near irrigation tanks, the Western tribes could move around. "The primitive character of the tribe may be broken by the movement of history or migration; the tribe may remove from its original place of settlement and occupy *foreign* soil, thus entering new conditions of labor and developing the energies of the individual further. The more such factors operate . . . the more do conditions arise which allow the individual to become a *private proprietor* of land–of a particular plot–whose special cultivation belongs to him and his family."[66] The primitive communities own the land, but they assign a plot to each family, and the families pass it on through inheritance. Private property in land slowly emerges.

Thus out of primitive communism emerges "ancient communal"[67] or "ancient classical"[68] production, a transitional form between communism and the ancient mode.[69] This transitional form appears with "the union of several tribes into a city by agreement or by conquest."[70] The city-state will be the economic unit of ancient society.[71]

The community lives on in the form of the city-state;[72] "union in the city gives the community as such an economic existence."[73] The community, as a city-state, owns all the land; the land is, for example, *Roman* land. The state sets aside part of this as common land for everyone's needs–pasture, firewood, hunting–and distributes the rest to individual families as private property. Every Roman by birth has a claim to so many units of land, and also a right to the common land. The community is based on the fact that its members are working owners of land, small peasant cultivators.[74] State and private property coexist: a man has a farm because he is a Roman, yet the farm is his.[75] The city-state turns democratic, and Rome becomes the classic example of a free farmers' republic.

As this ancient classical form rises out of tribal communism, social classes take shape, and society splits into rich and poor. "The nature of tribal structure leads to the differentiation of kinship groups into higher and lower, and this social differentiation is developed further by the mixing of conquering and conquered tribes."[76] Patricians and plebeians appear and begin the class struggle that runs like a red thread through Roman history.

In this ancient classical society, each peasant owns his plot and tills it. The community rests on this economic foundation of free peasants.[77] But the base is shaky, for the peasant can *lose* his property.[78] In time, most Roman peasants *do* lose their property, and the community dissolves into the ancient mode of production. How did this loss of property come about?

The community was always at war.[79] Many wars were defensive,[80] but others were offensive: as the population expanded, colonization of foreign lands began.[81] Wars meant the capture of slaves,[82] and slavery broke up the peasant farming on which the community rested.[83] The tendency to war drove the community beyond the limits of a free farmers' republic into empire.[84] While the Italian peasants were away fighting for the empire, the rich bought up their farms and built ranches run by slaves, the slaves captured in war. Marx quotes Appian: "Thus the powerful men drew all wealth to themselves, and all the land swarmed with slaves."[85] Italy turned into a land of slave estates producing a cash crop for the urban market. The peasants drifted to the city of Rome, where they became a lumpenproletariat, a proletariat-in-rags. (*Lumpen* means "rags" in German.) The community had vanished, and the ancient mode of production, based on slavery, was grinding out luxury goods for the lucky few.[86]

Though in Rome there was a proletariat and big money to invest, capitalism could not develop there.[87] The slave mode of production excluded capitalism. The surplus wealth was amassed in the hands of a few people "in the ancient mode of production which depended on slavery," writes Marx. "But the ancients never thought of transforming the surplus product into capital. . . . They used a large part of the surplus product for unproductive expenditure on art, religious works and public works."[88] There was no class of investors, for rich Romans did not use money to make more money–they spent it. Their aim was enjoyment, and this included the arts and sciences.[89] Slave labor provided them with the leisure to pursue civilization.

Since there were no machines, slaves had to do the work. "If," dreams Aristotle, the greatest thinker of the ancient world, "if every tool could do its work by itself, just as the creations of Daedalus moved of themselves or the tripods of Hephaestos went of their own accord to their sacred work, then there would be no need . . . of slaves for the lords." Thus Marx quotes Aristotle's defense of the ancient mode of production: there were no machines, and slaves had to work so a few could carry on civilization. "Oh! those heathens!" continues Marx. "They perhaps excused the slavery of one because it was a means to the full development of another. But to preach slavery of the masses so that a few crude and half educated parvenus might become 'eminent spinners,' 'extensive sausage makers,' and 'influential shoe black dealers,' to do this they lacked the bump of Christianity."[90] There is no excuse for wage slavery under modern capitalism, but Marx and Engels think that slavery was a necessary base for Greco-Roman civilization.[91]

Yet slavery was a brake on further economic evolution. The slave carried on passive resistance by mistreating animals and breaking tools. So the masters gave slaves only heavy, clumsy implements, difficult to damage; slave labor was a costly process.[92] Economic evolution ran its course in the slave mode of production, and a regression began. Rome slowly declined. Why?

Historians have given different answers: decline of Roman virtue, decrease of the population, increase of social conflict, barbarization of the ruling class, two centuries of drought, a crisis of authority, a law of civilization and decay, dilution of the racial elite, collapse of the idea of citizenship, a series of historical accidents, the murderous barbarians, the immorality of the pagans, the rise of the Christian religion. Marx says little about Rome's decline, but he undoubtedly saw it as economic decay. Writing after Marx's death, Engels developed their explanation stressing the economy.

All the slave societies of the ancient world, he says, suffered from a contradiction in the economic system, a cancer that doomed them to death.[93] The following words sum up his general view: "Wherever slavery is the main form of production it turns labor into servile activity. That makes labor dishonorable for freemen. Thus the way out of such a mode of production is barred, while on the other hand slavery is an impediment to more developed production, which urgently requires its removal. This contradiction spells the doom of all production based on slavery and of all communities based on it."[94]

Let us examine this hypothesis about slavery's decline. Engels accepts Marx's thesis that slaves express their hatred by mistreating animals and breaking tools, thus forcing the masters to give them only implements difficult to damage.[95] And cheap slaves obviously make labor-saving inventions unnecessary. Engels draws the inevitable conclusion: slavery was a brake on further economic evolution, an impediment to more developed productive forces. But no revolutionary class could arise to overthrow the slave system and reorganize production. "Antiquity did not know any abolition of slavery by a victorious rebellion."[96] The slaves were crushed and helpless; how could they carry on a revolutionary struggle? They were "deprived of rights and of their own will and the possibility to free themselves, as the defeat of Spartacus had already proved."[97] And slavery made all labor seem disgraceful, turned it into "servile activity," so that the free poor fled from it. They become not wage laborers, says Marx, "but a mob of do-nothings more abject than the former 'poor whites' in the South of the United States."[98] Freemen transformed into "poor whites" could not make a revolution. "Between slaves and poor whites, two classes equally unfit for self-emancipation," says Engels, "the old world went to pieces."[99] The slave mode of production had run into a "blind alley."[100]

The Italian slave estates were parceled out and leased in small lots to those who paid a fixed amount annually, were attached to the land, and could be sold together with the plots. These *coloni* were forerunners of the medieval serfs. Thus freemen slipped down toward serfdom, while slaves moved up toward it.[101]

What happened in Italy usually occurred throughout the Western Empire. "Social relations in the provinces came nearer and nearer to those obtaining in the capital and Italy."[102] Slavery no longer paid, so it died out.[103] The Roman world slid toward natural economy, in which people produce for their own use, "a low stage of agriculture, and of industry as well."[104]

The German barbarians poured down across the Roman Empire. "Only barbarians are capable of rejuvenating a world laboring in the throes of a dying civilization."[105]

Engels, then, sees the breakup of the ancient mode as a process lasting centuries: gradual economic decay, the dying out of slavery, and the disappearance of the Empire under a flood of Germans. But Soviet Marxism offers a different interpretation of Rome's fall: according to official Marxism, the ancient mode exploded in a revolution, a transition to a higher social formation. This revolution was a step up the ladder of progress toward communism. In *Fundamentals of Marxism-Leninism* Otto Kuusinen describes the fall of Rome as follows:

> More and more insistently the needs of the development of the productive forces demanded the abolition of the old production relations. This could only be accomplished by a social revolution. The classes and groups that suffered most from the slave system and therefore had most to gain from its abolition formed the driving force behind that revolution. For the most part, they were slaves and the poorest section of the freemen. . . .

In the end, under the combined blows of the uprisings of the working classes and the attacks of neighboring barbarian tribes, which the slave-
owning state, weakened by internal contradictions and conflicts, could
no longer resist, the slave system crumbled. It was replaced by a
new formation–feudalism. (p. 158)

The view has interest, but it is not that of Marx and Engels: nowhere do they
call the fall of Rome a social revolution. In *The German Ideology* they sometimes mention Rome's decline. In discussing it, they speak of the "powerful
mechanical shocks to which the Roman world power was subjected as a result
of its division among several Caesars and their wars against one another,
as a result of the colossal concentration of landed property in Rome and the
fall in the population of Italy caused by this, and as a result of the pressure
of the Huns and Germans."[106] They note that agriculture declined, industry
decayed for want of a market, and trade died out.[107] In a crossed-out sentence,
probably deleted for expository purposes, they say that "finally the Hellenic
and Roman world perished, mentally in Christianity and materially in the migration of peoples."[108] There is nothing about social revolution.

While official Marxism holds that the barbarian invasions ended the slave
system, most historians agree with Engels that slavery died out before the
barbarians arrived. Engels argues that before and after the German invasions,
economic conditions remained roughly the same.[109]

Marx and Engels accept the common view that the Western Empire went
through a long decline: when the barbarians came, Rome was a worn-out
frame, a society gone to sleep, a dying civilization.[110] It would have died a natural death, but the barbarians murdered it.

The Feudal Mode

According to official Marxism, the feudal mode of production and distribution
once covered the planet. It was a universal social formation, spanning the
continents and the centuries, and its breakup was a slow and uneven process.
Some nations, according to official Marxist statements, are still in this formation. For many countries of the underdeveloped world, the cause of backwardness and stagnation is feudalism.

This is not the view of Marx and Engels. For them feudalism is above all
a West European development: they specifically exclude the Orient from feudalism. "In the whole of the Orient, where the village community or the state
owns the land, the very term landlord is not to be found in the various languages," writes Engels (in a work approved by Marx). "It was the Turks who

first introduced a sort of feudal ownership of land in the countries conquered by them in the Orient."[111] India and China, for example, were never feudal: they belonged to the Asiatic mode.

This does not mean that feudalism was found only in Western Europe. Marx observes that Japan had a purely feudal organization of landed property;[112] and Engels says that wherever conquerors make the original inhabitants work the land for them, serfdom tends to appear, as it did "very early" in Thessaly.[113]

For Marx and Engels serfdom is a defining characteristic of feudalism. Relations of personal dependence that bind people to the land as serfs–these define feudalism.[114] Serfdom, a relation of production, implied that those who tilled the soil belonged there as surely as the fences and animals until death separated them from it. The other relation of production that defines feudalism is "lordship."[115] The lord's power flowed from inheritance of land, which was not bought and sold, but handed down from father to son.[116] And the serfs were passed along with the soil; the power of a feudal lord was measured by the number of his subjects.[117] Feudalism for Marx and Engels is neither a network of cultural institutions nor a special political system. It is a mode of production.

In Western Europe feudalism from the ninth to the eleventh century was an economy without markets, but this was not a defining characteristic of the system. Though medieval manors producing for their own use hardly ever brought forth a cash crop, feudal systems in Latin America have sold goods on the market. Feudalism does not *necessarily* imply a withdrawal from the circulation of goods into economic self-sufficiency on the manor or hacienda. Feudalism is a mode of *production*. "The real science of modern economics first begins," writes Marx, "where the theoretical treatment passes from the circulation process to the process of production."[118]

A number of Marxists, however, are now saying that feudalism implies a closed natural economy, while capitalism is identified with money and markets. They reason that since Europe was already drawing Asia, Africa, and Latin America into a world market 500 years ago, capitalism has dominated the planet for five centuries–it was not feudalism that caused developmental problems for areas like Latin America, we are told, but capitalism.*

For Marx, however, feudalism is a mode of production; the question of whether a system produces for the market is irrelevant to its definition. And

*See Andre Gundar Frank, *Latin America: Underdevelopment or Revolution*; Ronald Chilcote and Joel Edelstein (eds.), *Latin America: The Struggle with Dependency and Beyond*; and Immanuel Wallerstein, *The Modern World-System*. It is doubtful that the views of these writers are fully Marxist. For a Marxist critique of their definition of feudalism, see Ernesto Laclau, "Feudalism and Capitalism in America," *New Left Review*, no. 67 (May–June 1971): 19–55.

he clearly says that the presence of money and markets does not imply capitalism.[119]

In general Marx said little about the origin of feudalism, while Engels said more, some of it during Marx's lifetime in *The Mark* and some of it later in *The Origin of the Family*. There is no reason to think that Marx would have disagreed with what Engels wrote after his death.

From the ruins of the Roman Empire feudalism slowly grew up in Western Europe. "The first form of property . . . in the Middle Ages," write Marx and Engels, "is tribal property."[120] The German barbarians poured down over the Western Empire, bringing tribal communism with them, and set up their primitive communities in the conquered lands. In this situation feudalism came into being. Its emergence was a long process, lasting from the fifth to the ninth century. "The formation of an original aristocracy, as in the case of . . . the Germans," writes Engels, "took place on the basis of common ownership of the land, and at first was not based in any way on force, but on voluntariness and custom."[121] The economic conditions found in the conquered empire influenced this development.[122]

For centuries the soil in the conquered lands had been private property. The barbarians brought their communities into these economic conditions, which slowly penetrated their communities and dissolved primitive communism. They ceased periodic redistribution of the land, and each family passed on its plot through inheritance. Private property emerged. Although the village communities survived, only pasture and woodland were held in common.[123]

Thus the conquest shook up the tribal communities and set in motion the wheels of economic change. "The invasion drew Western and Central Europe into the course of historical development."[124] The conquest pushed the tribes toward nationhood: tribal organization based on kinship could not administer the conquered lands, could not replace the Roman government; so the barbarians elected kings–that is, they put states in place of the Roman Empire.[125]

After the invasion, the Germans took for themselves two-thirds of the conquered lands. They distributed part of the land among their village communities; but since they were few in number, most of the land remained the property of the German people.[126]

France provides a model of what happened next. "The first thing the king of the Franks, transformed from an ordinary military commander into a real monarch, did was to convert this property of the people into a royal estate, to steal it from the people and to donate or grant it in fief to his retainers."[127] But he not only gave land to his military retainers and army commanders. He gave large grants to educated slaves and Roman Gauls in his court; he handed forests to bishops and abbots; he laid the basis for a landed nobility at the expense of the people.[128]

Centuries of war, terror, and disorder followed, wars that exhausted and ruined the free peasants.[129] By the ninth century France was in chaos. "The ravages of the Northmen's invasions, the eternal wars between kings, and feuds between nobles, compelled one free peasant after another to seek the protection of some lord."[130] Village communities sought the safety of a fortified manor; the peasants gave up their land in return for protection. "Ruined by war and plunder they had to seek the protection of the new magnates or the Church, for the royal power was too weak to protect them."[131] But the peasants paid dearly for this safety: they lost their freedom and became serfs.[132] The lord often took the common land—pasture and woods—from the village. The lord forced the serf to pay rent, till his fields, and chop his wood. He reserved hunting for himself. If the serf married, the lord had the right of the first night with the bride.[133]

Thus, in the ninth century, anarchy and disorder did not lead to the triumph of invading Northmen and Moslems, but to feudalism.[134] Feudalism was based on natural economy: towns, manufacture, trade, merchants, and money were gone; and people everywhere produced for their own use. Engels describes the productive unit of the age:

There was scarcely any room for money in a model feudal farm of the early Middle Ages. The lord obtained all he needed from his serfs, either in the form of labor or as ready produce; the women spun and wove flax and wool and produced the clothing; the men tilled the fields; the children tended the lord's cattle and gathered the fruits of the forest, birds' nests and straw; besides, the entire family had still to turn in grain, fruit, eggs, butter, cheese, fowl, domestic animals, and countless other things. Every feudal manor was self-sufficient; even military dues were demanded in kind; commerce and barter were nonexistent and money was superfluous.[135]

Here Engels' description expresses the historical outlook of his day, but a century of research has shown that there was more exchange of commodities in the Middle Ages than nineteenth-century scholars supposed. Yet if we allow for exaggerations of manorial self-sufficiency, Engels' basic picture is correct. Thousands of manors dotted the map of Europe, and the feudal system spread from France to other countries.[136]

In Europe the foundation of feudal ownership of land was the fief. The landlord granted large fiefs to his vassals in return for military service, and they divided their grants into smaller fiefs for vassals of their own. Feudalism covered Europe with a network of these fiefs, rising from the knight's fee at the bottom to the huge holdings of the real owners at the top. "Here," writes Marx, "we find everyone dependent, serfs and *seigneurs*, vassals and lords, laymen and clergy. Personal dependence here characterizes the social relations of production just as much as it does the other spheres of life organized on the basis of that production."[137]

In France, says Marx, the division of the great feudal territories into countless tiny fiefs reached an extreme. By the fourteenth century there were 100,000 of them, and each little "lord" had rights of jurisdiction over the people who lived on his soil. "The oppression of the agricultural population under all these petty tyrants can be imagined. There were in France 160,000 judges, where today 4,000 tribunals are enough."[138]

What sort of law did these judges apply? There were local customs, of course, but codified feudal law finally appeared, with a strong respect for property rights. When feudalism passed into decline its customs crystallized into fixed forms. This was the end of a thousand-year process that began with the breakdown of Roman civilization.

As the Roman Empire slowly cracked apart (300 A.D.–800 A.D.), shoots of feudalism grew up here and there among the spreading ruins. Feudalism had a hundred variations in time and place, but its most characteristic evolution came in France. "It is evident," Marx writes, "that tradition must play a dominant role in the primitive and undeveloped circumstances on which these production relations and the corresponding mode of production are based. . . . The constant reproduction of the basis of the existing order and its fundamental relations assumes a regulated and orderly form in the course of time. . . . It entrenches itself as custom and tradition and is finally sanctioned as an explicit law."[139] This codification happened near the end of the thirteenth century when the feudal age was drawing to a close, and in parts of France and Germany feudal codes continued to regulate the property relations of lords and vassals for several centuries.

Scholars consider the problem of the origins of feudalism the most interesting part of the subject. The founders of Marxism only sketch some ideas on the problem; these can hardly count as an explanation. Already in later life Engels admits that he tended to overemphasize the importance of military conquest in the emergence of medieval serfdom.[140]

The simple account of Marx's and Engels' views on feudal origins given here, however, is enough to show that they do not see the rise of feudalism as a revolution from below against Rome. The feudal mode of production, like previous modes, arose out of primitive communism. The ancient mode had arisen out of the breakup of the primitive community. Private property, write Marx and Engels, develops "out of the disintegration of the natural community. With the Romans the development of private property . . . had no further industrial and commercial consequences, because their whole mode of production did not alter. With modern peoples, . . . there began with the rise of private property . . . a new phase, which was capable of further develop-ment."[141] The feudal mode developed into a higher system, the bourgeois mode of production.

Conclusion

For Marx, world history is a process of individualization. "The further back we go into history, the more the individual and, therefore, the producing in-dividual seems to depend on and constitute a part of a larger whole: at first it is, quite naturally, the family and the clan, which is but an enlarged family; later on, it is the community growing up in its different forms out of the clash and the amalgamation of clans."[142] The individual is everywhere submerged in the tribal community. Land, water, seed, tools, animals, skins, weapons–these are held in common. People have the same needs, the same tasks, the same skills. They work and live together: the primitive human is a communal being.

The motors of economic evolution start up and snap the umbilical cord that binds each person to companions in the primitive community–individualization begins.[143] Various modes of production evolve out of tribal communism. "Slav-ery and serfdom are . . . simply further developments of property based on tribalism. They necessarily modify all its forms. This they are least able to do in the Asiatic form."[144] In the Asiatic form, slavery and serfdom cannot arise on a large scale. Individuals in this form never become owners, explains Marx, for they are at bottom themselves the property of the Oriental despot.[145] Every-one bows down to the king: the Asiatic mode remains a sea of communities under the sway of the despot.

But around the Mediterranean many communities give birth to private proper-ty, and city-states grow up. Individualization, based on property, develops in-side the city. The community survives in the city-state for a time. But the city-state takes up empire building, and the community disappears in the ancient mode of production based on slavery. The slave society fosters intense indi-vidualization: crafts, manufacture, division of labor, expansion of the market, trade and exchange, aristocratic luxury. Then the slave economy, weakened by internal pressures, cracks and crumbles into ruin. Tribal barbarians finish off ancient civilization.

There begins a new evolution out of the tribal community, a new individuali-zation of communal humanity. "In the case of the nations which grew out of the Middle Ages, tribal property evolved through various stages–feudal landed property, corporative movable property [of the guilds], capital invested in man-ufacture–to modern capital, determined by big industry and universal compe-tition, that is, pure private property that has thrown off all semblance of the community."[146] In the bourgeois mode of production the community has vanished, and people are individualized. "When the narrow bourgeois form has been peeled away," says Marx, we find "the universality of needs, capacities, enjoyments, productive powers of individuals produced in universal exchange."[147]

This individualism is taken up and transformed in a new and higher community—the communist. Under communism the division of labor disappears: each worker moves from one task to another, from the workshop to the garden, from the garden to the writing table, from writing to the hunt, from hunting to the factory, from the factory to the kitchen, from cooking to brick laying, from building to art, from painting to the scientific laboratory.[148] This abolition of the division of labor, write Marx and Engels, "is not possible without the community. Only in community with others has each individual the means of cultivating his gifts in all directions; only in the community, therefore, is personal freedom possible."[149] There is perfect individualism in "the community of revolutionary proletarians";[150] the communist community follows a plan that allows all people to develop themselves in any direction they wish.[151] "In the real community the individuals obtain their freedom in and through their association."[152]

III. Capitalism

The Rise of Capitalism

During the early Middle Ages thousands of manors covered the face of Europe, and serfs on the manor produced most of the things needed by the lord: food, shelter, clothing, furniture, tools, weapons. In the later Middle Ages there was a revival of trade, towns, and crafts: workshops in the medieval city became centers of production. In his workshop a craftsman employed a few helpers or journeymen; the workshops banded together in handicraft guilds. "Peasant agriculture on a small scale, and the carrying on of independent handicrafts," says Marx, "together form the basis of the feudal mode of production."[1] But these handicrafts were signs of the coming transition to a new economic order.

If for Marx the property relations of a society define its mode of production,[2] then the craftsmen were heralds of important changes. "The chief form of property during the feudal epoch consisted on the one hand of landed property with serf labor chained to it, and on the other of the labor of the individual with small capital commanding the labor of journeymen."[3] The individual craftsman, owning raw material and tools, hired two or three journeymen to help in his workshop. The crafts thrived in the towns. In the leather crafts, for example, there were skinners, tanners, cobblers, harnessmakers, saddlers, and makers of fine leather goods. In carpentry there were chestmakers, cabinetmakers, boatbuilders, wheelwrights, coopers, twiners. There were scores of crafts, and each formed a guild to protect its interests.

As feudalism matured, land and the emerging craft workshop were the main productive forces. Marx holds that a transformation of productive forces initiates fundamental economic change, a gradual shift toward a new mode of production.[4] Thus an advance in productive forces would cause feudalism to evolve toward capitalism.

Work relations, modes of cooperation, tools, and techniques are some of the basic elements in the productive forces. (This concept is fully explained in chapter 6.) From 1400 to 1800 A.D. these elements changed as the craft workshop gave way to manufacture, a word Marx uses in a special way. For Marx manufacture is an extension of handicraft techniques: a capitalist or bourgeois brings many craftsmen under one roof, supplies raw materials, pays wages, and sells the product. The capitalist, for example, brings dozens of clothmakers together and divides up the labor among them. Each clothmaker does one thing: one cards, another spins, another weaves, another draws, another dresses, another presses and packs. Each craftsman does his job over and over again. He becomes an expert at it, and this saves time and speeds up production. This expansion of the productive power of handicraft techniques Marx calls *manufacture* (*manu*, by hand + *factura*, a making = a making by hand). Throughout this book the word will have this Marxist meaning: a capitalist extension of *handicraft* techniques through division of labor.

In Europe manufacture began in some places as early as the thirteenth century: in a few towns some bourgeois invested in the new system, and manufactories increased the production of certain articles, especially cloth. Through the centuries the gradual shift from crafts to manufacture was a great advance in productive forces. Manufacture is a new mode of cooperation, a new set of work relations, and this division of labor creates specialized tools and techniques. The expansion of productive forces is revolutionary.[5]

The old craft workshop was a productive force that flourished in the heyday of feudalism. The craft produced for a local market, the town and its surroundings. Feudal laws kept competitive goods out. Guild laws limited the number of master craftsmen in the area, and of journeymen to a master. Laws discouraged competition in quantity of production and price of product. Feudalism encouraged quality, monopoly, and a "just price."

The new productive force, manufacture, clashed with these feudal laws. Bourgeois manufacture produced an enormous quantity of goods, employed large numbers of workers, and thrived on competition and trade. Manufacture broke all the laws of the guild monopolies in the towns. "The new manufactures were established at sea ports or at inland points beyond the control of the old municipalities and their guilds."[6] Manufacture produced for a wide market, and traders carried the goods everywhere. Expanding trade clashed with feudalism. Traders hated the guild monopolies on sales, the hundreds of petty states with different weights and currencies, the tolls for entering ports, crossing bridges, using roads or canals or rivers. There were, for example, sixty-two toll stations on the Rhine alone; merchants paid sixty percent of their cargo to carry it on that river. Manufacturers and traders struggled to weaken feudalism.

Manufacture existed mainly in northern Italy and the Low Countries during the fourteenth and fifteenth centuries, but spread elsewhere during the sixteenth, seventeenth, and eighteenth centuries, especially in England and

France.[7] The Low Countries, England, and France were the economic leaders of Europe. Around 1500 the discovery of sea-lanes to India and America shifted the world trade route to the Atlantic seaboard, and this accelerated the development of these leading European countries during the following centuries.[8] "Holland, England, and France conquered the leading positions in world trade, founded colony after colony and developed the manufacturing industry to the highest pitch of prosperity."[9] The dramatic advance in productive forces was followed by political revolutions in the Low Countries (sixteenth century), in England (seventeenth century), and in France (eighteenth century).[10] Feudalism was declining and the bourgeois mode of production was growing stronger.

These bourgeois political revolutions were the outcome of a long process of social and economic development; they made it possible for that development to continue at a more rapid pace. Engels describes the revolutions as follows:

> At a certain stage the new productive forces set in motion by the bourgeoisie–in the first place the division of labor and the combination of many detail laborers in one general manufactory–and the conditions and requirements of exchange developed through these productive forces became incompatible with the existing order of production handed down by history and sanctified by law, that is to say, incompatible with the privileges of the guild and the other personal and local privileges . . . of the feudal order of society. The productive forces represented by the bourgeoisie rebelled against the order of production represented by the feudal landlords and the guild masters. The result is known: the feudal fetters were smashed, gradually in England, at one blow in France.[11]

The bourgeois revolutions smashed kings, priests, aristocrats, guilds, and feudal laws; in their place sprang up republics promoting further growth of the capitalist mode of production and distribution.

In the sixteenth century a bourgeois revolution swept through the Low Countries (1568–1609). It started as a religious revolt. The Low Countries belonged to feudal Spain, and the Spanish set up an Inquisition there. The Low Countries began one of the bloodiest struggles for freedom in world history. They fought under the banner of Protestantism, but though the form of the revolution was national and religious, the content was bourgeois.[12] The triumph of the revolution in the northern provinces resulted in a republic and commercial expansion. "Holland," writes Marx, "in 1648 stood already at the acme of its commercial greatness. It was 'in almost exclusive possession of the East Indian trade and the commerce between the southeast and northwest of Europe. Its fisheries, marine, manufacture, surpassed those of any other country. The total capital of the Republic was probably more important than that of all the rest of Europe put together.'"[13]

In the seventeenth century a bourgeois revolution swept over England (1640–1689). The privileges, guilds, corporations, and regulations of the Middle Ages no longer corresponded to the new productive forces of manufacture and trade. "Under the protection of the regime of corporations and regulations, capital was accumulated, overseas trade was developed, colonies were founded. But the fruits of this would have been forfeited had people tried to retain the forms under whose shelter these fruits had ripened. Hence burst two thunder claps–the Revolutions of 1640 and 1688. All the old economic forms, the social relations corresponding to them, the political system which was the official expression of the old civil society, were destroyed in England."[14] The English killed the king, proclaimed a republic, suffered a dictatorship, and returned to limited monarchy; they endured decades of civil war, bloodshed, violence, and revolution. Calvinism provided the ideological costume for the English bourgeoisie's performance on the stage of world history.[15]

The eighteenth century produced the Great French Revolution (1789–1814). This time the bourgeoisie threw off the religious disguise and took the philosophy of materialism for a theoretical flag.[16] Bourgeois revolutionaries hammered at the feudal basis of society.[17] They cleared away "all manner of medieval rubbish, seignorial rights, local privileges, municipal and guild monopolies and provincial constitutions."[18] The aristocracy was destroyed.[19] Napoleon reworked the economic basis with the *Code Civil*, created the conditions for an expanding capitalism, and attacked feudalism beyond French borders.[20]

None of these bourgeois upheavals happened overnight; each was "an epoch of social revolution."[21] The Dutch Revolution, the English Revolution,[22] and the French Revolution[23] were long processes of social and political change. The struggles lasted for more than a generation and passed through several political stages: absolute monarchy, republic, dictatorship, restoration, constitutional monarchy. "Everywhere the transition from the absolute to the constitutional monarchy is effected only after severe struggles and after a republican form of government has been gone through," writes Marx.[24] "History is thorough and goes through many phases as it conducts an old form to the grave."[25] In each revolution the bourgeoisie hammered at the feudal forms throughout a historical epoch and worked toward a new society. "Unheroic as bourgeois society is, it nevertheless took heroism, sacrifice, terror, civil war and battles of peoples to bring it into being."[26]

Revolution is a chain of actions and reactions. Once the social equilibrium is disturbed, the whole society begins to totter, and the masses are drawn into the struggle. Society seesaws back and forth between revolution and counterrevolution. After a series of oscillations, a new center of gravity is attained.[27]

This is how Engels analyzes bourgeois revolutions:

> The common form of all these revolutions was that they were minority revolutions. Even when the majority took part, it did so–whether it knew it or not–only in the service of a minority; but because of this, or even simply because of the passive attitude of the majority, this minority took on the appearance of being the representative of the whole people. As a rule after the first great success, the victorious minority divided; one half was satisfied with what had been gained, the other wanted to go still further, and put forward new demands, which partly at least were also in the real or apparent interest of the great mass of the people. In individual cases these more radical demands were actually forced through, but often only for the moment. The more moderate party would regain the upper hand, and what had last been won would wholly or partly be lost again; the vanquished would then shriek of treachery or ascribe their defeat to accident. In reality, however, the truth of the matter was largely this: the achievements of the first victory were only safeguarded by the second victory of the more radical party; this having been attained, and with it what was necessary for the moment, the radicals and their achievements vanished once more from the stage.[28]

Bourgeois revolution is a complicated process.

Classic bourgeois revolutions swept through Holland, England, and France, transforming people and things, creating a new order of society. These revolutions were great social earthquakes. Centuries of subterranean changes had gradually run fault lines through the economic foundations of feudalism; revolutionary convulsions tore away old political forms; and feudalism waned before rising capitalism. The classic bourgeois revolutions were nodal points in world history, transitions to a new age.

But not all bourgeois revolutions followed this pattern, not all of them swept away the feudal state in a single epoch. In many countries the revolutionary movement broke out again and again without success. Through the centuries the revolutionary tide ebbed and flowed, but failed to wash away the feudal fortress. Sometimes the revolution made a breach in feudalism, then interrupted itself to return to its starting point. Through many starts and stops the bourgeoisie abolished the feudal political structures gradually.

Germany is an example of this kind of development. In the thirteenth, fourteenth, and fifteenth centuries the merchant bourgeoisie grew powerful in Germany, which lay along the world trade route from India to Scandinavia. Industry flourished, and the Hanseatic League united the bourgeoisie against the feudal barons.[29] In the sixteenth century a bourgeois revolution broke out under the flag of Protestantism (the German Reformation).[30] But the revolution failed,[31] and the development of the bourgeoisie was arrested.[32] In the Rhineland it revived under the impact of the French Revolution.[33] "No sooner had the armies of the Revolution conquered the Left Bank of the Rhine than all the old rubbish vanished as at the stroke of an enchanter's wand— corvée service, rent dues of every kind to the lord, together with the noble lord himself."[34] For twenty years the Rhineland was part of France (1795–1814). The guilds, the internal customs, the small states—all this disappeared: the *Code Napoléon* weakened feudalism, and a great industrial advance began.[35] The whole Left Bank of the Rhine was French in outlook when the Germans marched in again in 1814.[36]

Prussia was another part of Germany that felt the impact of the French Revolution. Though Prussia fought the French armies, the war had a regenerative character.[37] To gain support from the masses, the Prussians abolished the most shameful privileges of the nobles, at least on paper;[38] from 1808 to 1813 the Prussians carried out antifeudal reforms.[39] The rest of Germany, however, remained divided and feudal. During the 1840s industrial growth in Berlin, Silesia, Saxony, and the Rhineland[40] was followed by an antifeudal revolution in 1848. This bourgeois revolution was a failure, but it further weakened feudalism,[41] and a great industrial advance took place in the 1850s and 1860s.[42] "The existence of a mass of petty German states with their many differing commercial and industrial laws was bound to become an intolerable fetter on this powerfully developing industry and on the growing commerce with which it was linked—a different rate of exchange every few miles, different regulations for establishing a business, everywhere, literally everywhere, different kinds of chicanery, bureaucratic and fiscal traps, even in many cases still, guild restrictions against which not even a license was of any avail."[43] The civil war of 1866, in which the German states were further unified, was the beginning of Bismarck's Revolution from Above.[44] In the Franco-Prussian war of 1870, Bismarck continued his work for the German bourgeoisie: he united all Germany.[45] For a generation he carried on his Revolution from Above, gradually weeding out feudalism until Germany had become a modern nation.[46]

In the thirteenth and fourteenth centuries Italy lay along the world trade route, and the bourgeoisie in its northern cities grew rich and strong. Capitalist manufacture blossomed in Florence; Venice controlled Europe's commerce with the East. In the sixteenth century the trade route shifted to the Atlantic seaboard. Italy's capitalism collapsed; her cities deindustrialized; and the bourgeoisie weakened. For centuries the Italian states were governed by foreign powers. Only in the nineteenth century did the bourgeois revolution flare up to unify and free Italy. Thus the Italian bourgeoisie, the first to begin the long march out of feudalism, was among the last to finish.[47]

During the nineteenth century in Spain the bourgeois revolution flickered on and off–like a broken light. In the struggle against Napoleon the bourgeoisie set up a radical constitution (1812), but at war's end the country lapsed into feudal reaction. The revolution returned to the attack, and the Spanish army became its driving force. As the century rolled by, the liberal army revolted again and again, yet the bourgeoisie was too weak to transform society, and each attempt ended in exhausting civil wars. In 1873 a republic emerged, but collapsed the next year. There were five periods of civil war and revolutionary struggle: 1808–1814, 1820–1823, 1834–1843, 1854–1856, and 1868–1874. The bourgeois revolution dominated the history of nineteenth-century Spain, but could not conquer the country.[48]

Even the great revolution in seventeenth-century England, though it broke the political bonds of feudalism, ended in compromise between the bourgeoisie and a fraction of the nobility (1689). This fraction ruled England in the interest of the bourgeoisie. For a century the compromise underwent gradual changes in favor of the bourgeoisie, but only in 1832 did the industrialists win direct political power. In this sense the English Revolution had a gradualist character.[49]

Thus in Europe the bourgeois revolution differed from country to country. The passage from the feudal to the capitalist epoch developed slowly, produced occasional violence, and dragged on for centuries. "Epochs in the history of society," Marx writes, "are no more separated from each other by hard and fast lines of demarcation than are geological epochs."[50]

In Europe as a whole the transition from feudalism to capitalism spanned centuries of historical evolution. Engels sees this as a single gigantic process: from the twelfth to the nineteenth century the revolution rose in wave after wave, each stronger than the last, until it flowed over the walls of feudal society. In the French towns of the twelfth and thirteenth centuries the Albigenses struggled against the Catholic Church, the international center of feudalism. In the fourteenth century the movement broke out with greater force in England: the Wycliffites launched powerful attacks on the feudal Church. In the fifteenth century the Hussite movement in Bohemia became a national revolt against the feudal power of Catholicism. Finally in the sixteenth century the first success came in Germany–the Lutheran Reformation broke the Church. The Reformation spread across Europe, and triumphed in Switzerland, Holland, England, Scotland, Denmark, and Sweden. This was the first triumph of the bourgeois revolution, though only of its religious form. In the seventeenth century came the breakthrough of the bourgeois content: the Puritan Revolution in England, a revolution that ended in compromise. In the eighteenth century the French Revolution was the greatest triumph of the bourgeoisie. It smashed the Church, and undermined feudalism in other parts of Europe. The nineteenth century saw the dying down of bourgeois political revolution before a threatening proletariat: German business groups begged the Hohenzollern government to finish the modernization of the country from above. This was done, and capitalist economic evolution accelerated.[51]

Why did the bourgeois revolution take the form of attacks on the Catholic Church in the early centuries? The Church united Western Europe into one political system opposed to both Byzantium and Islam; it crowned feudal institutions with a halo of divine blessing; it had organized its own hierarchy along feudal lines and had become the most powerful feudal lord, for it owned at least one-third of the land of Catholic Europe.[52]

The first revolts against feudalism *were bound to be attacks on the Catholic Church*.[53]

The bourgeois plebeian heresies had two aims: the reform of the Church and the reform of society. First, the heretics wanted to reform the Church by getting rid of popes, cardinals, bishops, and monks. This would make the Church cheaper to run, and the bourgeois could pocket the savings. Second, the heretics wanted to reform society by bringing back primitive Christian equality. For nobles, peasants, bourgeois, and plebeians there was to be equality before the law and even some equality of property.[54]

The bourgeois plebian movement of the Middle Ages had two wings: a moderate wing of bourgeois, and a radical wing of plebeians and peasants. (The plebeians were the day laborers, servants, and unemployed of the towns–the preproletariat; the peasants were the mass of the population.) The moderate bourgeois wanted only the first reform, a cheaper Church; the plebeians and peasants wanted this and the second reform as well–primitive Christian equality.[55]

The first great outbreak of the bourgeois plebeian movement was the Albigensian heresy.[56] In the twelfth and thirteenth centuries this heresy spread through southern France, Italy, and the Balkans; the French towns were its stronghold. The Albigenses wanted to abolish the Catholic Church and create equality.[57] The Church crushed the movement.

In the fourteenth century the next outbreak of the bourgeois plebeian movement took place in England: the Wycliffites attacked the Church. The moderate bourgeois wanted to abolish the costly Church hierarchy–and that was all. The plebeian peasant wing split off and became an independent party in Wat Tyler's Rebellion (1381). This mass rebellion failed, and the Wycliffites suffered cruel persecution.[58]

In the fifteenth century the Hussite Revolt, the next outbreak of the bourgeois plebeian movement, took place in Bohemia. This was the great heresy of the century and became a national revolution. The movement soon split into a bourgeois moderate wing and a plebeian revolutionary one: the Calixtines wanted a cheaper Church, and the Taborites wanted communism. This split ruined the movement.[59]

In the sixteenth century the next outbreak of the bourgeois plebeian movement occurred in Germany–the Reformation. For the first time the movement had some success–the triumph of its religious form. (The bourgeois content did not triumph.) Germany's strong economic position caused this breakthrough: at the beginning of the sixteenth century, the world trade route from India to Scandinavia still lay across Germany, and the gold and silver mines were booming there. Thus the Germans had some success where the English and the Bohemians had failed.[60]

The Reformation in Germany soon split into the bourgeois moderate and plebeian peasant wings,[61] and that weakened it.[62] The world trade route slowly shifted from Germany to the Atlantic seaboard; this broke the power of the bourgeoisie and the German Reformation.[63] But it dealt powerful blows to the feudal Church.

In the form of the Reformation, the bourgeois plebeian movement spilled out of Germany and flowed across Europe. The religious form triumphed in several countries: Switzerland, Holland, England, Scotland, Denmark, and Sweden.[64] The European Reformation–the first great success against feudalism–was Bourgeois Revolution No. 1.[65] The religious wars that raged across Europe were class wars.[66] The Catholic Church, the bulwark of feudalism, was shaken to its foundations and abolished in several countries.

With the shift of the world trade route to the Atlantic, the revolution surged up again in Holland and England, where it once more assumed a religious form. But for the first time the bourgeois content scored a success.[67] The Great Puritan Revolution in seventeenth-century England was Bourgeois Revolution No. 2.[68] The usual split between the bourgeoisie and the plebeian radicals[69] did not ruin the movement. The bourgeoisie allied itself with the modern nobility against the monarchy, feudal nobility, and established Church.[70] The feudal political order weakened, and the revolution resulted in a compromise between the bourgeoisie and the modern nobility: the modern nobility ruled the country in the bourgeoisie's interest, and the state Church was further Protestantized.[71]

Bourgeois Revolution No. 3 was the Great French Revolution of the eighteenth century.[72] The most powerful revolution in history threw off the religious disguise–freethinkers attacked the Church. For the first time the revolution dealt mortal blows to feudalism.[73] The plebeian radicals gained the mastery during the Reign of Terror,[74] and the bourgeoisie took refuge from them in Napoleon's despotism.[75] The revolution reached out to Belgium, Holland, Germany, Switzerland, and Italy: it was a revolution of European scope.[76] In the reaction that followed (1815–1830), the French bourgeoisie lost political power, but regained it in the revolutions of 1830 and 1848.[77]

France and England, then, had completed their bourgeois political revolutions by the nineteenth century. These were revolutions in which the bourgeoisie fought its way to power, and they were the last of their kind. After 1830 the bourgeoisie was frightened by the growing proletariat: it shrank from starting a revolution that the plebeian radicals might finish. In the revolutions that swept Europe in 1848, the bourgeoisie everywhere betrayed the antifeudal movement. After that year the frightened bourgeoisie turned against revolution, and monarchial governments began to pull out the weeds of economic feudalism from above. The age of bourgeois political revolution was drawing to a close.[78]

In Engels' historical vision, the bourgeois revolution is a process that develops through 800 years. It begins in the Middle Ages with the emergence of the towns, the cradle of the bourgeoisie. It rises in wave after wave, each stronger than the last, and breaks against the feudal barrier. Finally it sweeps away feudal political forms in the leading countries of Western Europe, then slowly subsides in the nineteenth century.

To make Engels' historical view clear I have simplified it, and it may appear too schematic: each revolution seems merely a bourgeois thrust toward power. But Engels sees every revolution as a complicated affair in which many classes took part. The peasantry did most of the fighting.[79] A fraction of the nobility always joined the bourgeoisie against die-hard aristocrats, princes, and priests.[80] In each revolution the bourgeoisie found allies in the mass of plebeians and peasants, but at a certain stage most bourgeois drew back in fear, and a radical minority drove the revolution onward with mass support.[81]

Religious heresy, Protestantism, national liberation struggles—the bourgeois plebeian movement assumed many *forms*. But the movement was bourgeois in *content*. What does this mean?

First, under feudalism there was only one kind of ideology: religion. And so the economic aspirations of the bourgeoisie assumed a religious form. Since all people fed at the trough of religion, their material interests found expression as religious beliefs. The Calvinists thought they wanted a republicanized Church, but what they really desired was a capitalist republic.[82]

Second, the whole historical movement was in the hands of the bourgeoisie. As the modern world emerged from the Middle Ages, there were many battles against the old order: religious reformations, national movements, economic struggles. The enemy was always feudalism; every attack on feudalism favored the bourgeoisie, and the fruits of every victory fell to the bourgeoisie. It was the class that held the future in its hands.[83]

But the bourgeoisie, though an active class in every revolution, was not always its driving force. In the Great French Revolution, for example, the plebeian radicals drove the revolution forward and fought the main battles against the old regime: the Bastille, the October Days, the storming of the Tuilleries, and the defense of Paris. They fought for the bourgeois slogan of *Equality*, and after the revolution they learned what this meant: equality before the law, and exploitation of the masses. With the triumph of the bourgeois content, equality turned into its opposite. This is the irony of history.[84]

Bourgeois revolution is no simple affair, and we may ask how Marx's concept of revolution applies to it. Let us look at the model he sets forth in the preface of 1859. There he writes of the productive forces, the relations of production corresponding to them, and a superstructure of legal and political institutions surrounded by ideologies. At a certain stage of their development, he says, the productive forces clash with the relations of production. Then follows an epoch of social revolution. The changes in the economic foundation of society bring about a gradual transformation of the superstructure.[85]

The French Revolution suggested this abstract model to Marx. During his formative period he had immersed himself in French history, especially the study of the Great Revolution. Engels later describes that formative period as follows: "All of us, as far as our conceptions of the conditions and the course of revolutionary movements were concerned, were under the spell of previous historical experience, particularly that of France."[86] Marx and Engels view France as the "typical country" for the political development of Europe.[87] "The center of feudalism in the Middle Ages, the model country of unified monarchy resting on estates since the Renaissance, France demolished feudalism in the Great Revolution and established the rule of the bourgeoisie in a classical purity unequalled by any other European land."[88]

Marx used this abstract model to study several revolutions, but it best fits the French Revolution and the future Communist Revolution. Marx knew this; he did not apply his model to all revolutions in a schematic way.

We have seen that Marx and Engels often applied it in a flexible manner. In analyzing a nation's passage from feudalism to capitalism, they didn't always find one climactic moment, *the* revolution. They described a cumulative, epochal process, with more than one critical transition. They never became slaves of the model.

Like all historical thinkers, they needed a conceptual framework for their

studies; so they developed this model of historical change. As they studied
the rise of the bourgeoisie in modern history, they used the model to analyze
the crest of the world revolutionary wave coming out of the Middle Ages:

$$
\begin{array}{ccc}
 & 1789 & \\
1648 & & 1830 \\
1525 & & 1848 \\
1415 & & \\
1381 & &
\end{array}
$$

"The bourgeoisie, historically, has played a most revolutionary role," writes
Marx. "An oppressed class under the sway of the feudal nobility, an armed
and self-governing association in the medieval commune; here independent
urban republic (as in Italy and Germany), there taxable 'third estate' of the
monarchy (as in France), afterwards in the period of manufacture proper,
serving either the semifeudal or the absolute monarchy as a counterpoise
against the nobility, and in fact cornerstone of the great monarchies in general, the bourgeoisie has at last, since the establishment of modern industry
and of the world market, conquered for itself in the modern representative
state exclusive political sway."[89] Modern history is the story of the bourgeois
revolution against feudalism.

What caused the breakdown of feudalism?

In Marx's analysis a growth of productive forces caused a shift from feudalism toward capitalism: crafts diminished before manufacture, and bourgeois
political revolutions followed (1500 to 1800), paving the way for the emergence
of mature industrial capitalism. For the beginnings of capitalism, Marx and Engels stress the importance of the Great Discoveries—the sea-lanes to America and the East (c. 1500).

Europeans discovered civilizations in the Americas, enslaved them to work
the silver mines, and shipped bullion home for a century. "The treasures captured outside Europe by undisguised looting, enslavement, and murder,"
writes Marx, "floated back to the mother country and were there turned into
capital."[90] The capital went into trade and manufacture, especially in the Low
Countries and England. In the sixteenth, seventeenth, and eighteenth centuries there was a growth of manufacture in Europe.

The Great Discoveries led to colonies, an expanding market, and demand
for manufactured goods. Manufactures in certain seaboard nations thrived and
grew, for they were countries geared to trade. "In the period of manufacture
properly so called," says Marx, "it is trading supremacy that gives industrial
predominance."[91] The trading nations lived for the new world market. This mar-

ket steadily broadened; it stretched out from Borneo to Peru, it cried for European goods. The guilds could not meet demand, and manufacture pushed them aside.

What quickened manufacturing capitalism during this period? Why did urban guilds decay while manufactories appeared in the countryside? What accelerated the growth of the new work relations, modes of cooperation, and division of labor? Marx lists three accelerators of the rise of manufacture: the formation of capital by looting the planet, the expansion of the market through colonization, and the appearance of a proletariat in Europe.[92] Again and again Marx and Engels mention these factors working toward the transformation of feudalism into capitalism.[93] The first two factors, capital formation and market expansion, resulted mainly from the Great Discoveries: in the sixteenth century the Europeans, armed with compass and gunpowder, sailed onto the seven seas to conquer.

The Great Discoveries cannot be repeated; they changed the world forever. The bourgeoisie looted the world and industrialized Europe. They "made barbarian and semibarbarian countries dependent on the civilized ones, nations of peasants on nations of bourgeois," writes Marx.[94] "They also forcibly rooted out in their dependent countries all industry."[95] They changed the economic relationships of the planet for hundreds of years.

If Marx's conception of the original accumulation of capital in Europe is correct, it means that much of modern Development Economics is on the wrong track. Marxists like Ernest Mandel in his essay "Die Marxsche Theorie der ursprünglichen Akkumulation und die Industrialisierung der Dritten Welt" claim that modern research has fully confirmed Marx's idea. But this is an exaggeration, for not much research has been done on the subject. What research there is tends to confirm Marx's view that huge sums flowed to Europe from sixteenth-century Mexico and eighteenth-century India.

In analyzing the growth of productive forces in Europe during the sixteenth, seventeenth, and eighteenth centuries, we must remember this: the world situation of that time is not repeatable. We can't transfer Marx's analysis to other ages. His analysis of the rise of capitalism points to the conflict between productive forces and feudal relations. This analysis can throw light on civilizations beyond Europe only if we remember the different relations of production, the different forces at work in them, *and the different world contexts*.

The Great Discoveries did not *cause* the shift from feudalism toward capitalism. The Discoveries, says Marx, were only an accelerator.[96] Before them capitalist manufacture had already arisen in the Low Countries.[97] Then came the Discoveries (c. 1500 A.D.) to spur the growth of this capitalism in Flanders and Holland. In the sixteenth century the Flemish metropolis of Antwerp became the center of infant European capitalism; in the seventeenth century there was more capital in the Dutch Republic than in the rest of Europe put together.[98] Holland's empire reached around the globe, and it completed its bourgeois political revolution in the seventeenth century. By contrast, feudal Portugal started in 1500 with a fabulous empire but no manufacture. Portugal lost her eastern empire to the Dutch. And the gold and silver of the Americas leaked out of medieval Spain to the European bourgeoisie in Amsterdam.[99]

Continuing Revolution

We have seen how from 1500 to 1800 capitalist manufacture put down some roots in the leading countries of Western Europe, and bourgeois revolutions exploded the feudal political forms. During this period the advance in productive forces resulted in a shift toward a new mode of production. A centuries-long social revolution began its triumphant march toward a new order–feudalism gradually evolved toward capitalism.

Only in the eighteenth century did the capitalist mode of production and exchange really become dominant, and this happened only in England. "In 1735 John Wyatt brought out his spinning machine, and began the industrial revolution of the eighteenth century."[100] Throughout the century in England steam and the new machines were changing manufacture into modern industry. This transformed the foundation of bourgeois society. The slow developmental tempo of the manufacturing period turned into a mad gallop toward industrialization.[101]

The transition from craft manufacture to machine industry was a dramatic advance in productive forces, and in the nineteenth century these new forces outgrew the capitalist mode of production and distribution.[102] Marx and Engels argue that the productive forces of machine industry were rebelling against the capitalist mode:

> Just as at a definite stage of its development manufacture came into conflict with the feudal order of production, so now large-scale industry has already come into conflict with the bourgeois order of production established in its place. Tied down by this order, by the narrow limits of the capitalist mode of production, this industry produces, on the one hand, an ever-increasing proletarianization of the great mass of the people, and on the other hand, an ever greater mass of unsalable products. Overproduction and mass misery, each the cause of the other–that is the absurd contradiction which is its outcome and which calls for the libera-

tion of the productive forces by means of a change in the mode of production.[103]

This change in the mode of production can come only through socialist revolution: capitalism must pass into communism. And who will make this revolution? The new class of wage laborers, the class of propertyless workers–the industrial proletariat. The factory-employed working class will create communism.[104]

The proletariat is the class with no means of production, no income-producing property. It divides into factions: the lumpenproletariat of unemployed beggars, thieves, prostitutes, and tramps; and the industrial proletariat employed in railways, mines, and factories. Throughout the nineteenth century, Marx and Engels argued that the agency of socialist revolution was the industrial proletariat. Through all their writings runs the theme that socialism must be the work of the laborers themselves.[105] In an international revolution the workers will overthrow the ruling classes and begin the construction of communism. "This act of universal emancipation is the historical mission of the modern proletariat."[106]

Why did the founders of Marxism see the factory proletariat as revolutionary, a view that some Marxists no longer hold? The answer is clear: during the nineteenth century, social conditions drove the proletariat toward revolution, while in the twentieth century these conditions have often disappeared (though a few may reappear if capitalism sickens in the closing decades of this century). For Marx's description of these conditions see the appendix.

Marx and Engels thought that the proletarian class, not a political party, would be the agent of revolution. But not even the class would really *make* the revolution, for revolutions are not made–they happen.[107] "Revolutions are not made intentionally and arbitrarily," writes Engels in 1847, "everywhere and always they have been the necessary consequence of conditions which were wholly independent of the will and direction of individual parties and entire classes."[108] He and Marx counted on a spontaneous European revolution.

For thinking about the European revolution they developed two strategical categories–the concept of mass revolution and the concept of continuing revolution. These concepts complement each other. In their political writings the founders of Marxism use first one concept, now the other, depending on the area under analysis, England or the Continent.

The concept of mass revolution applies to the key capitalist country of the nineteenth century: England. The center of international capitalism, the despot of the world market, and the owner of an empire, England finished its industrial revolution by 1850. There the productive forces of machine industry had first rebelled against the capitalist mode of production: economic crises shook England (and world capitalism) to its foundations. Machine industry produced too many goods; poorly paid workers could not buy them; and factories shut down.[109] Engels describes the usual crisis thus: "Commerce is at a standstill, the markets are glutted, products accumulate, as multitudinous as they are unsalable, hard cash disappears, credit vanishes, factories are closed, the mass of the workers are in want of the means of subsistence, because they have produced too much of the means of subsistence; bankruptcy follows upon bankruptcy."[110] These crises were getting worse.[111] On the one hand, this industry proletarianized the great mass of the people, and on the other hand, it produced more and more products no one could buy.[112] In every crisis the proletariat grew larger.[113] The economic crises, write Marx and Engels in the *Manifesto*, periodically return to threaten the very existence of bourgeois society, each commercial collapse more terrible than the last.[114] Marx and Engels have a vision of the final crisis: "Simultaneously the working classes revolt because of underconsumption and the upper classes go bankrupt through overproduction."[115] The process of capital accumulation was working toward a mass revolution. Marx's model of capitalist development splits this process into its parts and shows the relations between them.

(1) The period of competitive capitalism opens with three main classes on the scene: the bourgeoisie (big owners), the petty bourgeoisie (small owners), and the proletariat (nonowners). The bourgeoisie is the class of capitalists, owners of factories, banks, lands, mines, buildings, and railways.[116] The huge petty bourgeoisie is the class of small owners: the shopkeepers with their bit of capital, the artisans with their tiny workshops, and the peasants with their plots of ground.[117] The proletariat is the class with nothing at all—the workers in factories, mines, and plantations.[118]

(2) The size of each class changes. The bourgeoisie grows smaller and smaller, as the capitalists drive one another out of business: "one capitalist always kills many."[119] The petty bourgeoisie grows smaller and smaller, for the shopkeeper can't compete with big stores, nor the artisan with factories, nor the peasant with agribusiness.[120] The petty bourgeoisie is doomed. "The individual members of this class are being constantly hurled down into the proletariat. . . . They will completely disappear as an independent section of modern society."[121] The size—and the misery—of the proletariat steadily increases.[122] Marx sums up in a sentence: "Thus the proletariat is recruited from all classes of the population."[123]

(3) "The middle classes must increasingly disappear until the world is divided into millionaires and paupers."[124] Capitalist society winds up with two classes directly facing each other: a handful of bourgeois and a sea of proletarians.[125]

A social revolution begins. "We have the expropriation of a few usurpers by the mass of the people."[126] This mass revolution is the work of the proletarian majority–the people rise spontaneously. "The proletarian movement is the self-conscious, independent movement of the immense majority, in the interests of the immense majority. The proletariat . . . cannot raise itself up without the whole superincumbent stratum of official society being sprung into the air."[127]

(4) With the overthrow of the bourgeoisie, we are left with an association of workers in a classless society.[128]

This idea of majority revolution applied to England, the advanced capitalism of the nineteenth century. England was one hundred years ahead of the Continent. In the 1840s when Marx and Engels developed their theory, France and Germany began industrialization as England brought its industrial revolution to completion. In England the peasants were gone and the proletariat was enormous: the country seemed near mass revolution. But in France and Germany the peasants made up most of the population.[129]

This situation continued through the second half of the nineteenth century. During the lifetimes of Marx and Engels, the concept of majority revolution fit only England. "It is the only country where there are no more peasants and where property in land is concentrated in a few hands," writes Marx in 1870. "It is the only country where the great majority of the population consists of wage laborers."[130] This was still true in 1894: peasants formed the majority in every country on the Continent.[131] There could be no mass revolution of the proletariat there.

For the countries of the Continent, Marx and Engels developed another concept of minority or continuing revolution. (On a few occasions they spoke of this revolution as "permanent."[132]) In this conception the revolution explodes in a backward country and attacks the remains of feudalism. But the revolution does not stop halfway; it keeps on going until emergent capitalism also disappears. In France and Germany it passes from one stage to another and brings the proletarian minority to power. The proletariat leads the nation toward a new world: the revolution continues straight into communism.

The revolution has an international character: it blazes up in one country after another, until all Europe is in flames. Here the tradition of the French Revolution–the greatest revolution that history had ever produced[133]–was again the formative influence on the political thought of Marx and Engels.[134] This revolution surged up in France and spilled across Europe, smashing feudal institutions everywhere and transforming the Continent. The revolutionary epoch lasted through twenty-five years and embraced uprisings, terror, civil war, and battles of peoples.[135]

From the 1840s onward, Marx and Engels expected the Communist Revolution to be like that, but on a larger scale: it would be the biggest revolution history had yet seen.[136] It would open in France.[137] Once the republicans had begun the revolution, the Paris proletariat would seize power.[138] The revolution would sweep on across Europe, infecting one country after another.[139] In Germany the bourgeoisie would smash feudalism, and then fall victim to an uprising of the young proletariat.[140] The revolution would leap over the channel to ignite England: in the most advanced country, the proletariat would rise *en masse* and begin the construction of communism.[141] In feudal Europe –Poland, Hungary, Austria, Bohemia, Croatia, Wallachia, Moldavia–democrats and nationalists would tear down the old empires and set up republics. "The big agrarian countries between the Baltic and the Black Seas can free themselves from patriarchal feudal barbarism only by an agrarian revolution which turns the peasants who are held down or liable to labor services into free landowners, a revolution which would be similar to the French Revolution of 1789 in the countryside."[142] All revolutionary countries would unite against Russian tsarism: an international crusade against the Gendarme of Europe must guarantee the freedom of the peoples–through a world war.[143] All revolutionaries hated tsarism in the 1840s.

On the Continent there would be a long period of disorder. If there were Russian victories, aristocrats and bourgeois might stage uprisings against proletarian governments, just as counterrevolutions had flamed up in France in the 1790s.[144] The proletariat must confiscate the property of all emigrants and rebels,[145] put down Vendées and Girondist revolts wherever they occur, and gradually force the bourgeois from the banks, factories, mines, shipyards, and railways.[146]

The proletariats of Germany and France, at the helm of the revolution on the Continent, would struggle to build up the productive forces.[147] They would even organize industrial armies.[148] England, an advanced country with a communist government, could offer material aid.[149] Once communism had taken root in Western Europe, it would draw the rest of the world into its orbit by economic force alone.[150]

During the years 1789 to 1795, the height of the Great French Revolution, one party followed another into power, each more radical than the last, until the Jacobins seized control. For a year this "Party of the Mountain" represented the Paris proletariat (1793–94). It smashed feudalism and struggled for a centralized republic. Then the Mountain crumbled into ruin, for the proletariat was too weak to rule. But in the 1840s the proletariat had grown stronger, reasoned Marx and Engels, and could revolutionize the old society once and for all. First a democratic revolution would sweep kings and priests from Europe; then bourgeois radicals would clear away the debris of feudalism;

and finally the proletariat would take power. "In all civilized lands," writes Engels in 1847, "the democratic movement strives in the last instance for the political rule of the proletariat."[151] And Marx is just as hopeful: "The Jacobin of 1793 has become the Communist of our day."[152] The two men see an analogy between the Jacobin phase of the French Revolution and the proletarian phase of the Permanent Revolution: "During the short time that the proletariat sat at the helm of state in the French Revolution, during the rule of the Party of the Mountain, it carried through centralization with all means, with cartridges and with guillotine. The democratic proletariat—when it once again takes power—will not only have to centralize each country in itself, but as soon as possible must centralize all civilized countries together."[153] The communist regime would fuse all nations in a classless society, in a universal brotherhood and sisterhood of the proletariat.

In the year 1848, revolution broke out in France and swept through Austria, Hungary, Germany, and the Italian states. The founders of Marxism thought that the Great Communist Revolution had begun. But the revolutions of 1848 did not fulfill the vision of Marx and Engels. In France the bourgeoisie crushed a proletarian insurrection; in Germany a section of the bourgeoisie went over to the feudal reaction; in Austria-Hungary a Russian invasion returned the reaction to power. The revolutions fizzled. They would have fit the Marxist vision "only if they had not been the conclusion but the starting point of a long revolutionary movement in which, as in the Great French Revolution, the people would have developed further through its own struggles and the parties become more and more sharply differentiated until they had coincided entirely with the great classes, bourgeoisie, petty bourgeoisie, and proletariat, and in which the separate positions would have been won one after another by the proletariat in a series of battles."[154]

But Marx and Engels did not despair: they expected the revolution to break out again, stronger than ever. The year 1848–49 seemed only the first stage of the continuing revolution. In 1849 Marx draws an analogy between it and the English Revolution of the seventeenth century: "The struggle in England lasted over twenty years [1640–1660]. Charles I came out on top several times and ended up on the scaffold." And the present revolution? "We have seen only the first act of the drama."[155] The next act, better than the first, must soon follow.

Marx and Engels looked for this event in 1850. According to their expectation, the proletariat would seize power in France, then the bourgeois revolution would flare up again in semifeudal Germany,[156] where two parties would lead the revolution—the democrats and the communists. The democratic party would represent revolutionary bourgeois and the vast petty bourgeoisie; the

Communist League would guide the small proletariat.[157] Marx lays down the communist strategy for the German revolution:

> While the democratic petty bourgeois wish to bring the revolution to a conclusion as quickly as possible . . . it is our interest and our task to make the revolution permanent, until all more or less possessing classes have been forced out of their position of dominance, until the proletariat has conquered state power, and the association of proletarians, not only in one country but in all the dominant countries of the world, has advanced so far that competition among the proletarians of these countries has ceased and at least the decisive productive forces are concentrated in the hands of the proletarians. . . . Their battle cry must be: The Revolution in Permanence.[158]

In this passage lies the whole concept of continuing revolution. In backward Germany the aristocracy will be overthrown by the bourgeoisie, but the revolution does not stop halfway: the bourgeoisie will then be overthrown by the proletariat. The revolution must continue across Europe until the proletariat is in power "in all the dominant countries of the world." This means war. Proletarian communism in Germany and France can survive only by spreading the revolution to England. "The class war within French society turns into a world war, in which the nations confront one another. Accomplishment begins only at the moment when, through the world war, the proletariat is pushed to the head of the people that dominates the world market, to the head of England."[159] How does this come about? The English bourgeoisie declares war on revolutionary France. The war provides the English Chartists with conditions for a successful rising, and the proletariat takes power.[160] The revolutionary nations then unite to destroy tsarist Russia or be destroyed by her–the world war rages on. Everything hangs in the balance "until the proletarian revolution and the feudalistic counterrevolution measure swords in a *world war*."[161]

With the proletarian majority revolution in England the Great Communist Revolution will only have begun. "The revolution, which finds here not its end, but its organizational beginning, is no short-lived revolution. The present generation is like the Jews whom Moses led through the wilderness. It not only has a new world to conquer, it must go under in order to make room for the men who are able to cope with a new world."[162] War, revolution, counterrevolution, popular struggles, social reorganization, industrial development, and the remaking of circumstances and people lie ahead. Through generations of struggle they advance toward the communist society.

This was Marx's and Engels' revolutionary perspective in early 1850. It was not borne out by events: the Communist Revolution failed to come, and by the summer of 1850 Marx realized that it would not come right away.[163] But he did not abandon his vision; he believed that the revolution had merely been postponed.

He decided that the revolution could arrive only during an economic crisis. An economic crisis, he reasoned, must always begin in England, the workshop of the world, the heart of world capitalism. From England the crisis would spread to the backward capitalism of the Continent. Capitalism was unstable in these areas, and insurrections must break out on the Continent. These insurrections would cause a reaction in England and trigger mass revolution there.[164]

In the 1850s the Tai Ping Rebellion in China caused chaos in England's eastern market. Marx thinks this might hasten the economic crisis in England: "If one of the great markets suddenly becomes contracted, the arrival of the crisis is necessarily accelerated thereby. Now the Chinese rebellion must for the time being have precisely this effect upon England."[165] Sparks from the Chinese Revolution, falling upon faraway England, must "cause the explosion of the long-prepared general crisis, which, spreading abroad, will be closely followed by political revolutions on the Continent."[166]

The economic crisis came in 1857. It was a tremendous crash, yet not severe enough to cause revolution. This event disappointed Marx. But he clung to the view worked out in 1850: sooner or later a great crisis would trigger an all-European revolution.[167]

The 1850s were a period of political reaction, but in the 1860s there was an upsurge of the workers' movement. "When the working class of Europe had again gathered sufficient strength for a new onslaught upon the power of the ruling classes, the International Working Men's Association came into being. Its aim was to weld together into *one* huge army the whole militant working class of Europe and America."[168] In 1864 Marx drew up the rules for the First International, in which he reaffirms the principles of continuing revolution: "The emancipation of labor is neither a local nor a national, but a social problem, embracing all countries in which modern society exists, and depending for its solution on the concurrence, practical and theoretical, of the most advanced countries."[169] The movement of the 1860s reached a climax in the proletarian insurrection of 1871–the Paris Commune. Standing alone, the Commune soon collapsed. Marx sees this as another confirmation of his thesis that the revolution must be universal: "The revolution needs solidarity, and we have a great example of it in the Paris Commune, which fell because a revolutionary movement corresponding to that supreme rising of the Paris proletariat did not arise in all centers, in Berlin, Madrid, and elsewhere."[170]

When Marx died, Engels continued to defend his basic ideas. In the 1880s he reaffirmed the strategy of the continuing revolution.[171]

In the 1890s Engels preached international revolution to the French. "If the revolution breaks out in France first, say in 1894, then Germany follows suit at once and then the Franco-German proletarian Alliance forces the hand of England," writes Engels to the chief theoretician of French Marxism, "then we have a revolutionary war against Russia–if not even a revolutionary echo from Russia."[172] This was the vision that Marx and Engels had entertained for half a century. "It would mean the achievement of what we have foreseen and predicted for many years. The French give the signal, open fire, and the Germans decide the battle."[173] That is, the Germans would decide the battle in Western Europe. "Neither France nor Germany will ensure final victory so long as England remains in the hands of the bourgeoisie. Proletarian emancipation can be only an international deed."[174]

Marx and Engels clung to the concept of continuing revolution throughout their lives. Only in his last months did Engels modify the concept.[175]

In his masterwork, *Capital*, Marx hardly mentions social revolution, and even then talks only of majority revolution. Most readers take the two pages on majority revolution in the first volume[176] as final, and apply the concept to all nations. They forget that *Capital* is the beginning of a work many, many volumes long, a work Marx did not finish: only a fraction of his system appears there.[177] Elsewhere we learn that the concept of majority revolution applies to England, while a concept of continuing revolution covered all Europe.

Continuing revolution is based on what Marx calls "the international character of the capitalist regime."[178] Marx and Engels never tire of repeating that the capitalist system is not made up of independent national capitalisms existing in isolation; capitalism is an international system.[179] In fact, the integrating force of the world market has drawn all the peoples of the earth into the capitalist network.[180]

We have seen how the first beginnings of manufacturing capitalism were accelerated by the Great Discoveries of sea routes to America and Asia, discoveries that created the world market.[181] "At one stroke the size of the world had increased nearly tenfold. Instead of only a quadrant of a hemisphere the whole globe was now open to the gaze of the West Europeans who hastened to take possession of the other seven quadrants."[182] Western Europe soon owned large pieces of the globe, and its navies, outposts, and trading stations were everywhere.

The emergence of industrial capitalism three centuries later increased the international organization of production, international division of labor, and international exchange.[183] In the *Manifesto* Marx explains it like this:

> All old established national industries have been destroyed or are daily being destroyed. They are dislodged by new industries, whose in-

troduction becomes a life and death question for all civilized nations, by industries that no longer work up indigenous raw material but raw material drawn from the remotest zones, industries whose products are consumed not only at home but in every quarter of the globe. In place of the old wants satisfied by the productions of the country we find new wants requiring for their satisfaction the products of distant lands and climes. In place of the old local and national seclusion and self-sufficiency we have commerce in every direction, universal interdependence of nations.[184]

The framework of the capitalist economy is the world market.[185]

In Marx's time the center of this market was England, "the country that turns whole nations into her proletarians."[186] In 1849 Marx describes the European economy as follows: "Industrial and commercial relations within each nation are governed by its trade with other nations and depend on its relations with the world market. But the world market is dominated by England. . . ."[187] Around England, the hub of the British Empire, revolved a global economy. "England cannot be treated simply as one country among a number of other countries," writes Marx in 1870. "She must be treated as the metropolis of capitalism."[188] Near this metropolis lay satellite countries where industrialization was only beginning–France, Germany, Belgium; and beyond these were the colonies and semicolonies: India, Indonesia, Canada, Australia, China, Japan, Latin America.[189] In their analysis of revolution Marx and Engels focus on this world system, the capitalist social formation.

For them, internal conflicts drive every social formation toward a higher mode of production and distribution. The productive forces, Marx explains in the preface of 1859, explode the relations of production and initiate an era of social revolution. "No social formation ever perishes before all the productive forces for which there is room in it have developed; and new, higher relations of production never appear before the material conditions of their existence have matured in the womb of the old society itself. . . . or are at least in the process of forming."[190]

In these famous lines Marx is not talking about a single country; he has in mind a social formation. How do his theoretical principles apply to the formation of international capitalism? In that system a high level of productive forces already existed, for its center was England–a developed industrial area. The conflict between productive forces and relations of production spread from England throughout the formation of European capitalism, even into backward countries like Germany.

Semifeudal Germany was a backward country, but the international conflict between productive forces and relations of production was driving it toward proletarian revolution. In 1845 Marx and Engels give an explanation for this:

All collisions in history have their origin, according to our view, in the contradiction between the productive forces and the [relations of production]. Incidentally, to lead to collisions in a country this contradiction need not necessarily have reached its extreme limit in this particular country. The competition with industrially more advanced countries brought about by the expansion of international commerce is sufficient to produce a similar contradiction in countries with a backward industry (for example, the latent proletariat in Germany brought into view by the competition of English industry).[191]

Germany was trapped in the network of international capitalism, entangled in the meshes of the world market, and exposed to English competition. Power looms in England forced Germany to use machines in its weaving industry; and many workers in Silesia, dependent on hand weaving for a living, were driven by hunger to revolt. According to Marx, the Silesian Weavers' Revolt was the debut of the German working class on the stage of history. In Germany, he writes in 1847, "the political misery of the absolute monarchy still exists with an entire appendage of decadent half-feudal relations and classes. But because of industrial development and Germany's dependence on the world market, there already partially exist the modern antagonisms between bourgeoisie and working class and the resulting struggle. Examples of this struggle are the worker revolts in Silesia and Bohemia."[192]

The revolt of the Silesian weavers in 1844 greatly impressed Marx. "The Silesian uprising begins precisely where the French and English labor revolts end, with the consciousness of the nature of the proletariat," he writes in 1844. "The action itself bears this superior character. Not only the machines, the rivals of the workers, are destroyed but also account books and titles to property. While all other movements were directed first of all against the visible enemy, the industrial lord, this movement is at the same time directed against the hidden enemy, the banker."[193] The Silesian revolt, thinks Marx, is a foretaste of proletarian revolution.

Thus in backward Germany as in advanced England, economic development was driving society toward proletarian revolution. All the productive powers for which there was room in the world capitalist organism had developed in its heart. "The English have all the material requirements for the social revolution."[194] And once "the metropolis of capital"[195] had fallen, capitalism would die everywhere, for England was the "country where every revolution in its economic conditions must cause a direct reaction in the entire world."[196]

The concept of continuing revolution fits a social formation containing ripe capitalism (England), budding capitalism (France, Germany), and pockets of feudalism (East Prussia). In the area of ripe capitalism the level of productive forces rises to the danger point–the forces conflict with the mode of production and distribution. The conflict spreads throughout the formation, which becomes unstable: any good shock, such as an economic crisis, may detonate it.

The weakest parts of this unstable system are the backward areas on the Continent. Industrialization creates a growing bourgeoisie. The bourgeoisie breaks out in antifeudal revolution, then collapses before an uprising of the youthful proletariat. Proletarian revolution sets off a chain reaction in the social formation. The disintegration of the economic basis spreads from one country to another, causing explosion after explosion, until the system is burned up in a vast revolutionary conflagration. (See the diagram for a visual image of this chain process of revolution.) The international economic basis "makes each nation dependent on the revolutions of the others."[197] The revolution is international or it is nothing; the dominant nations can only reach communism if they struggle toward it at the same time.[198]

England	Germany	France
◄ − −	− − − − −	− −

Once the revolution has triumphed in the dominant countries of Europe, the rest of the planet must drift into the communist orbit.[199] "Big industry has brought all the people of the earth into contact with each other, has merged all local markets into one world market, has spread civilization and progress everywhere and has thus ensured that whatever happens in the civilized countries will have repercussions in all other countries."[200]

Thus for Marx and Engels there can only be a world revolution. Marx says that the French Revolution was a revolution of a *"European* pattern."[201] And in fact it had a universal impact, as the following description by the historian Eric Hobsbawm in *The Age of Revolution* shows:

> At the peak of their power (1810), the French directly governed, as part of France, all Germany left of the Rhine, Belgium, the Netherlands and North Germany eastwards to Luebeck, Savoy, Piedmont, Liguria and Italy west of the Apennines down to the borders of Naples, and the Illyrian provinces from Carinthia down to and including Dalmatia. French family or satellite kingdoms and duchies covered Spain, the rest of Italy, the rest of Rhineland-Westphalia, and a large part of Poland. In all these territories (except perhaps the Grand Duchy of Warsaw) the institutions of the French Revolution and the Napoleonic Empire were automatically

applied, or were the obvious models for local administration: feudalism was formally abolished, French legal codes applied and so on. . . . In fact, it can be said with little exaggeration that no important continental state west of Russia and Turkey and south of Scandinavia emerged from these two decades of war with its domestic institutions wholly unaffected by the expansion or imitation of the French Revolution. . . . No country was immune from it. The French soldiers who campaigned from Andalusia to Moscow, from the Baltic to Syria–over a vaster area than any previous single military force in Europe except the Norsemen–pushed the universality of their revolution home more effectively than anything else could have done. (pp. 89–90)

The revolution shook the Continent, and we know that this universal event was a fountain of theoretical inspiration for nineteenth-century radicals. From its stream of political and strategical ideas Marx and Engels took material for their own social thought.[202]

In the early stages of the French Revolution, the Commune of Paris believed that the kings of feudal Europe would not rest until they crushed France; so the Commune urged a propagandist war to liberate the nations. The only hope for revolutionary France, argued the Commune's leaders, lay in the republicanization of Europe: a war to the bitter end was necessary. Robespierre sent them to the guillotine. Their deaths were tragic, think Marx and Engels, for the Commune's leaders were right.[203] Later France took up the Commune's program, fought a series of wars, and set up satellite republics. The French legislative body soon grew corrupt. "The French people in the person of Bonaparte dissolved the legislative body," writes Marx.[204] "The energetic Napoleon took the revolutionary work into his own hands," writes Engels, "he identified the Revolution with himself."[205] He embarked on a policy of conquest and domination that pushed the revolution across Europe. "He brought his law book with him into the conquered lands, a law book which was endlessly applied to everything existing and which in principle recognized equality."[206] His target was feudal privilege. "The French were able to win the recognition and sympathy even of the countries to which they came as enemies."[207]

The revolution conquered Western Europe, penetrated Central Europe, and raised echoes in Eastern Europe–but tsarism remained. The French armies marched on Moscow. They met defeat, and the pendulum of history began to swing back. Napoleon retreated before the tsar's hordes. The Russians arrived in Paris. Soon political darkness settled over Europe: from 1815 to 1848 the might of tsarism backed the Holy Alliance of Russia, Austria, and Prussia. Tyrants, soldiers, bureaucrats, gendarmes, priests, censors, and informers thrived on the Continent. In Western Europe the weight of the tsar pressed down everywhere: all rebels saw Russia as the enemy. The next revolution must be a war of the peoples against tsarism to free Europe forever. Throughout the Continent rebels continued to work for the revolution; they prepared for the end of the great work begun by the French in 1789. In 1846 Engels writes that "the whole European social movement of today is only the second act of the Revolution, only the preparation for the end of the drama that began in Paris in 1789 and now has all Europe for a stage."[208]

Engels describes the coming revolution in these words: "It is a universal revolution and will accordingly have a universal range."[209] He is not expressing an especially Marxist idea: in the generation before 1848 all revolutionaries believed that the revolution must blaze across Europe, consuming one king after another, and then sweep on toward Russia to defeat tsarism in a world war. Nationalists, democrats, and patriots believed in "the European revolution and the various republics that went with it as a matter of course."[210] What Marx and Engels did was to give the "European revolution" a communist interpretation: the revolution would not only thunder across Europe and smash the tsar; it would pass from the bourgeois republic to communist society.

Decade by decade the history of the nineteenth century implied the all-European revolution. The French Revolution first showed that rebellion could spread across the Continent. In 1820 the Spanish Revolution indirectly provoked uprisings in Portugal, Naples, and Piedmont. (The Holy Alliance reacted with brutal suppression.) The year 1830, says Engels, was a historical turning point: revolutionary Paris sent shock waves through Europe as Belgium revolted against Holland, Poland rose against Russia, the Italians rebelled in the Papal States, insurrections occurred in the Germanies, radical bourgeois campaigned in Switzerland, and the Reform Bills were pushed through in England.[211] (Again the Holy Alliance hit back with force.) In 1848 a great conflagration roared across the Continent: revolution broke out in France and swept away the "bourgeois king"; the fires of rebellion spread to Austria, Hungary, Croatia, Bohemia, Moravia, Galicia, Dalmatia, Transylvania, and Poland, burned through the Germanies to Berlin, ignited revolts in the Italian states; there were large disturbances in Spain, Denmark, and Romania; unrest appeared in Greece and Britain; an uprising occurred in Ireland. The all-European revolution that Marx and Engels expected had taken place. The Holy Alliance temporarily collapsed before the onslaught of the revolution, and Russia slowly mobilized its forces against it. Although it soon burned out, this revolution left a permanent mark on the vision of Marx and Engels.

They believed that the revolution would blaze up again, a thousand times brighter, and transform all Europe. The revolutions of 1848 were tokens of what was coming. Marx says in 1856: "The so-called Revolutions of 1848 were but poor incidents–small fractures and fissures in the dry crust of European society. But they revealed the abyss. Underneath the apparently solid surface they showed oceans of liquid matter, only needing expansion to tear into fragments continents of hard rock."[212]

The revolutions of 1848 passed away, and after a year or two society returned to its original condition: Russia put down the revolt in Hungary; Prussia reverted to military despotism; France turned into a dictatorship; and the Hapsburg Empire was governed as before. Not much had changed on the Continent, and the idea of continuing revolution–so alive during the years of the Holy Alliance–seemed just as valid for Europe in the years after 1850.

But conditions changed dramatically in England. After 1850 the English bourgeoisie's attitude toward the proletariat became altogether different. In the late nineteenth century Engels describes the transformation of the bourgeoisie's attitude toward the English working class after 1850: "A gradual change came over the relations between the two classes. . . . Trade Unions, up to now considered inventions of the devil himself, were now petted and patronized as perfectly legitimate institutions and as useful means of spreading sound economic doctrines among the workers. . . . The Reform Acts of 1867 and 1884 make a near approach to 'universal suffrage.' . . ."[213] The English bourgeoisie's affection for the proletariat troubled Marx and Engels, but they considered it a passing phase.

Up to 1850 the English proletariat showed revolutionary feeling, but in the second half of the nineteenth century it became reformist. Marx and Engels were aware of this fact; their correspondence brims with complaints about the English proletariat. It had become "bourgeois," "Christian," "sheeplike," "slavish," "cringing," "narrow-minded," "demoralized," "corrupted," "a tail of the Liberals."[214] The founders of Marxism always thought this a temporary condition, and waited for its end. "How soon the English workers will free themselves from their apparent bourgeois infection one must wait and see," Marx writes to Engels.[215] The two men retained the strategical views worked out in the 1840s; continuing revolution on the Continent would trigger mass revolution in England. A commercial and financial crisis had preceded every serious revolution in European history,[216] and Marx and Engels predicted periodic crises for England: they believed that capitalism continued to suffer internal conflicts, that underconsumption and overproduction must vent themselves in economic crises.[217] Might not capitalism be moving toward a final crisis?[218] Sooner or later the English proletariat would become revolutionary again. The crisis would spread to the Continent and cause insurrections there: these would then draw the English proletariat into the European revolution. "No revolution in Western Europe can win conclusively," writes Engels in 1875, "as long as the present Russian state exists beside it."[219] To the end he and Marx believed that Russian tsarism would fall before a crusade of the nations.

Besides the theoretical statements cited in note 217, the Marx-Engels correspondence is filled with expectations of economic crises. For a generation after 1850 crises shook England, but the proletariat remained bourgeoisified. So about the time of Marx's death, Engels developed a supplementary theory to explain this bourgeoisification, a theory he defended to the end. He argued that empire and a monopoly of the world market brought great profits to English industry, that labor aristocracies received high wages, and that the proletariat's living conditions improved temporarily. Thus the proletariat lost its revolutionary passion. But Germany and Austria would soon break England's monopoly of the world market, profits would shrink, wages fall, and the proletariat again become revolutionary.[220] In chapter 8 of *Imperialism, The Highest Stage of Capitalism* (1916), Lenin revived this theory, and it remains a cornerstone of Leninist thought to this day: the United States, Japan, and Western Europe use multinational corporations to suck superprofits from the Third World in order to buy off the proletariats at home.

During Marx's lifetime he and Engels retained their faith in an international rising of the working class. Europe was sitting on a volcano, they thought, and past events proved it: 1789, 1820, 1830, 1848. On those dates the surface of society cracked open, and the two men stared into the fissures. We saw oceans of liquid lava, says Marx, ready to blast away the surface of hard rock.[221]

This vision of a social volcano governed Marx's thinking through the nineteenth century: he often heard the "crater of revolution"[222] rumble, he felt the Continent shaking, and he awaited the vast explosion. For decades Marx's and Engels' correspondence reflected their expectations of revolution.

They expected the economic crisis of 1857 to end in revolution.[223] Marx writes that he was working madly through the nights to finish *Capital* before the flood came.[224] Engels planned to lead a force of revolutionary cavalry, and he trained himself daily: in horseback riding, fox hunting, tactical studies.[225] In 1862 Marx writes to Kugelmann: "We are obviously approaching a revolution—which I have never doubted since 1850. The first act will include a by no means refreshing repetition of the stupidities of 1848–1849."[226] But the other acts would follow, leading to a communist transformation of Europe. In 1863 the Polish insurrection broke out, and Marx hails it as the first blast of the volcano: "So much is certain, the era of revolution has once again opened in Europe. . . . Hopefully this time the lava will roll from East to West."[227] From 1864 on, Marx struggled to build up the First International. "Things are moving," he writes to Engels. "And in the next revolution, which is perhaps nearer than it appears, we (that is, you and I) will have this powerful engine *in our hands.*"[228] In 1873 Marx writes that "the contradictions inherent in the movement of capitalist society" must periodically vent themselves in a "universal crisis. That crisis is once again approaching. . . ."[229] He expects it to trigger the European revolution. In 1881 he speaks of the "disintegration of the dominant order of society continually proceeding before our eyes and the evergrowing fury into which the masses are lashed by the old ghostly governments."[230] Revolution is imminent. In 1890 Engels surveys the political scene and finds Europe rushing toward the "world revolution."[231]

In *From Marx to Hegel*, George Lichtheim, an influential historian of socialist thought, argues that after 1848 Marx became "an ex-Communist" (pp. 85–86). The reformist Eduard Bernstein, we are told, was a true Marxist. In chapter 6 of his brilliant work *Marxism: An Historical and Critical Study*, Lichtheim maintains that the failure of the revolutions of 1848 disillusioned Marx and Engels. This Social Democratic scholar supposes that our two revolutionaries turned to mass politics and reduced the goal of all political struggles, whether violent or peaceful, to a democratic republic. After 1848, we are told, Marx and Engels postponed the struggle for communism to an indefinite future when triumphant democracy could peacefully evolve toward socialism.

Lichtheim believes that Marx and Engels became Social Democrats like himself, but his widely accepted view is mistaken. During the nineteenth century in every political emergency, in each economic crisis, our two theoreticians saw the revolutionary eruption beginning, and they continued to believe that the democratic revolution would telescope into proletarian uprisings. Though the usual interpretation holds otherwise, the *Marx-Engels Correspondence* does not support it.*

To the end Marx and Engels held this revolutionary perspective: (1) economic crisis, (2) insurrections on the Continent, (3) mass revolution in England, (4) revolutionary war against Russia, and (5) construction of communism. There were variations on this theme, and the most important was the change in Marx's conception of Russian society. Russia was the citadel of counterrevolution. In the 1860s the founders of Marxism realized that the Russian intelligentsia was becoming an internal opposition to the tsar. In the 1870s

---

*Lichtheim's influential interpretation misses the mark, but for the grain of truth in his Social Democratic view of Marx see the appendix. A survey of the correspondence in the *Marx-Engels Werke*, volumes 27 to 39, revealed the following passages backing up the interpretation in the present work: 27:137; 28:116, 118, 226, 302–303, 578–581; 29:9–10, 28–29, 76, 86, 112, 117, 153, 211–212, 225, 254, 303–304, 309, 360, 551, 561, 572, 605; 30:287, 324, 327, 333, 353–354, 641; 31:204, 212, 226–227, 293, 342–343, 378; 32:443, 596–597, 610, 620; 33:140; 34:87, 162–163, 296, 366, 368, 433; 35:276, 283; 36:38, 54–55, 73, 106, 117, 120, 253, 290, 304–307, 350, 374, 379, 391, 634, 636, 638, 641, 713; 37:6, 25, 359–363, 371, 416, 513–514; 38:153, 188–189, 545–546, 564–565; 39:89, 141, 255, 384, 421.

this opposition took on a revolutionary color; so the two men learned Russian and corresponded with Russian radicals. "Russia undoubtedly is on the eve of a revolution," writes Engels in 1875. "Here all conditions of a revolution are combined, of a revolution that . . . must be rapidly carried beyond the first constitutional phase by the peasants, of a revolution that will be of the greatest importance for the whole of Europe if only because it will destroy at one blow the last reserve of the entire European reaction."[232] Marx watched Russia with growing interest. "Russia . . . has long been standing on the threshold of an upheaval; all elements of it are prepared," he writes in 1877. "All sections of Russian society are in full decomposition economically, morally, and intellectually. This time the revolution begins in the East, up to now the unbroken bulwark and reserve army of counterrevolution."[233] And if a great revolution broke out in Russia, might it not spread to the West? Under the impact of such a tremendous event there could be a revolutionary upsurge in Germany, where the proletarian minority might seize power.[234] This is Marx's and Engels' view in 1882: "Events . . . are maturing in Russia where the vanguard of the revolution will engage in battle. This and its inevitable impact on Germany is what one must in our opinion wait for, and then will come the time of a grand demonstration."[235] Russia could throw a lighted torch into the powder keg of Western Europe and set off a series of proletarian revolutions; then with aid from the West it might move from backwardness toward socialism. "If the Russian Revolution becomes the signal for a proletarian revolution in the West, so that both complement each other, the present Russian common ownership of land may serve as the starting point for a communist development."[236] In 1894 Engels again emphasizes that Russia could leap from backwardness toward socialism only if it were aided by a victorious West European proletariat.[237] To the end, this portentous principle remained a cornerstone of Marxist thought.

The Russian Revolution indeed arrived in the generation after Engels' death. Its Marxist guides, leading a young proletariat, hoped to set off permanent revolution in the West. The Russian uprising gave the signal, but insurrections in Central Europe soon collapsed, and the revolution was isolated in Russia. The Marxists then attempted to build socialism in this backward country.

In 1853 Engels discussed revolution thus isolated. He speaks of "a backward country like Germany, which possesses an advanced party" and reasons that "the advanced party must get into power at the first serious conflict and as soon as actual danger is present, and that is, in any event, *ahead* of its normal time." The communists might drive from backwardness toward socialism without aid from advanced England: "driven by the proletarian populace, bound by our own printed declarations and plans—more or less falsely interpreted, more or less passionately thrust to the fore in the Party struggle—we shall be forced to undertake communist experiments and perform leaps the untimeliness of which we know better than anyone else. In so doing we lose our heads–only physically speaking, let us hope–a reaction sets in. . . ."[238] This drama was enacted in the twentieth century: many revolutionaries in isolated Russia lost their heads in the Great Purge, and the bureaucratization of the revolution set in.

In 1858 Marx, too, worried about the question: What if the revolution is isolated in a backward area? What if the revolution triumphs on the Continent in France and Germany while advanced England remains capitalist? The English proletariat was bourgeoisified–or so Engels writes to Marx in 1858–and the revolution in England might be delayed.[239] Marx accepts this, and admits that capitalism is still expanding in England and the world market (America, India, China, Australia, Japan). Then he notes anxiously: "The difficult question for us is this: on the Continent the revolution is imminent and will immediately assume a socialist character. Is it not bound to be crushed in this little corner, considering that in a far greater territory the movement of bourgeois society is still in the ascendant?"[240]

In 1845 Marx and Engels argued that expansion of international capitalism would "abolish local communism. Empirically, communism is only possible as the act of the dominant peoples 'all at once' and simultaneously."[241] And if the revolution–isolated in a backward area–managed to survive, it would soon degenerate. Backwardness, scarcity, and poverty would change communism into a competitive struggle for necessities and reproduce all the "shit" of the old society.[242]

For Marx and Engels socialism in one country was unlikely. Throughout the nineteenth century they argued that the revolution would have a universal range. In the 1840s Engels asks the question, "Will it be possible for this revolution to take place in one country alone?" and he answers in a word: No.[243] Not even advanced England could build socialism alone. "The triumph of the European working class does not depend upon England alone," writes Engels in 1892. "It can only be secured by the cooperation of, at least, England, France, and Germany."[244] The revolution would be nothing if not international: it must continue in permanence to transform the planet.*

Marx embraced communism in 1844. He worked out his theory of history

---

*"If this interpretation of Marx is correct," a neo-Stalinist friend once told me, "it would be impossible for socialism to emerge in one country, yet Stalin built it in Russia and Mao in China." It did not occur to him that Marx either erred or was analyzing conditions that no longer held in the twentieth century. Stalin himself, in the conclusion of his *History of the Communist Party of the Soviet Union (Bolsheviks)*, argued that Marx's analysis applied only to nineteenth-century conditions. But would the socialism actually built in Russia or China be approved by Marx? That question will continue to be debated.

in 1845 and 1846; in a book on Proudhon he developed his economic views in 1847; in the *Manifesto* he summed up Marxism in 1848. Marx and Engels endorsed the principles of the *Manifesto* forty years later;[245] and in *The Historical Destiny of the Doctrine of Karl Marx*, Lenin reaffirmed the *Manifesto* as a statement of Marxism in 1913.

Thus the Marxist historical outlook was forged by 1848. Marx and Engels labored on for forty years and produced an enormous *oeuvre*, but it was an elaboration of principles laid out in the 1840s.

Most interpreters of Marx fail to study his thought in this historical context, and their mistake produces a distortion of his meaning. To show this we now sum up his development in the nineteenth century. The summary will contrast nineteenth-century conditions with the situation in the twentieth century, and that may suggest questions for Marxist analysis today.

In the 1840s Europe lay under the heel of the Holy Alliance–Russia, Austria, and Prussia. Marx called them the Powers of old Europe: the pope and the tsar, Metternich and German police spies.[246] There was no democracy. In France a handful of people had the vote, elsewhere no one had it. The Continent was a vast tsarist prison: no parliaments and no reforms, but kings and priests everywhere. The only way out seemed a *European revolution*.

In Paris the spirit of the revolution was a living force. The memory of 1789, "the most colossal revolution that history had ever known,"[247] smoldered in the minds of the people. The revolution of 1830 toppled the Bourbons and brought a new constitution–and a new king. The masses began to stir. Blanquist communists struck at the state in uprising after uprising. The bourgeoisie wanted a republic, and the workers thirsted for socialism.

During the 1840s socialism and communism were the topics of the day in Paris. People discussed them everywhere: in the great newspapers, in cafes, in pamphlets, in clubs, in the street–everywhere. No one doubted that the revolution would come; the only question was what to do when it came. Revolutionaries and exiles from old Europe gathered in Paris–the Red Babylon–and at night the cafes simmered with discussion and debate. They argued and plotted and dreamed. In Paris lived 100,000 German workers, and communist ideas caught fire in that tinderbox. Paris was the capital of Europe.

During the 1840s Marx and Engels were in and out of Paris, arguing with the ideologists, studying revolutionary history, and learning communist theory. The French scene shaped their thought. They came to believe that the night of tyranny was over, they saw a red dawn breaking–the revolution. It would grow brighter and brighter, warming the nations, transforming people until the sun of communism had risen over Europe. The revolutionary process might last a generation, pass through many stages, and dissolve whole classes of society. But it would remake humanity.

When the revolutions of 1848 swept the Continent, Marx thought this process had begun. France, Italy, Austria, Hungary, and Germany caught fire. These revolutions fizzled, but Marx expected the revolution to break out again stronger than ever. His hope simmered during the 1850s. As the years stretched out he withdrew into economic studies, but he never changed his mind about the revolution: always that vision worked in his brain, the communist transformation of Europe before the century ran out.

In 1869 the vision brightened. The decade of the 1860s had created the First International, strike waves in Europe, and rebel feeling in Paris. In 1869 revolutionary clubs appeared in that city; radical agitation against the emperor began. The proletariat grew restless. "A very interesting movement is going on in France," Marx writes in 1869. "The Parisians are making a regular study of their recent revolutionary past, in order to prepare themselves for the business of the impending new revolution. . . . And so the whole historical witches' cauldron is bubbling."[248] Marx expected a gigantic "1848." The revolution would break out in France and spread across Europe. The proletariat had grown stronger; now in 1870 it could drive toward communism–and win.

The year 1870 came. The Franco-Prussian war turned revolutionary feeling into nationalism and ended in the tragedy of the Paris Commune. That massacre of the proletariat dimmed the vision of revolution. But the vision shaped Marx's thought to the end, twelve years later.

On the cover of Fischer-Bucherei's tiny edition of his works there is a biographical sketch, a summary of his life in a paragraph. It mentions his birth in Trier, traces his revolutionary activities in the 1840s, and ends with the sentence: "In August 1849 he had to go into exile in London, where he died in 1883."

Massive biographies also focus on the 1840s, for those years provided Marx with revolutionary experience, while thirty years in exile were a reflection on it. In the 1840s industrialization was taking place in Paris, Lyons, and Marseilles, in Berlin, Saxony, Silesia, and the Rhineland. The horrors of the early factory system persisted in England; the European proletariat seethed with revolt. Outlawed unions, no vote, poor pay, low status, no education, slum housing, police beatings–the workers had nothing to lose but their chains. The middle classes were restless; they wanted to break out of the prison in which Metternich had locked them. They demanded a parliament. The intellectuals fumed and raged: a century after the Enlightenment they found Europe ridden with priests; they had to write with an eye on the censor. That was Europe in the 1840s, which the English called The Hungry Decade.

By 1900 this scene was changing. Through technological advance and imperialist expansion, capitalism stepped up the output of goods and pulled wages slowly upward. The proletariat had the vote and unions; the middle class had their parliaments; and the intellectuals had free speech.

Marx was dead, but the workers had spread his ideas across the Continent. In Western Europe they still spoke of revolution. That was how they *talked*. They raised their fists and threatened, while they used votes and unions to demand reforms within capitalism. And the reforms slowly came: better wages, shorter hours, social security, state medicine.

In Eastern Europe the scene was different. The tsar ruled a vast domain with the noose and the knout, the priest and the censor, the gendarme and the Cossack. The "feudal-patriarchal-absolutist-bureaucratic-priestly Reaction"[249] that Engels saw in Western Europe during the 1840s still ruled Eastern Europe at the turn of the century. The conditions for a great social revolution were maturing in the East. Amid a sea of angry peasants emerged industrial islands: Moscow, Baku, Petersburg, Warsaw, Lodz, the Donets Basin, the towns in the Urals. The Russian proletariat, passing through rapid industrialization, gathered itself for a leap toward utopia, for a revolutionary surge that would change the history of the world.

IV. Communism

The Socioeconomic Structure

From the seventeenth century on, a number of social thinkers advocated common ownership of the means of production. The land and the tools, the mines and the factories, the ships and the stores, argued these thinkers, should be owned and operated in common. Winstanley, Mably, Morelly, Babeuf, Cabet, Thompson, and Owen preached communism.

Marx and Engels accepted their vision of the future society, but rejected their methods for arriving at it. The founders of Marxism condemned these methods as utopian. By them communists tried to persuade the ruling class to reorganize society, they tried to convert the rich by peaceful means: model communities, socialist experiments, cooperative factories, communist colonies, propaganda novels, and blueprints for the future. Against appeals to the ruling class Marx and Engels argued for proletarian revolution. Efforts to convert the capitalists were utopian; the proletariat would have to rise against capitalism, capture state power, and build communism.[1]

Communist writers, says Marx, "while in their criticism of present society clearly describing the goal of the social movement, the supersession of the wage system with all its [economic] conditions of class rule, found neither in society itself the material conditions of its transformation nor in the working class the organized power and the [consciousness] of the movement."[2] The communists were right about ends but wrong about means: they struggled for the goal through persuasion instead of revolution.

By criticism of existing institutions the communists described their goal; they called for abolition of the difference between town and country, private ownership of factories and land, the wage system, the family, and the state.[3] Marx and Engels accepted these proposals for the future society and preached them for a lifetime: concerning final goals they agreed with the communists of their age, people like Robert Owen.

In communist society, say the founders of Marxism, the difference between town and country must disappear. This is basic in their vision of the future; they repeat the idea throughout their writings.⁴ They believe that factories will move out of cities, where swarms of people are huddled together. People will break up the cities, scatter the factories over the fields, and build communities combining industry with farming.

Thus communism will end the curse that plagued civilization for thousands of years–the split between town and country.⁵ Isolation in the country away from art and science made people stupid; crowding into huge towns with dirty air made them sick.⁶ The "town animal" became an emasculated dwarf, while the "country animal" remained a clownish boor.⁷ Both must disappear in communities distributed over the countryside: people will work in factories and fields, develop culture in groups, and breathe freely again.

"It is true," admits Engels, "that in the huge towns civilization has bequeathed us a heritage which it will take much time and trouble to get rid of. But it must and will be got rid of, however protracted a process it may be."⁸ To decentralize the cities is not utopian, argue the founders of Marxism, but a necessity of life.⁹ "It has become a direct necessity of . . . public health. The present poisoning of the air, water, and land can be put an end to only by the fusion of town and country."¹⁰

Each communist community will be such a fusion. What will these communities look like? In a draft of the *Manifesto* Engels says that in the future society there will be "construction on public lands of great palaces as communal dwellings for communities of citizens engaged in both industry and agriculture and combining in their way of life the advantages of urban and rural conditions while avoiding the one-sidedness and drawbacks of each."¹¹ This concept of communal palaces comes from Robert Owen. Owen's proposals, Engels explains elsewhere, are the most practical and developed of all communist plans. "Owen proposes that in place of our present cities and villages with their isolated dwellings that get in one another's way we should erect enormous palaces, which, built in a square 1650 feet long and wide, will enclose a great garden and comfortably lodge about two or three thousand people."¹² Fields and workshops will surround each palace.

The communal palace is like a great apartment building in the country, in which each family has its rooms. The palace contains communal kitchens, laundries, nurseries, storehouses, and committee rooms for the use of all. Gardens, orchards, fields, and workshops are minutes away. The palace will simplify heating, lighting, cleaning, and cooking. Instead of countless people running to market, using many kitchens, serving separate families, instead of individual cooking, the palace will have communal eating places that feed everyone in a third of the time. No longer will one person do the housework in a home: work teams will sweep out the palace in short order. A thousand smoky stoves to be fueled, cleaned, and watched—all that disappears, for the palace provides steam heat. Instead of a city with miles of pipes carrying gas to the rich, there is the palace with gas light for all.[13]

The communal palace is not a beehive. The aim of communal kitchens and laundries is to free men and women from drudgery, not to drown the individual in collective life. The palace provides everyone with a suite of rooms; privacy is available for all. People can go to their apartments when they wish, and they will certainly go there to sleep. Marx and Engels ridicule communal sleeping as "barracks room communism."[14]

In *The German Ideology* Marx and Engels note that throughout history communal living was rare. The low level of productive forces made communal living difficult, for great buildings were always cold and dark: there was no gas lighting, no steam heating, and no running water. Communal life was a Spartan affair, and it thrived only in prisons, barracks, and monasteries. Comfortable living meant a house, a hearth, a garden, a well.[15]

"The setting up of a communal domestic economy presupposes the development of machinery, of the use of natural forces and of many other productive forces—for example, of water supplies, gas lighting, steam heating, the removal of the antagonism of town and country."[16] Machine industry, say Marx and Engels, has provided the material basis for communal life.

Communal living simplifies housework; cooperation reduces labor time in fields and workshops. There is more leisure for art and science, because communal economy becomes a new productive force.[17]

From the 1840s to the end, Marx and Engels held this vision of communist society. In 1878 Engels (in a work endorsed by Marx) still approves of Owen's proposal "that the population should be scattered through the country in groups of 1,600 to 3,000 persons, each group occupying a gigantic palace with a household run on communal lines in the center of their area of land."[18] The communal palace, surrounded by factories and farmland, remained the ideal communist community of the future.

Charles Fourier, whom Marx called a "patriarch of socialism,"[19] had also preached breaking up the cities into small communities scattered over the countryside. Each community would surround a giant hotel where everyone lived. Such communitarian socialism was widespread in the 1840s, the decade that made Marxism. During this period England and America contained many successful communist communities. "Communism—social life and production with community of goods—is not only possible, but is in many American communities and in some places in England already realized, and with the best results, as we shall see." Thus in 1845 Engels opens his "Description of the Communist Settlements That Have Arisen in Modern Times and Still Exist."[20]

Fourier and Owen shaped Marx's and Engels' vision of *the rough outlines of the communist future*. But Owen's social experiments, his faith in peaceful persuasion, and his obsession with the details of the future society–all this annoyed Marx and Engels. They called him a utopian.[21] He was forever dreaming of perfect communities, working out model societies, and drawing up social blueprints. He imagined different kinds of communal organization. Like all such plans, "the more completely they were worked out in detail, the more they could not avoid drifting off into pure fantasies."[22] He loved to make plans like the one he presented in his *Report to the Committee for the Relief of the Manufacturing Poor*:

> The drawing exhibits in the foreground an establishment with its appendages and appropriate quantity of land; and at due distances other villages of a similar description. Squares of buildings are here represented sufficiently to accommodate about 1,200 persons each. . . . The central buidling contains a public kitchen, mess rooms, and all the accommodation necessary to economical and comfortable cooking and eating. To the right of this is a building, of which the ground floor will form the infant school and the other a lecture room and a place of worship. The building to the left contains a school for the elder children and a committee room on the ground floor; above a library and a room for adults. In the vacant space are enclosed grounds for exercise and recreation: these enclosures are supposed to have trees planted in them. It is intended that three sides of each square shall be lodging houses chiefly for the married, consisting of four rooms in each; each room to be sufficiently large to accommodate a man, his wife, and two children. . . . At the other side are offices for washing, bleaching, and so forth, and at a still greater distance from the squares are some of the farming establishments with conveniences for malting, brewing, and corn mills, and so forth; around these are cultivated enclosures, pasture land, the hedges of which are planted with fruit trees.

Marx and Engels thought such plans useful criticism of existing society, but as blueprints for the future they raised a smile. People must create the future society through revolutionary struggle. The details of that society could not be foreseen, and Owen's passion for them marked him as utopian.

Yet the outline of the future was clear enough. The split between town and country, the basis of all division of labor,[23] would be overcome: everyone could take part in both industry and agriculture, could work outdoors part of the day.

In outdoor work the division of labor must further disappear. "In communist society," write Marx and Engels, "where nobody has one exclusive sphere of activity but each can become accomplished in any branch he wishes, society regulates the general production and thus makes it possible for me to do one thing today and another tomorrow, to hunt in the morning, fish in the afternoon, rear cattle in the evening, criticize after dinner, just as I have a mind, without ever becoming hunter, fisherman, shepherd or critic."[24] In factory work, too, divided labor will vanish under communism. People can learn to run different machines and move from one machine to another.[25] They will have to learn this, for science and industry constantly develop new techniques, and new machines replace old ones.[26] "Modern industry," writes Marx in *Capital*, "compels society under penalty of death to replace the detail worker of today, crippled by lifelong repetition of one and the same trivial operation, by the fully developed individual fit for a variety of labors, ready to face any change of production, and to whom the different social functions he performs are but so many modes of giving free scope to his own natural and acquired powers."[27] Abolition of the division of labor, far from utopian, is necessary for modern industry.

Under capitalism, says Marx, automation pushes physical labor out of one branch of production after another, and people find themselves tending machines. "Labor does not seem anymore to be an essential part of the process of production. The human factor is restricted to watching and supervising the production process."[28] Watching and tending machines in a mill, for example, is a simple affair: "it allows of a rapid and constant change of the individuals burdened with this drudgery."[29]

Communism will end the worker's "labor of Sisyphus." The Greek gods condemned Sisyphus to rolling a rock to the top of a mountain, watching the rock fall back of its own weight, and beginning the task again. There is no more dreadful punishment, thought the gods, than futile and hopeless labor. Yet precisely this, say Marx and Engels, is what people suffer under capitalism. "The miserable routine of endless drudgery and toil in which the same mechanical process is gone through over and over again is like the labor of Sisyphus. The burden of labor, like the rock, keeps ever falling back on the worn-out laborer."[30] The laborer needs change and rest, rotation of work, both physical and intellectual effort. Abolition of the division of labor will bring this about under communism.[31]

Marx and Engels were not utopians; they never outlined the work day of the future or wrote recipes for ending divided labor. They smiled at Fourier, who drew up schedules for the rotation of work in his droll utopia. Here is an example of Fourier's fantasies in his *Le nouveau monde industriel et sociétaire*:

Hours. Sleep from 10½ at night to 3 in the morning.
At 3½   rising, getting ready.
At 4   court of public reveille, news of the night.
At 4½   the *délité*, first meal, then the industrial parade.
At 5½   attendance at the hunting group.
At 7   attendance at the fishing group.
At 8   *breakfast*, newspapers.
At 9   attendance at an agricultural group under cover.
At 10   attendance at mass.
At 10½ attendance at the pheasantry group.
At 11½ attendance at the library.
At 1   DINNER
At 2½   attendance at the group of cold green houses.
At 4   attendance at the group of exotic plants.
At 5   attendance at the group of fish ponds.
At 6   *luncheon* in the fields.
At 6½   attendance at the group of shepherds.
At 8   attendance at Change.
At 9   SUPPER, fifth meal
At 9½   attendance at court of the arts, ball, theater.
At 10½ bed time.   (p. 68)

Marx and Engels consider Fourier a mad genius, whose fantasies stimulated the sociological imagination: "We can leave it to the literary small fry to solemnly quibble over these fantasies, which today only make us smile, and to crow over the superiority of their own plain reasoning as compared with such 'insanity.' For ourselves we delight in the grand thoughts and germs of thought that everywhere break out through their fantastic covering and to which these philistines are blind."[32]

Fourier thought he could transform work into play, could make labor amusing, and for this Marx sharply criticizes him.[33] Marx believes that labor means struggle—and sometimes painful effort. Even the labor of an artist involves the agony and discipline of creation. "Really free labor, the composing of music for example, is at the same time damned serious and demands the greatest effort."[34] Work in fields and factories is more demanding still. But in communism people face it with a new attitude, and divided labor vanishes forever.

Yet labor remains. "Just as the savage must wrestle with Nature to satisfy his wants, to maintain and reproduce life," says Marx, "so must civilized man, and he must do so in all social formations and under all possible modes of production."[35] Under communism, too, people must wrestle with nature for their daily bread. But their labor has dignity: they cease to suffer as beasts and begin to suffer as humans.

Marx's conception of labor is central in his vision of communist society. Labor for the common good, labor no longer divided, labor combining physical and intellectual effort–this creates Communist Man and Woman. In his draft for the *Manifesto* Engels sketches the new society in broad strokes:

> The division of labor as it has been known up to the present will completely disappear. . . . Just as the peasants and manufacturing workers of the last century changed their whole way of life and became quite different people when they were impressed into big industry, in the same way communal control over production by society as a whole and the resulting new development will both require an entirely different kind of human material. People will no longer be, as they are today, subordinated to a single branch of production, bound to it, exploited by it; they will no longer develop one of their faculties at the expense of all others; they will no longer know only one branch of production as a whole. Even industry as it is today is finding such people less and less useful. Industry controlled by society as a whole and operated according to a plan presupposes well-rounded human beings, their faculties developed in balanced fashion, able to see the system of production in its entirety. The form of the division of labor which makes one a peasant, another a cobbler, a third a factory worker, a fourth a stock market operator has already been undermined by machinery and will completely disappear. Education will enable young people quickly to familiarize themselves with the whole system of production and to pass from one branch of production to another in response to the needs of society or their own inclinations. It will therefore free them from the one-sided character which the present-day division of labor impresses upon every individual. Communist society will in this way make it possible for its members to put their comprehensively developed faculties to full use. . . . A corollary of this is that the difference between city and country is destined to disappear.[36]

The cities will be broken up and distributed over the country in thousands of communities combining industry with agriculture.

The communities will not be all alike. "Alpine dwellers will always have different conditions of life from those of people living on plains."[37] There will be mining communities in the mountains, fishing communities in the harbors, lumbering communities in the forests. Most people will live in the valleys and plains, where fields and factories surround centers of communal life.

But can the communities, scattered over the countryside, carry on industrial production? Industry requires coal and raw materials. Factories rise near coalfields, iron mines, and sources of ore. In Pennsylvania, in the Ruhr, in England giant industrial towns have grown up. These areas are an insult to nature, for "the factory town transforms all water into stinking manure."[38] Such population centers, with their pollution of air and water and earth, are a threat to human life, but aren't they inevitable?

Marx and Engels argue that industry need not grow up in this spontaneous way. Certain trends under capitalism show that industry can exist far from fuel and ore. The textile industry works up imported raw materials; Spanish iron ore is processed in England and Germany. Every coalfield supplies fuel to an industrial area beyond its own borders, an area that widens year by year. Steamships and railways allow factories to exist miles from raw materials and markets.[39]

The key to decentralization of industry is economic planning. "Only a society which makes it possible for its productive forces to dovetail harmoniously into each other on the basis of one single vast plan can allow industry to be distributed over the whole country in the way best adapted to its own development and to the maintenance and development of the other elements of production."[40] This planning and direction of economic life is basic in communism.

But who are the planners? Who draws up the "single vast plan" that governs the economic life of the country? Who assigns one community to produce watches and another steam engines? Who directs distribution among the communities? The founders of Marxism answer that "society" makes the plan.[41]

Does this mean society organized as the political state? Not exactly, for under communism a good deal of the state dies out, and Marx and Engels identify what is left with society. What's left is the organization that administers the common affairs of the nation. This organization, which becomes the planning body under communism, expresses the will of the people. For thinking about the communist future, says Marx, the question to answer is this: "What social functions will remain in existence there that are analogous to present functions of the state?"[42]

Throughout history the state had social functions and political functions. The social functions of the state include relief of the poor, maintenance of roads and canals, and administration of the common affairs of society. Engels says that the "social function was everywhere the basis of political supremacy; and further that political supremacy has existed for any length of time only when it discharged its social functions."[43] Some social functions of the state survive under communism.

But the essence of the state was its political function: to hold down the masses for the ruling class. Political power meant kings, armies, police, judges, courts, prisons–in a word, force. Political force was an instrument of class rule;

the ruling class controlled the state and used it to keep down the working masses.[44]

After the communist revolution there will be "a political transition period in which the state can be nothing but *the revolutionary dictatorship of the proletariat*."[45] The proletariat uses political force–revolutionary tribunals, people's prisons, Red Guards–to suppress the bourgeoisie. Then soldiers, tribunals, and prisons disappear. What remains of the state is an administration that runs the national economy: planners, accountants, bookkeepers, statisticians, economists, engineers, and technicians. The social function of the state survives, while the political function dies out.

Under communism, says Marx, "the public power will lose its political character. Political power, properly so called, is merely the organized power of one class for oppressing another."[46] Engels explains that "public functions will lose their political character and be transformed into the simple administrative functions of watching over the true interests of society."[47] This is the "conversion of political rule over men into an administration of things and a direction of processes of production."[48]

According to Marx, the Paris Commune, before its fall, planned such a transition to communism. "While the merely repressive organs of the old governmental power were to be amputated, its legitimate functions were to be . . . restored to the responsible agents of society," writes Marx. "Universal suffrage was to serve the people, constituted in Communes, as individual suffrage serves every other employer in the search for the workmen and managers in his business."[49] Assignment of the administrative functions through elections would become a business affair.

In communist society, then, the state in the traditional sense dies out. There is no more government. "The government of persons is replaced by the administration of things."[50] But a society without a government is in a condition of anarchy. And that is exactly what communism is, according to Marx and Engels: a system of anarchy. This is how they put it: "All socialists understand by Anarchy the following: once the goal of the proletarian movement–the abolition of classes–has been reached, then the power of the state disappears (a power that served to hold the great producing majority under the yoke of a tiny exploiting minority), and the governmental functions are transformed into simple administrative functions."[51] A national planning body carries out these administrative functions for the common good.

But isn't the administrative apparatus, elected by the people, a sort of political authority? Don't the people elevate the planners to authority through an election? And doesn't the word *election* suggest the political state? "The character of an election does not depend on the word itself," answers Marx, "but on the economic basis, on the economic relationships of the voters; and as soon as the functions have ceased to be political, then (1) there are no more governmental functions, (2) assignment of the administrative functions becomes a business matter, which gives no political authority, and (3) elections no longer have a political character."[52]

I have been quoting Marx and Engels at length to show how they are using the word *political* in a new way. Their usage has caused much confusion about their concept of "the withering away of the state." Under communism elections don't put people in command of police and soldiers, courts and prisons, guards and executioners. Elections decide who serves society as planners, technicians, and administrators. Through elections administrators can rotate, and everyone may take part in the general affairs of society.[53] "Every member of society," says Engels, "will be enabled to participate not only in production but also in the . . . administration of social wealth."[54]

Under communism "production has been concentrated in the hands of a vast association of the whole nation."[55] Railways and telegraphs connect the communities with the planning center and with one another. Each community produces for the plan.

The planners will calculate how much labor time every product contains. They will reckon how many hours of labor go into a bushel of wheat, into a steam engine, or into a hundred square yards of cloth of a certain quality. They will estimate the number of products society needs and assign different communities to produce them.[56]

The planners will divide the total social product into an accumulation fund, a reserve fund, and a consumption fund. The accumulation fund provides for replacement, maintenance, and expansion of the productive forces. The reserve fund is insurance against earthquakes, storms, droughts, floods, and plagues. The consumption fund provides communal services and goods for personal use.[57]

A great deal of the consumption fund goes for communal services, including housing and food. Medicine, education, and books come from the community.

The rest of the consumption fund supplies articles for personal use. There will be individual ownership of such articles under communism.[58] People will have their own clothes, their own furniture, their own typewriters, their own watches, their own toothbrushes.

In communist society there will be no money, no market, and no exchange: "within the cooperative society based on common ownership of the means of production, the producers do not exchange their products."[59] The consumption fund supplies products to all: if someone needs a towel, a fountain pen, or a pair of shoes, he or she goes to the communal storehouse. The planners make sure that such articles are there. The planned economy provides for everyone according to need, and material abundance is the basis of communal life.[60]

Communal living, maintain Marx and Engels, creates a higher form of the family. The bourgeois family must disappear with capitalism; under communism new relationships between the sexes, new ways of caring for children, and new moral attitudes emerge.[61]

There is no such thing as the family *as such*, say Marx and Engels, there are only historical forms of it.[62] Sometimes in the extended family of primitive society (a family containing many couples and their children) the work of women in running the communist household matched food-getting by the man. Society valued both kinds of work, and on this economic basis equality flourished between men and women. But with civilization came the patriarchal family, in which men dominate their wives and children (the man is the property owner or breadwinner, and his wife a servant).[63] In world history the patriarchal family takes on many forms: as social structure changes from one epoch to another, the organization of the family varies.[64] The following forms made a series in historical development: (1) the Eastern form, with the husband holding his slave wives in a harem, (2) the ancient Greek form, with the wife in seclusion while her husband enjoyed social life, courtesans, and boys, and (3) the ancient Roman form, in which the wife gained some equality with her husband.[65] Bourgeois marriage is the last phase of the patriarchal family, for under communism the family assumes a higher form.

In the bourgeois form of the patriarchal family, argue the founders of Marxism, boredom and money are the binding link.[66] The man may marry for love, but the woman marries for security: unlike a prostitute who hires out her body from time to time, a wife sells it once and for all.[67] A husband's love may lapse into boredom.[68] Thus in the morals of bourgeois marriage two prostitutions make one virtue.[69] The man is the breadwinner, and this gives him power over the woman: "in the family, he is the bourgeois, the wife represents the proletariat."[70] She depends on her husband for a living.

The economic relation, the existence of children, and the structure of modern towns—these are the basis of the bourgeois family. In every town there are thousands of houses, each with a wife in it; she stays home to watch the children.[71]

Because of children, bourgeois marriage is a legal institution: the law binds man to wife, for child care must not depend on arbitrary whims. Without children in mind two people would hardly make a legal arrangement to live together; nor would society forbid their separation.[72]

Throughout their writings Marx and Engels argue that in the proletarian class these bourgeois family relations are dissolving. In the nineteenth century rapid industrialization weakened the family: the demand for labor pulled men, women, and children into factories; women earned their bread; and children strayed or worked. There was a breakdown of the patriarchal family. The decline of this family form, the employment of women and children in industry, the eclipse of the powerful father–all this was laying the basis for a higher type of family, says Marx, for under communism the father's dominance vanishes into equality between men and women, and everyone in the family works.[73]

What sort of family emerges in communist society? Marx and Engels tell us that education is "social,"[74] that child care is "a public matter,"[75] that it takes place "on a communal basis,"[76] and that it begins as soon as the child can leave its mother.[77] Engels speaks with approval of the "infant schools" that Robert Owen set up in his social experiment at New Lanark. "At the age of two the children came to school, where they enjoyed themselves so much that they could scarcely be got home again."[78] Today many would consider this a year or so too soon, but the principle is clear enough: communal nurseries, run with affection, have an important place in the future society.

Older children *live in communal schools.*[79] There is "a combination of work and instruction in socialist society, which is to ensure an all-round technical education as well as a practical foundation for scientific training."[80] Robert Owen's proposals for education, says Marx, are realized under communism: there is instruction combined with work and play "as the only method of producing fully developed human beings."[81] Children work from the age of nine on (with careful supervision, safety measures, and time limits).[82]

Communal education revolutionizes the family, for child care ceases to occupy man and wife. Society no longer fixes their relationship, binds them with laws, and forbids their separation. Communism "will transform the relations between the sexes into a purely private matter which concerns only the persons involved and into which society has no occasion to intervene. It can do this since it does away with private property and educates children on a communal basis."[83]

In communist society, housework does not fall upon women alone; it becomes, as Engels puts it, a public industry.[84] In the communal palace public kitchens prepare food, and work teams clean every apartment in the building –these tasks are distributed to all.[85] Communal living transforms the role of women. No longer domestic servants, they become the equals of men and share in productive labor.[86] Again and again Engels repeats this theme, which will interest the feminist movements of our time: "With the passage of the means of production into common property, the individual family ceases to be the economic unit of society. Private housekeeping is transformed into a social industry. The care and education of the children becomes a public matter."[87] Freed from child care, men and women build new love relationships.

What are these relationships like? They are not promiscuous; free love is not the way of the new society. A few communists preached free love and community of sexual partners, but the founders of Marxism reject them.[88] "It is a curious fact that with every great revolutionary movement," says Engels, "the question of 'free love' comes into the foreground."[89] He and Marx disown the advocates of casual sex.

They also attack the old world and its ways and mock "the miserable amorous and patriarchal illusions of the domestic hearth."[90] The best that bourgeois marriage produces is "a wedded life of leaden boredom, which is described as domestic bliss."[91]

In communist society all unions are based on love alone. Engels traces the evolution of sexual love through history and finds gradual progress. Romantic love emerges late in history. This highest form of love has three traits: it is mutual love between man and woman; it is intense and persistent; and it justifies sexual intercourse (in modern eyes). Such is the basis of free unions in communist society. If the love fades or disappears before a new passion, then separation is a blessing. Thus Engels foresees an increase of freedom in the relations between men and women under communism.[92]

But the founders of Marxism are not utopians. Their vision of love in communist society is no dogma, nor do they paint future relationships in detail. Coming generations, warns Engels, will develop sexual relationships and moral attitudes beyond our experience. "Once such people appear, they will not care a rap about what we today think they should do."[93] The nineteenth century was a romantic age, and Marx and Engels absorbed its values. Their view of sex may strike many of us as old-fashioned. They would find nothing surprising in this.

The Transition Period

We have examined Marx's and Engels' vision of the communist society. How does this society come into being? Through proletarian revolution. The revolution is not an event but a process—it takes years.

The proletarian revolution does not suddenly unveil a new society. "Between capitalist and communist society lies the period of the revolutionary transformation of the one into the other."[94] In this transformation the seizure of political power is only "the first step,"[95] and the transition to communism may last a long time. The transition period brings about two things: a tremendous increase in productive forces and a gradual abolition of private property.[96] To accomplish this, the proletariat "will have to pass through long struggles, through a series of historic processes, transforming circumstances and men."[97]

After the revolutionary seizure of power, the workers organize a new state—"the dictatorship of the proletariat."[98] In our century the word *dictatorship* suggests the rule of one person or a junta, but this is not what "the dictatorship of the proletariat" means to Marx and Engels. They do not think of it as the rule of a dictator, a committee, or a party: it is the rule of "the entire revolutionary class."[99] "The first step in the revolution by the working class," says the *Manifesto*, "is to raise the proletariat to the position of ruling class, to win the battle of democracy."[100]

How is the "class dictatorship of the proletariat"[101] organized? What form of state does it assume? Engels suggests the "single, indivisible Republic."[102] But Marx believes that the Paris Commune foreshadowed the state form of the transition period,[103] though in a pessimistic mood he judges the Commune differently.[104] Marx sees the proletarian government as a federation of free communes, in which the governing officials are elected by universal suffrage, paid workers' wages, and controlled by total recall.[105]

Thus the dictatorship of the proletariat is democratic: the working masses run the state through recall and elections. The state is not an instrument of the revolutionary intellectuals. Anarchists charged that it would be a rule of the scholars over everyone else, but Marx denies this.[106] State officials are "working men or acknowledged representatives of the working class."[107]

In what sense, then, is the state a dictatorship? It is a dictatorship of the proletariat over the bourgeoisie; the state suppresses the political rights of the bourgeoisie and breaks its hold on the economy. The bourgeois will not release their proletarian slaves without resistance. The proletariat will take "the organized political force of the state and with this aid stamp out the resistance of the capitalist class and reorganize society."[108] But this takes time, for the capitalist slaveholders rebel against the proletarian communes. "Once communal organization is firmly established on a national scale, the catastrophes it might still have to undergo would be sporadic slaveholders' insurrections, which, while for a moment interrupting the work of peaceful progress, would only accelerate the movement by putting the sword into the hand of the Social Revolution."[109] Again and again the bourgeois attack the proletarian state, resaid its decrees, sabotage its actions. It suppresses these rebels and confiscates their property.[110]

The workers' state struggles to expand the productive forces and build an economy of abundance. The state establishes "industrial armies, especially for agriculture."[111] What does this mean? Think of an army of 500,000 people employed in construction rather than destruction. Instead of burned villages and ruined provinces we have fields cultivated, trees planted, canals dug, and aqueducts built. If the old society could recruit armies for destruction, the new society can draw millions into the projects of the future: construction of dams and harbors, reclamation of swamps and deserts, and extension of roads and railways.

The state nationalizes the banks. With credit and money in its hands, it can play a central role in the economy.[112] The state sets up national factories and workshops, takes over the industries of rebel bourgeois, and buys out many capitalists.[113] The state sector of the economy grows while the capitalist sector weakens. The result is "gradual expropriation of landowners, industrialists, railroad magnates and shipowners, partly through competition by state industry, partly directly through compensation in the form of bonds."[114]

The state abolishes inheritance and further weakens the capitalists with a graduated income tax.[115] The capitalists find themselves hedged in by laws, "factory owners, insofar as they still exist, being obliged to pay the same high wages as those paid by the state."[116] The expanding state sector chokes out private property. "Finally, when all capital, all production, all exchange have been brought together in the hands of the nation, private property will disappear of its own accord, money will become superfluous. . . ."[117]

As money dies out, society passes from the transition period into the first phase of communism. In this phase money vanishes, but material incentives still operate, for society has not reached the stage of economic abundance, nor have all learned the duty of productive labor. People receive paper checks for their labor, and with these they draw consumers' goods from the public stocks. The checks are not money: they don't circulate.[118]

People working longer than others receive more checks, says Marx, and people without children find their checks going further. Equal consumption has not arrived. "But these defects are inevitable in the first phase of communist society as it is when it has just emerged after prolonged birth pangs from capitalist society."[119]

Reeducation of aristocrats and bourgeois takes place for, as the *Manifesto* puts it, there is "equal liability of all to labor."[120] Anyone who won't work gets no checks, and without them starves. The ethic preached by St. Paul (ignored by Christians) becomes the social norm: "He who does not work shall not eat" (2 Thessalonians 3:10).

The economy rapidly expands: the search for private profit is no longer its driving force, overproduction and crises no longer its disease. "Big industry, freed from the pressure of private property, will undergo such an expansion that what we now see will seem as petty in comparison as manufacture seems when put beside big industry of our own day. This development of industry will make available to society a sufficient mass of products to satisfy the needs of everyone. . . . In this way such an abundance of goods will be produced that society will be able to satisfy the needs of all its members."[121] Slowly the higher phase of communism is reached, and society can write on its banners: "From each according to his ability, to each according to his needs!"[122]

Society no longer makes people work for paper checks. Moral incentives to work replace material incentives—everyone labors for society. "Production will so expand and man so change that society will be able to slough off whatever of its old economic habits may remain."[123] Communist society is an economy of abundance: if people want something they go to a communal storehouse and help themselves.

To sum up, Marx expects a long transition period between capitalist and communist society, a period in which growing communism struggles with dying capitalism and wages and markets exist beside industrial expansion and economic planning. Once communism is reached, the new society divides into stages: a lower phase containing hangovers from capitalism, and a higher phase of abundance. Most Leninists call Marx's lower phase of communism *socialism* and confuse it with the transition period. This error is so widespread that we must spell out the postrevolutionary phases with care. After the revolution there is first the transition period, then the lower phase of communism, and finally the higher phase of communism.

Marx's outline of the transition period applies to an advanced country like England. But during the lifetimes of Marx and Engels the countries of the Continent were peasant nations with a backward industry. For such countries the transition period presents special problems.

When proletarian revolution takes place in a peasant country, the urban workers may be isolated among hostile peasants. The peasants cling to their patch of land and look upon the proletariat with suspicion: communists plan to abolish private property.[124] But the proletariat must win the peasants for the revolution, for they are the majority of the nation. The proletariat's revolutionary song, says Marx in a striking image, must obtain a peasant chorus: a solo song of the proletariat turns into a swan song in all peasant countries.[125] Marx wrote this in 1852, after the French peasants voted for the death of the revolution. In 1874, after the peasants had abandoned the Paris Commune to its fate, Marx writes in a personal notebook:

Where the peasant exists *en masse* as a private owner; even where he is in a more or less considerable majority as in all the states of the West European continent; where he has not disappeared and been replaced by agricultural day laborers (as he *has* been replaced in England); in these situations the following conditions occur: either the peasant hinders the revolution, wrecks it, as he has done up to now in France, or the proletariat must apply government measures that immediately improve the peasant's condition, that win him for the revolution.[126]

Marx goes on to explain that these measures must lead the peasants toward the transition from private to collective property, make the transition easy for them, create conditions that move them through it of their own free will. Such measures must not alienate the peasants, as nationalization of their land would surely do. On the other hand, they must not feed their craving for property by dividing up plantations among small holders.[127]

Marx and Engels are clear about the plantations, whether feudal estates or giant capitalist farms. The state sends the landowners packing and hands the plantations to the rural proletariat, the class that works the land. The plantations become cooperatives. These cooperatives show the peasants the advantages of large-scale agriculture, and the peasants persuaded by such examples try to form cooperatives themselves.[128]

"Marx and I have never doubted," Engels writes to Bebel in 1886, "that cooperatives must be used on a wide scale as an intermediate step in the transition to a full communist economy. Only the thing must be arranged so that . . . the special interests of the cooperatives (against society as a whole) cannot gain a footing."[129] In cooperatives or collective farms, the peasants pool their resources, till the soil together, send the produce to market, and divide up the profit. They produce for profit, not for a national plan, and they may develop special interests against society as a whole. The proletarian state must work to prevent the transitional cooperatives from hardening into fixed social forms.

Society must never take away the peasants' land, nor force them into collective farms, says Engels, rather society should attract them by examples, by persuasion, by aid to cooperatives.[130] Big farming through cooperatives means using agricultural machinery, and machinery makes the work of most peasants superfluous. Society must help these peasants to organize major industries in the villages.[131]

For communist revolution to succeed, writes Marx in his notebooks of 1874, the proletariat must be able to do something for the peasants. The proletariat should be able to do as much for them as the bourgeoisie did in the French Revolution–though different things. To do these things, the proletariat must play a significant role in the economy. In peasant countries where a growing proletariat exists (Belgium, France, Germany), communist revolution can take place. The peasant countries of Eastern Europe have no proletariat: there communism is impossible.[132]

Marx and Engels, in brief, believe that communist revolution can happen in peasant countries if two conditions are present: there is a growing proletariat in the cities and the revolution is international (so that an advanced nation helps the backward countries). The revolution, writes Engels in 1847, "will develop in each of these countries more or less rapidly insofar as one country or the other has a more developed industry, greater wealth, a more significant mass of productive forces. So it will go slowest and will meet most obstacles in Germany, most rapidly and with the fewest difficulties in England. It will have a powerful impact on the other countries of the world and will radically alter the course of development which they have followed up to now, while greatly stepping up its pace. It is a universal revolution and will accordingly have a universal range."[133] For Marx's conception of the role of the peasant in the continuing revolution of the nineteenth century, see the appendix.

The Future Society

Communist society, says Engels, "is not something finished once and for all. Like other social conditions, it should be thought of as undergoing continual change and transformation."[134] Marx and Engels do not think of communism as a perfect society. "Just as knowledge is unable to reach a complete conclusion in a perfect, ideal condition of humanity, so is history unable to do so; a perfect society, a perfect 'state,' are things which can only exist in imagination."[135] Communism is not a utopia beyond suffering, an Eden without conflicts, a heaven of equality.

"The idea of socialist society as the realm of *equality* is a one-sided French idea," remarks Engels.[136] Socialism spreads across the planet to unite all communities in one family–but inequality remains. "There are no two countries which furnish an equal number of the necessaries of life in equal plenty and with the same quantity of labor," Marx quotes an English writer.[137] Countries differ in climate, contour, and position. Tundra, desert, jungle, and mountain are not as productive as forest and plain. Marx mocks the anarchist communists who want to reduce everyone to the same level, who want to make all people equal: "And the difference between lowland and highland, river basins, climate, soil, coal, iron, acquired productive forces–both material and spiritual, language, literature, technical capacities, and so forth?"[138] Though planned trading will eliminate many inequalities, people in different countries will have unequal conditions of life. Engels notes that this also holds inside each country: "Between one country and another, one province and another and even one locality and another there will always exist a *certain* inequality in the conditions of life. . . ."[139] Unequal conditions may create conflicting interests, but under communist institutions people find rational solutions for these conflicts.

To solve international conflicts people no longer resort to war. The triumph of communism means abolition of standing armies.[140]

Nor will people resort to violence in social conflicts. In communist society, says Marx, there will be no more revolutions, only social evolution. Conflict results in argument, discussion, and debate, and people settle their differences by a vote. Revolution has come to an end.[141]

What about personal conflicts? Will there be crimes of passion, like murder? No, only class society, based on exploitation and violence, breeds murderers.[142] But there will be personal disputes, says Engels. The community sets up courts of arbitration, and judges (*Schiedsrichter*) settle such disputes.[143]

In communist society the population is still made up of human beings: they have their joys and fears, their quarrels and loves, their failures and achievements. And they have their work. Labor, even under communism, can be a painful discipline. "The realm of freedom actually begins only where labor which is determined by necessity and everyday needs ceases; thus in the very nature of things it lies beyond the sphere of actual material production."[144] Under communism, economics becomes a question of "reducing the necessary labor of society to a minimum. The counterpart of this reduction is that all members of society can develop their education in the arts, sciences, and so forth, thanks to the free time and means available to all."[145] As more and more free time becomes available in a communist society, people get down to the real business of life—the creation of beauty and the search for knowledge. In the life of art and science they find true freedom.

And yet in communist society, Marx maintains, there is some freedom for people struggling in material production:

> Freedom in this field can only consist in socialized man, the asso-
> ciated producers, rationally regulating their interchange with Nature,
> bringing it under their common control instead of being ruled by it as by
> the blind forces of Nature, and achieving this with the least expenditure
> of energy and under conditions most favorable to their human nature. But
> it still remains a realm of necessity. Beyond it begins that development
> of human energy which can blossom forth only with this realm of
> necessity as its basis. The shortening of the working day is its basic
> requirement.[146]

What does freedom in the field of material production, though limited, consist of? Scientific mastery of nature, rational regulation of production, and control of the products through a common plan.[147]

Through planning the workers gain control of their products again. Under capitalism, explains Marx in *Capital*, people see their products as "alien," something they make not for themselves but for capitalists.[148] The miner digs out gold, and the capitalist carts it off; the weaver produces silk, and the capitalist takes it away; the worker builds a palace, and the capitalist moves into it: what the workers do has no meaning for them, their product vanishes, their activity is pointless–except to bring in a wage.[149] Their labor is a labor of Sisyphus, a meaningless torment.

Under communism all this changes, for men and women no longer produce for others, but for themselves. Production follows a social plan, and all people know they work for the common good. Scientific administration of production becomes an exercise in freedom–labor turns into free activity. "The labor concerned with material production can only have this character if (1) it is of a social nature, (2) it has a scientific character and at the same time is general work, that is, if it ceases to be human effort as a definite, trained natural force, gives up its purely natural, primitive aspects and becomes the activity of a subject controlling all the forces of nature in the production process."[150]

People find freedom in the labor process because they control it. In every factory the workers themselves solve the questions that arise, "whether they are settled by decision of a delegate placed at the head of each branch of labor or, if possible, by a majority vote."[151] The old labor discipline (threats, fines) becomes unnecessary, for all are working for themselves.[152]

In communist society there will be a tremendous increase in productive power, as society plans production not for profit but for all, as war and crises and waste disappear, as playboys, speculators, middlemen, lawyers, soldiers, and priests vanish or go to work: all this "will suffice with everybody doing his share of work to reduce the time required for labor to a point which measured by our present conceptions will be small indeed."[153] When everyone has plenty of free time, when leisure fills much of the day, when people live for science and art, then the human being becomes a different creature and labor takes on a new meaning.

Free time–which includes leisure time as well as time for higher activities–naturally transforms anyone who enjoys it into a different person, and it is this different person who then enters the direct process of production. The person who is being formed finds discipline in this process, while for the person who is already formed it is practice, experimental science, materially creative and self-objectifying knowledge–this person already commands the accumulated wisdom of society. Both of them find exercise in it, to the extent that labor requires practical manipulation and free movement, as in agriculture.[154]

In productive labor for society, the new person of leisure finds discipline, physical exercise, and a chance to apply scientific knowledge.

But who will do the dirty work in communist society? Who will collect the garbage? Won't everyone shirk such tasks? Under communism three things solve this problem.

First, in the new society manual work loses its stigma, and necessary tasks like collecting garbage become respectable.[155] Next, society gets rid of much dirty work by using machinery (like steam cleaning dishes in communal kitchens).[156] Finally, abolishing divided labor means that no one does disagreeable work all day: people rotate from dreary jobs to interesting ones.

Does abolishing division of labor mean that specialists disappear? No, Marx and Engels are aware that a civilization needs specialists (physicists, statisticians, engineers, geologists, planners, navigators, accountants, astronomers, surgeons, teachers, painters, chemists, architects).[157] But a specialist will also be ready to do manual work. An architect, says Engels, may give instructions as an architect for half an hour, and then act as a brick carrier for a while until the architectural knowledge is needed again. Everyone does a little manual labor.[158]

Overcoming the division of labor does not mean ending specialization; it means ending specialization *in one activity*. The architect may also be engineer, doctor, and teacher. A painter may be sculptor and architect as well. "With a communist organization of society," write Marx and Engels, "there disappears the subordination of the artist to . . . some definite art, thanks to which he is exclusively a painter, sculptor, and so forth, the very name of his activity expressing the narrowness of his professional development and his dependence on division of labor. In a communist society there are no painters but at most people who engage in painting among other activities."[159] The name of Michelangelo–painter, sculptor, architect–comes to mind at once; and in fact Marx and Engels model Communist Man and Woman on the heroes of the Renaissance. What were the people of the Renaissance like?

Engels writes,

> there was hardly any man of importance then living who had not traveled extensively, who did not command four or five languages, who did not shine in a number of fields. Leonardo da Vinci was not only a great painter but also a great mathematician, mechanician, and engineer, to whom the most diverse branches of physics are indebted for important discoveries; Albrecht Dürer was painter, engraver, sculptor, architect, and in addition invented a system of fortification. . . . Machiavelli was statesman, historian, poet, and at the same time the first notable military author of modern times. . . . For the heroes of that time had not yet come under the servitude of the division of labor. . . . But what is especially characteristic of them is that they almost all pursue their lives and activities in the middle of the contemporary movements, in the practical struggle: they take sides and

join in the fight, one by speaking and writing, another with the sword, many with both. Therefore the fullness and force of character that makes them complete men.[160]

This hatred of mediocrity, this admiration of all-round development was common in socialist thought. Marx admired Fourier's "Gargantuan view of man."[161] In Fourier's utopia people got by on four hours' sleep a night, ate five meals a day, and learned to do all things well—from hunting to writing.

Marx and Engels themselves were giants. Marx knew eight languages and Engels twice as many; they investigated a dozen fields of knowledge: philosophy, physics, theology, law, anthropology, sociology, history, economics. They wrote on all these subjects, and they wrote on them well. Marx left reams of mathematical manuscripts, and Engels a work on the philosophy of science. Marx read world literature, memorized the classics, and devoured the novels of his day; Engels studied military strategy and tactics. Their encyclopedic minds never rested: they roamed over the sea of knowledge like hungry sharks and attacked every thinker in range. Yet they were not men of the study. They took part in the revolution of 1848: manifestos and pamphlets, speeches and articles, letters and programs flowed from their pens. Marx suffered prison and exile, Engels fought in the revolutionary war. In the 1840s they edited the greatest newspaper in Germany; in the 1850s they wrote the lead articles for a paper with vast circulation—The New York Daily Tribune; in the 1860s Marx guided the First International through a stormy decade, while Engels managed a factory in Manchester. As a student Marx drank beer and fought duels, finished a Ph.D. in philosophy, and found every university closed to him. He married a beautiful aristocrat and fathered several children—not all of them legitimate. (Engels kept mistresses.) The two men built the most remarkable friendship of all time. They tried to approximate the life they planned for people in the future communist society; they pursued the ideal of the Greeks, of the Renaissance, of the Humanists—"Total Man."

Marx and Engels never forgave the bourgeois for boring them. Their letters hurl curses at "bourgeois philistines"; their contempt for the ruling class is boundless. "The existence of a ruling class," warns Engels, "is becoming daily more and more a brake on the development of . . . science, art, and especially of forms of cultural intercourse. There never were greater boors than our modern bourgeois."[162]

But can Communist Men and Women come into existence? Won't the effort to create such beings end in utopia? Isn't the vision mocked by all we know about human nature?

Marx and Engels laugh at the concept of "Human Nature, of Man in general, who belongs to no class, has no reality, who exists only in the misty realm of philosophical fantasy."[163] Throughout *The German Ideology* they jeer at the philosophers' fixed "human essence." "The human essence is no abstraction inherent in each single individual," writes Marx. "In its reality it is the ensemble of the social relations."[164] It is silly to talk about humans outside a society. "*Man* is not an abstract being squatting outside the world," says Marx. "Man is *the world of men*, the state, society."[165] As we go from one society to another, from one class to another, from one age to another, human nature changes. The Greek aristocrat, the Roman plebeian, the French seigneur, the Russian serf, the Arab bedouin, the Chinese mandarin, the Hopi Indian, the Hindu yogi, the German bureaucrat, the Samoan native, the American business executive, the Mexican peasant–what do they have in common? "All history is nothing but a continuous transformation of human nature," writes Marx.[166] The only thing constant about human nature is that it changes.

Psychoanalysis, Christianity, existentialism, and other twentieth-century ideologies still worry about human nature. Aggressive instincts, original sin, anxiety, egoism–something is embedded in human nature and causes our behavior. "You can't change human nature," claim these philosophies, "and so you will never change society: we must give up looking for a world without exploitation, without injustice, without war." What do Marx and Engels reply to this sort of thinking? They admit that class struggle, oppression, and war run throughout history: people have always treated one another cruelly. Yet not wickedness made people cruel, say our two thinkers again and again, but economic scarcity. Throughout history people fought one another for a bone to gnaw. Today, however, scarcity can be overcome and society arranged so that human interests no longer dictate ruthlessness. Scarcity can vanish, if the productive forces of the industrial age function in a rational social system.[167]

When humanity overturns capitalist society in a mighty revolution, human nature will change. The acquisitive, stunted, cringing person of today will undergo a transformation. The revolutionary epoch will remake the European workers, though they will pass through a period of terrible struggles, through a series of revolutionary processes changing circumstances and people.[168]

But what is it in their nature that changes? Is it egoism? Do they lose their egoism and become obliging, self-denying people, ready to sacrifice themselves for the good of society? Is that what communism means? No–Marx and Engels write that communists "do not put to people the moral demand: love one another, do not be egoists, and so forth; on the contrary, they are very well aware that egoism, just as much as self-sacrifice, is in definite circumstances a necessary form of the self-assertion of individuals. Therefore the communists by no means want . . . to do away with the 'private individual' for the sake of the 'general,' self-sacrificing man."[169] In *The Holy Family* Marx affirms the Enlightenment tradition: he considers egoism healthy in a society arranged so that personal interests coincide with the general interest. Communism will be such a society.[170]

Then how will revolution change human nature? It will end the respect people feel for their "betters" and "superiors." The church trained them to kneel; the school made them conform; the factory taught them to obey. Under capitalism people are obedient, modest, and mediocre. Marx and Engels say that a revolution will change all that.[171] People will throw down their "betters," take over the factories, and make the decisions themselves.

Human nature changes through revolutionary struggle. The workers force out the capitalists, plan the economy, and develop communist consciousness. "For the production on a mass scale of this communist consciousness and for the success of the cause itself, the alteration of men on a mass scale is necessary, an alteration which can only take place in a practical movement, a *revolution*; this revolution is necessary, therefore, not only because the ruling class cannot be overthrown in any other way, but also because the class overthrowing it can only in a revolution succeed in ridding itself of all the muck of ages and become fitted to found society anew."[172]

The New Man and Woman emerge after generations of change. In communist society people show new attitudes. They think of the fields and factories as "ours"; only a madman wants to mark off a piece of ground as "his."[173] They laugh at descriptions of capitalism, of how the factories made things no one needed, and then tricked everyone into wanting them: lace, whiskey, top hats, chewing gum, china, tobacco. Marx describes the capitalist as follows: "He . . . excites in [the consumer] morbid appetites. . . . Every product is a bait with which to seduce away the other's . . . money; every real and possible need is a weakness that will lead the fly to the gluepot."[174]

Engels speaks contemptuously of "the useless and plainly ridiculous luxury that has its source only in the desire to show off" that will disappear under communism.[175] Waste and useless luxury vanish, but there is an increase in health services, higher education, scientific research, artistic development, public transport, popular tourism, and the circulation of books and ideas in general. "From [the revolution] will date a new epoch in history, in which mankind and all branches of its activity, especially natural science, will experience an advance before which everything preceding it will pale into insignificance."[176]

V. Classes

Definition of Class

In *Die Weltgeschichte ist das Weltgericht*, the historian A. G. Löwy tells a story about Nikolai Bukharin, the chief theoretician of world communism in the 1920s (p. 225). Bukharin once examined the original manuscript of the third volume of Marx's *Capital* in the Amsterdam archives. This final volume, composed from notes left by Marx, was published by Engels after the great economist's death. Bukharin began reading the last chapter of the manuscript, entitled "Classes." Hardly has this crucial chapter begun when it breaks off—unfinished! Bukharin reached this point, then looked out the window and said quietly, "Oh Karl, Karl, if only you had finished this."

All students of Marx have echoed this lament, for nowhere in the many volumes of Marx's writings is there a systematic treatment of class, nor even a clear definition of the concept. And yet Marx's writings abound with discussions of classes, their formation, and their role in history. What does the concept *class* mean to him?

The relation of a social group to the means of production, the relation of owning or not owning the means of production, is basic in Marx's conception of class. In capitalist society the bourgeoisie owns factories; the proletariat owns no means of production and lives off wages.[1] Classes are not income groups or status groups; classes are groups defined by their economic position, by how they make a living.[2]

A worker in Paris and a peasant in Provence may have the same income, but they belong to different classes: the worker owns no means of production, while the peasant owns land and tools. Though their education may be the same, the vineyard owner and the wine taster belong to different classes, for one has vines and the other nothing. A doctor owning a clinic and a professor drawing a salary have the same status—but they are in different classes.

On the other hand, a British lord and a Manchester upstart, if they both own factories, belong to the same class. An artist and a prostitute sharing a slum attic are in the propertyless class. A bookseller, a grocer, a cabinetmaker, a blacksmith, and a peasant belong to the class of small owners.

Functionalist sociology has criticized this conception of classes. Some sociologists deny that there are classes in capitalist society. Others accept Max Weber's distinction between class and status and emphasize status in their studies of social stratification. Class is defined by one's role in production, where one's money comes from; status is defined by how one spends the money, by one's life-style and prestige. At General Motors the welder and the clerk are both workers but each has a different status. Class and status are often different: the socialite rejects the *nouveau riche*, and the black millionaire cannot join the Kiwanis Club. Some sociologists stress status as the key to social stratification, and think this a great discovery, an advance over Marx's emphasis on class.

Marx and Engels were aware of the difference between class and status; they knew that people in an upper class may have low status. They discuss the English bourgeoisie's sense of inferiority, noting that the bourgeoisie allowed the aristocracy to govern for it, and they marvel at the inferior education that the bourgeoisie accepted. Yet it was the class that ruled England![3]

(In capitalist society the bourgeoisie rules economically, but does not always govern politically. An aristocratic class, a political elite, or a military junta often governs for it. Under capitalism there is government for the bourgeoisie, though not always by the bourgeoisie.)[4]

Why do Marx and Engels focus on class and ignore status? Because status seeking has little meaning for social change. Societies change, and class struggle is one mechanism of change. Marx and Engels are interested in social development, and the static models of the stratification theorists would have bored them.

For our two revolutionaries classes are rooted in property relations, and these change as society passes from tribalism through feudalism into capitalism. Class is a historical concept, and the definition of class must show this.

For the competitive capitalism of their day Marx and Engels see ownership of productive forces as the basic idea in class. The bourgeois or capitalists owned raw materials, machines, and factories: this gave them social and political power. The proletarians had their bare hands; they worked or starved. The bourgeois paid the workers a low wage and took home profits. They were overlords because they owned the means of production.[5]

But under feudalism the lords merely owned the land, says Marx, they did not really possess it. The serfs possessed the land. They were on the land plowing it with their tools. Why did they raise food for the lords? Not because of direct economic pressure. The serfs gave the lords food to be safe. And this was true of slavery: the masters held the slaves by force, not through economic pressure. In precapitalist societies a few people exploited many by force.[6]

Yet in every social system the property relations finally decide who commands and who obeys. The owners have social and political power based on property, and thus they force others to obey. The Roman aristocrat owned slaves, the feudal lord owned land, and the English capitalist owned factories. Those who obeyed owned little or nothing. "Whenever a part of society possesses the monopoly of the means of production," writes Marx, "the laborer, free or not free, must add to the working time necessary for his own maintenance an extra working time in order to produce the means of subsistence for the owners of the means of production, whether this owner be the Athenian aristocrat, Etruscan theocrat, Roman citizen, Norman baron, American slave owner, Wallachian Boyard, modern landlord, or capitalist."[7]

Societies always split into owners and workers, into ruling and laboring classes. This happened, argue Marx and Engels, because agricultural societies could not produce much, and their tiny surplus went to a ruling class. While the masses sweated in fields and workshops, the ruling class practiced law, politics, art, and science. The rulers piled burdens on the masses. Finally the industrial revolution offered the masses a chance to escape exhausting work. A social plan could raise production and free them from long labor: all might then take part in art and science in a society without classes.[8]

Class Fractions

With this powerful lens, the class concept, Marx and Engels surveyed the torrent of history since the Renaissance. They saw three currents swirling through it, three great classes of European society: landed aristocracy, bourgeoisie, and proletariat.[9] In the clash and flow of these forces they found the key to the development of society. In the *Communist Manifesto* they paint with sweeping strokes the pattern of historical motion, the bourgeois struggle against the nobility and the proletarian challenge to the bourgeoisie.[10] These currents stood out clearly, says Engels, and only the blind could not "see in the fight of these great classes and in the conflict of their interests the driving force of modern history—at least in the two most advanced countries."[11]

Marx and Engels racked up the lens for a close look at their own period, the epoch of competitive capitalism. They found classes and fractions of classes struggling with one another. The landowning aristocracy faded toward the background, but showed fight.[12] The bourgeoisie, the largest current, owned the ships and mines, the factories and banks, the stores and buildings of industrial society.[13] The petty bourgeoisie with crafts and shops steadily lost out to the big owners; the peasantry dwindled slowly, its small plots fusing into giant farms.[14] The industrial proletariat, the class that held the future in its hands, organized co-ops, unions, parties, marches, and strikes.[15] In the cities swarmed the lumpenproletariat, an army of unemployed: beggars, thieves, prostitutes, tramps, madams, pimps, pickpockets, gamblers, tinkers, organ-grinders, ruined bourgeois, decayed roués, drunken poets–the refuse and offal of all classes.[16]

Marx and Engels turned their lens on the classes one by one: aristocracy, bourgeoisie, petty bourgeoisie, and proletariat. Close-up views showed each class dividing into fractions, changing its composition, producing several parties, and fluctuating in consciousness. Each of the four classes had a long history; each divided into many parts.

(1) Through the centuries the landowning aristocracy experienced striking changes. In fifteenth-century England this class tore itself apart in the Wars of the Roses. Much of the aristocracy that grew up in its place had habits more bourgeois than feudal. These new landowners fully understood the value of money. To increase their rents they turned out the small farmers and replaced them by sheep growing expensive wool: their land produced for the European market.[17] A great part of English land was owned by the Catholic Church. In the Reformation, Henry VIII gave Church lands to favorites or sold them to bourgeois, and this enlarged the new bourgeoisified fraction of the landowning class.[18] Then in the English Revolution against king, Church, and old aristocracy, the new aristocracy joined forces with the bourgeoisie.[19] England was aiming at the impossible, a "bourgeois aristocracy."[20] In Parliament this aristocracy's representatives defended feudal traditions of monarchy and religion into the nineteenth century, but these Tories had bourgeois hearts worried about ground rent.[21] The English bourgeoisie never needed to launch a revolution against this fraction of the landowning class, for the landowners became more and more bourgeoisified.[22]

In France the Great Revolution (1789) either destroyed or transformed the landowning class. In his studies of the social struggles in nineteenth-century France, Marx considered the survivors of this class bourgeoisified. "Large landed property," he writes in 1852, "despite its feudal coquetry and pride of race, has been rendered thoroughly bourgeois by the development of modern society."[23] German landowners were meeting the same fate.[24] Modern history has seen the decline of the landowning aristocracy: bourgeois revolutions and advancing capitalism wipe out one fraction; the other fraction becomes more and more like the bourgeoisie. But these landowners don't all turn into capitalists in the strict sense, for they inherit the land from their parents and rent it to tenants.[25]

Bourgeoisie is a loose concept, *capitalist* a strict one. Even a medieval trader counts as a member of the bourgeoisie, but a capitalist is someone who owns lands, banks, mines, railways, or factories and exploits wage labor.[26] Only as capitalism matures does bourgeois become synonymous with capitalist.

(2) The bourgeois class divides into three fractions: the merchants, the financiers, and the industrialists. The merchant bourgeoisie—the middlemen and traders who buy in order to sell—is the oldest fraction of the bourgeois class. In the Middle Ages the merchants appear with the rise of towns and trade. "To buy cheap and sell dear is the rule of trade."[27] The merchants are experts at this cheating, and with the opening of the routes to India and America they learn plundering, piracy, and conquest as well. They become explorers, adventurers. As the capitalist system matures, the merchants fade into the background of the bourgeois class, where they carry on duller tasks—selling goods.[28] Other fractions of the class, such as the financial bourgeoisie, come to the fore. What is the financial bourgeoisie? The bankers, financiers, stock exchange kings, big moneylenders, and speculators on the money market.[29] Then comes the steam engine and a revolution in production. Another fraction of the bourgeoisie, the industrialists, pushes to the front of the class. The bankers move back; and the captains of industry, the great entrepreneurs, the princes of the manufacturing interests take charge of affairs, first in England, later in France.[30] Thus the fractions of the bourgeoisie struggle among themselves, and first one, now another, supplies the leading personnel of the class; it changes in composition as the centuries roll by. It hardens into a clearly defined social group as the capitalist system comes of age: bourgeois becomes synonymous with capitalist—a productive owner who exploits wage labor.

(3) The petty bourgeoisie, the class of small property owners, also experienced historical evolution. From the sixteenth century on, the petty bourgeoisie nestled in the declining guilds.[31] As the guilds collapsed, the petty bourgeoisie took on new forms; traders, shopkeepers, and artisans, fluctuating between bourgeoisie and proletariat, struggled to keep afloat in the storm of competitive capitalism.[32] An important fraction of the petty bourgeoisie is the peasantry—in several countries more than half the population.[33] In Western Europe the small peasants cling desperately to their patch of land.[34]

Though the petty bourgeois may hire an apprentice or farm hand, they draw the bulk of their income from their own labor rather than the sweat of others. Their mode of production, widespread in Europe from 1400 to 1800, is transitional between feudalism and capitalism. They are doomed to pass away.[35]

(4) The modern proletariat, the propertyless class, first appeared as a lumpenproletariat of unemployed with the collapse of feudalism. In the fifteenth and sixteenth centuries the breakup of feudalism drove millions of people from

their occupations; Europe swarmed with vagabonds and beggars.[36] As capitalism developed, part of the lumpenproletariat found employment and became the nucleus of an industrial proletariat. The masses of the lumpenproletariat, however, stayed in their misery. Forced off their lands, they still had a sound peasant nature, but through the centuries they became a demoralized fraction of the proletariat; they became beggars, thieves, and prostitutes.[37] They were "a mass sharply differentiated from the industrial proletariat,"[38] from the workers in mines, railways, and factories. In the 1840s the industrial proletariat was suffering the horrors of the early factory system. The proletarians created a political movement with noble leaders. "One must be acquainted with the studiousness, the craving for knowledge, the moral energy and the unceasing urge for development of the French and English workers," writes Marx, "to be able to form an idea of the *human* nobleness of that movement."[39] As industrialism matured in the second half of the nineteenth century, the factory proletariat itself divided into strata. Marx says that some proletarian militants were "bribed" by higher wages to support capitalism.[40] He and Engels describe a "working class aristocracy" of skilled laborers that benefited from English imperialism. These privileged workers supported the system, while many unskilled laborers fought it.[41]

Class is no simple idea. The changing composition of the bourgeoisie, for example, calls for careful analysis. The bourgeois arch stretches from the twelfth to the nineteenth century and includes Marco Polo, John Locke, and Friedrich Engels. The fractions of the bourgeoisie–merchants, bankers, industrialists–have often quarreled with one another. So Marx and Engels analyze classes into fractions,[42] into "subordinate gradations."[43] In time of danger the fractions come together; they concentrate into a class. Class concentration and fractionation make the rhythm of history.

What holds fractions together, what concentrates them into a class? No matter how much their interests clash, the fractions of the ruling class have a common bond: they want to guard the social system, to keep their class in power. In the eleventh century there was a war between some French knights and Norman knights, and the peasants rose in revolt; the knights immediately forgot their differences and concentrated on crushing the movement of the peasants.[44] In the French Revolution of 1848 the industrial bourgeoisie wanted to drive the financial bourgeoisie from its monopoly of government, but when the industrialists saw the working class rising from below, they made common cause with the financial bourgeoisie. The bourgeois fractions concentrated in a front against the workers. "Who is more directly threatened by the workers than the employer, the industrial capitalist?" asks Marx. "The manufacturer, therefore, of necessity became in France the most fanatical member of the party of Order. The reduction of profit by finance, what is that compared with the abolition of profit by the proletariat?"[45] As the revolutionary crisis deepened, all fractions of the bourgeoisie concentrated in a Party of Order against the people,[46] only to fractionize later on.

Modern history is a continual concentration and fractionation of the bourgeois class. In time of danger the fractions concentrate to defend the capitalist system, then divide again into opposing groups.[47] The fractions of the class understand their common interest and carry on their quarrels in the framework of that interest. They disagree on many matters, but one question is never at issue: the existence of capitalism. Disagreements about the constitution, about reforms, about policy, about ideology take place in this framework. Marx and Engels note that the ideologists of a class may fall out with its leaders, but that in time of danger these squabbles vanish like mist in the sun.[48]

The fractions of the petty bourgeoisie have a common interest, the safeguarding of small property in competitive capitalism.[49] The interest of the proletariat is to bring capitalism to an end.[50] When the proletariat is on the attack it grows in consciousness and unity.

Classes, Parties, Leaders

Several political parties may represent one class, each springing from a different fraction. In nineteenth-century France the Orleanists and the Legitimists represented bourgeois fractions with different interests in capital and land,[51] and so did Republicans and Democrats in the United States.[52] Sometimes parties reflect conservative and radical moods in the same class. Victorian England, Engels writes, provides an example, where "you have the real conditions of the rule of the whole bourgeois class, of parliamentarism in full blossom: two parties struggling for the majority and taking in turns the parts of Ins and Outs, of government and opposition. Here, in England, you have the rule of the whole bourgeois class; but that does not mean that Conservatives and Radicals coalesce; on the contrary, they relieve each other."[53] The proletariat may also have two parties, one revolutionary and the other reformist.[54]

There is a common belief that Marxism finds a one-to-one correspondence between social classes and political parties: each class is supposed to have a party, and behind every party must stand a class. But Marx and Engels don't teach a simple view of the relation between classes, parties, and leaders. One class can have several parties,[55] or one party may represent allied classes.[56]

Nor do the leaders and ideologists of a class always come from the class. In every society there are a number of "people of talent"–scholars, philosophers, writers, journalists, doctors, lawyers–who serve as spokespersons for the different classes.[57] Individuals are not always determined by their own class.[58]

In education and occupation, ideologists and leaders may be above the class they represent, but they express the viewpoint of that class.[59] The representatives of the petty bourgeoisie are not shopkeepers;[60] and the ideologists of the peasants are not plowing the land themselves: the peasants always draw their ideologists from the bourgeoisie or the plebeian priests.[61] Some people desert their class to lead another.[62] In the French Revolution nobles such as Mirabeau and Lafayette went over to the bourgeoisie; and in the nineteenth century, bourgeois like Marx and Engels joined the proletariat.[63]

In the storm of a revolution, mass moods change. Parties are in flux. A class may desert its leaders: sometimes a class accuses its leaders of abandoning principles, sometimes it accuses them of clinging to principles that have become useless.[64] A class may forget its real interest for a passing advantage, and turn upon leaders true to the party program.[65] Leaders may rush ahead of the class or fall behind it; in historical crises the relations between classes and leaders are fluid.

Revolutions sometimes catapult leaders into government too soon. Before their class can rule, the leaders find themselves in power. Circumstances force them to carry out measures against their principles.

In the 1850s Engels feared this would happen to the German communists.[66] Germany's weak proletariat had an advanced party, and the country seemed ripe for revolution. Engels writes about leaders ruling before their time:

> The worse thing that can befall a leader of an extreme party is to be compelled to take over a government in an epoch when the movement is not yet ripe for the domination of the class that he represents and for the realization of the measures which that domination implies. What he *can* do depends not upon his will but upon the degree of contradiction between the various classes and upon the level of development of the material means of existence, of the conditions of production and commerce. . . . In a word, he is compelled to represent not his party or his class but the class for whose domination the movement is then ripe. In the interests of the movement he is compelled to advance the interests of an alien class and to feed his own class with phrases and promises and with the assurance that the interests of that alien class are their own interests.[67]

This happened to Lenin. He found himself governing a country ruined by war and revolution. He represented the working class, a minority of the nation, and in the course of the Civil War this class weakened: workers were killed, died in famines and plagues, fled wrecked cities, or took posts in the new government. In 1921, after seven years of world war, revolution, and civil war, Russian industry was shattered and the proletariat dispersed or declassed. Lenin himself made this clear at the Bolsheviks' Tenth Party Congress (1921) in his speech of 9 March. The broken proletarian class could not lead the backward country into the modern world. So Lenin relied on an emerging bureaucracy until he sickened and died. During industrialization Stalin had to advance the interests of the bureaucracy, and to feed the working class with phrases and promises and with the assurance that the interests of the bureaucracy were the workers' interests.

In original Marxism there is a precedent for this view of the bureaucracy as an emergent ruling class. In the 1840s Engels argued that in Germany the aristocracy, the bourgeoisie, and the petty bourgeoisie were too weak to rule society and that the bureaucracy seemed the ruling class.[68] Today bureaucratic socialism has engulfed a third of the world. More and more Marxists now see it as a new social formation, humane because its planned economy meets everyone's needs for food, clothes, housing, education, medicine, and employment.

"There is never a political movement which is not at the same time social," writes Marx.[69] But the relation between political leaders and their social base is complex, and a class analysis of society requires research and skill. The following correlation is not a simple one: classes control parties, and parties are represented by leaders. The moods of the masses turn, shift, and flow; classes fractionize and concentrate; parties split into factions; leaders forget their principles and invent new ones. Class analysis is no easy task, and Marx offers no simple formulas for the study of society.

In the concept of *class* Marx stresses a social group's relation to the means of production, but he never clearly defines the concept. For Marx class is a subtle idea, more complex than many realize. A class is not homogeneous. It has fractions operating with autonomy in a context of basic class interest: a fraction's autonomy does not go beyond the limits of that interest, but within them it is real. Fractions often come together; they concentrate to assert the class interest, or as Marx puts it, the class becomes "for itself."[70]

In this last sense class is not a thing but a process. It happens as people begin to aim at class objectives, to feel they belong to a class, and to define their interests against other classes.

Over the centuries a class changes in sociological composition. The bourgeoisie, for instance, has changed a good deal. *Bourgeoisie* is not a rigid idea, but an elastic concept applying to many social groups, reaching through the centuries from Venetian traders to British capitalists. Traders, artisans, merchants, usurers, bankers, financiers, manufacturers, industrialists, middlemen, transporters, retailers, rentiers, stockbrokers, explorers, adventurers, and imperialists have made up the bourgeoisie. The class divides through space and time into many groups linked by family likenesses. *Class* can have no *simple* definition. Should it surprise us that this definition is missing in Marx? He was a pioneer in sociology, and in the beginning of every science some conceptual vagueness is inevitable.

Class Struggle

Marx and Engels open the *Manifesto* with a striking sentence: "The history of all hitherto existing society is the history of class struggles." Through the ages political thinkers have groped toward this basic thesis of Marxism. In germinal form it is as old as the Greeks.

In book 4 of *The Republic* Plato sees every city-state divided into "two cities"–"one the city of the poor, the other of the rich, the one at war with the other." According to Aristotle's *Politics*, economic classes determine the forms of state. Constitutions are the outcome of class struggles; revolutions result from changes in the military or economic power of the classes. In chapter 9 of *The Prince*, Machiavelli warns rulers to keep an eye on the struggling classes, because political power springs from this conflict. James Madison–the father of the United States Constitution–analyzed societies into propertied and nonpropertied classes with different interests, sentiments, and views. In an eternal struggle between these classes Madison saw the key to politics. Number 10 of the *Federalist* papers is the best statement of his views on class struggle.

In the first half of the nineteenth century, historians used the class struggle idea to study the evolution of modern Europe. The struggle between nobility and bourgeoisie explained a good deal of European history. Thierry, Guizot, Mignet, and Thiers considered it the key to understanding French history since the Middle Ages.[71] Up to 1850 John Wade and the English historians worked with this concept of class struggle.[72]

Utopian socialists were keen observers of the class struggle in history.[73] After 1830 the struggle between entrepreneurs and wage earners surfaced,[74] and socialist thinkers followed it with growing interest.

Classical economics dissected the classes and laid bare the latent civil war running through society. Marx names Malthus, Mill, Say, Torrens, Wakefield, McCulloch, Senior, Whately, Jones, and Ricardo as analysts of the class struggle. All these men, says Marx, showed that "the economic bases of the different classes are bound to give rise to a necessary and ever growing antagonism among them."[75] As Marxism took shape in the 1840s, class struggle hypotheses were commonplace.

Marx admits his debt to past writers. "No credit is due to me for discovering the existence of classes in modern society or the struggle between them," he writes. "Long before me bourgeois historians had described the historical development of this class struggle and bourgeois economists the economic anatomy of the classes."[76] But Marx goes beyond former historians: he argues that class struggle is not eternal, that it will come to an end.

The thesis that the class struggle is a motor of historical change is not uniquely Marxist; other thinkers developed this idea. But the linking of class struggle theory to Marxism has had curious results. Marxism often alarms academic sociologists. Many American sociologists have avoided class analysis of society, and some have denied that there are classes in America. Their work may be trivial, but they ensure that no one calls them radical.

Consider again the *Manifesto*'s famous line: "the history of all hitherto existing society is the history of class struggles." This sounds as if class struggles exist everywhere in space and time, that they rage throughout universal history. Engels surely seems to say that class struggles run through all history. He speaks of "the revolution brought about by [Marx] in the whole conception of world history. . . . Marx has proved that the whole of previous history is a history of class struggles."[77] Again, Engels writes that Marx made an "examination of all past history. Then it was seen that *all* past history, with the exception of its primitive states, was the history of class struggles."[78] Engels often makes statements like these.[79]

Are Marx and Engels claiming that class struggle theory is the key to ancient Egypt and Babylon, Aztec Mexico and Inca Peru, civilizations in India and China? Marxists have interpreted them in this way. "Marx's general philosophical and historical views," writes George Plekhanov in *Socialism and the Political Struggle*, "stand in exactly the same relation to modern Western Europe as to Greece and Rome, India and Egypt. They embrace the entire cultural history of humanity" (part 2). Soviet and Chinese Marxists accept this view and so do many Western Marxists. As Paul Sweezy puts it in *The Present as History*, the theory of class struggle applies "at any given time and place" (p. 306).

Marx's and Engels' statements on class struggle have misled their adherents. When the two men say in the *Manifesto* that the history of all past society is the history of class struggles they are talking about the history of Europe. They often speak of "world history," but this means the following sequence: ancient Greece, ancient Rome, the Middle Ages, and modern Europe. For them developments in Europe, above all the transition from feudalism to capitalism in Western Europe, fill the stage of world history. Other civilizations become a backdrop for the action in Europe.

The outlook of Marx and Engels was formed in the first half of the nineteenth century. They knew little about the history of other civilizations. This was true of Europeans throughout the period: the history of Europe was the history they thought important.

Consider how the world looked to Europeans at that time. Africa was the Dark Continent; good histories of India and China did not exist; and the Americas seemed mere outposts of European civilization. Western Europe controlled the planet: it owned large pieces of the globe (Canada, India, Australia, Indonesia), and its navies, colonies, and trading stations were everywhere. Among Europeans there arose a certain Europocentrism, and Marx and Engels shared it with everyone else. The history of Europe seemed the history that mattered.

Today our outlook has expanded a great deal: twentieth-century research lights up the tapestry of world history in detail. Archaeologists have dug up entire civilizations. Asian history, explored by an army of scholars, no longer appears stagnant. Prehistory and primitive society are better known. For us the tale of Europe's past is only one of a great collection, while for nineteenth-century Europeans it was the main story.

The first paragraphs of the *Manifesto* show that the class struggles Marx and Engels have in mind are European. There Marx begins with the ancient world, and takes Rome as the model. The struggle between patricians and plebeians dominates early Roman history. In the Republic there appears a struggle between freemen and slaves that continues into the Empire. The Empire collapses under the barbarian invasions, which Marx calls "the common ruin of the contending classes." In the Middle Ages there are class struggles between lords and serfs, guildmasters and journeymen. Feudal society is swept away in the French Revolution, which Marx calls "a revolutionary reconstitution of society at large." There remains modern bourgeois society and its warring classes.[80]

Marx and Engels rarely apply the concept of class struggle outside Europe.

And in fact class struggles may have been sharper in European history than in other parts of the world. Africa was mostly tribal. There may have been periods when Chinese society was such a continuous band between rich and poor that class struggle did not develop.

In India society was so rigidly divided into castes that interaction between them was lacking. Hindu religious ideology was woven into the social fabric, and Indians saw their castes as natural and good. Whatever their caste, even a low one, Hindus were proud of it.

The Sudras were as proud of their servant status as the Brahmans of their learning. Custom demanded, for instance, that Sudras wait in a different part of the house while the Brahmans ate. This treatment did not offend the Sudras: they waited patiently, and sometimes insisted upon eating only the leavings of the Brahmans. The lower castes did not question the right of the Brahmans to rule.

In Indian culture the idea of progress was missing. Class struggles hardly developed in India, for caste seemed the eternal order of the universe. Marx says that India's social condition remained unchanged for thousands of years.[81] His view is extreme, but he rightly stresses the difference between India and Europe.

Marx and Engels apply the concept of class struggle only to Europe. To find out whether the concept applies to countless other histories a Marxist must examine them. The founders of Marxism did not settle the question.

"The history of all hitherto existing society is the history of class struggles" –does this mean that all great events in European history are disguised class struggles? Does it mean that all wars, revolutions, reformations, invasions, insurrections, and crusades result from struggles between classes? Many readers take this as the meaning.* They say that Marxism reduces national and international relations to class antagonisms and explains *everything* by the class war. Engels himself, they point out, says that "all historical struggles" are class struggles.[82]

But Engels does not mean that the essence of *all* social strife is class conflict. Marx and Engels know that history contains many kinds of struggle. There was the great contest between Greece and Persia, the long struggle of Rome against Carthage, the conflict between pope and emperor, the Crusades of the eleventh and twelfth centuries–Christianity against Islam. These were world historical struggles of great importance, but they were not class struggles. The sixteenth-century struggle between England and Spain, the commercial wars of the seventeenth and eighteenth centuries, the Crimean conflict in the nineteenth century–these were mainly national struggles. True, in modern Europe smoldering class struggles flame up in revolutions, reformations, and wars, but Marx and Engels do not believe that *every* struggle in history is a class struggle.

They believe that many struggles are national struggles, struggles between nations. Though wars between nations may have a class content, in 1849 Marx can speak of "the present class struggles and national struggles" as if they are different.[83]

What, then, do Marx and Engels mean by their assertion? They mean that all struggles inside a developing nation-state are class struggles, that "all struggles within the state, the struggle between democracy, aristocracy, and monarchy, the struggle for the franchise, and so forth, are merely the illusory forms in which the real struggles of the different classes are fought out among

---

* Such an interpretation is widespread. The following scholars are examples of it: Bertrand Russell, *Freedom versus Organization*, p. 199; Karl Popper, *The Open Society and Its Enemies*, vol. 2, p. 116; George Cole, *What Marx Really Meant*, p. 39.

one another."[84] Examples of class struggles are the internal collisions in a country: the Peasant War in Germany, the Civil War between Puritans and Anglicans in England, the French Revolution.[85] Class struggle usually concerns the internal processes of society and not relations between societies.

Struggles between societies are generally lacking in class content. Sometimes, of course, international wars are also class wars, as every student of imperialism and revolution knows. Even religious wars between Protestant and Catholic nations were class wars (like the struggle of Holland against Spain in the sixteenth century).[86] In chapter 3 we saw that the Napoleonic Wars had a class content. But such wars are exceptional. World history is full of wars that are purely national struggles. Migrations, invasions, and conquests are movements of the tribe or nation.

For Marx and Engels the concept of class struggle has limitations, and the careful student keeps these in mind. The two men confine the class struggle to Europe and usually to affairs inside nation-states. And, as we have seen, they consider the main arena of class struggle to be the western half of modern Europe: Germany, Holland, France, Italy, and England since the Renaissance.

This means that Marxist students must apply class struggle theory with care. It may illuminate modern France more than ancient India. Only careful analysis of a nation's past can decide such a question.

Latent and Open Struggle

Marx uses Hegelian terms to distinguish two kinds of class, the *class-in-itself* and the *class-for-itself*.

Economic conditions create for a mass of people a common situation, common culture, and common interests. This mass is only a class-in-itself. It has no community, no national bond, and no political organization. Its members are scattered, out of touch, and not aware of their common interests. Only through struggle with another class can it become a class-for-itself, unified, organized, and conscious of its interests.[87]

In the Middle Ages there slowly grew up towns containing craftsmen and merchants. These towns were the gravitational centers of an emerging class. The bourgeois organized themselves in armed towns to save their skins, to protect themselves from the robber nobility. They had only local organization; they formed a class-in-itself. As the centuries passed, these town bourgeois got to know one another, discovered their similar interests, and joined together in wider organizations. The bourgeoisie struggled to organize itself nationally.

It grew into a class-for-itself. Finally it pushed aside the nobility and captured political power. The bourgeoisie as a class-for-itself then faced the proletariat.[88]

From the sixteenth century on, masses of people looked for work in the towns. After the industrial revolution they worked in factories. They were not yet aware of their common interests; they formed a class-in-itself. Their struggle with the bourgeoisie developed slowly. At first individual laborers protested their conditions of life, then local struggles in the factory developed. Strike waves led to trade unions, and the unions joined together in wider organizations. A political party formed. The proletariat became a class-for-itself carrying on a national struggle.[89]

When a class-in-itself becomes a class-for-itself Marx says that it has "constituted itself as a class,"[90] and this implies that in its inert state it was not yet a class. Even so, Marx also uses the term *class* for the class-in-itself. This loose usage has confused many of his readers, but the context often makes clear which meaning he has in mind.

Throughout history the class-in-itself was more common than the class-for-itself. Marx thinks of the class-for-itself as a latecomer in history: it fully formed in the French Revolution, though occasionally such classes appeared in ancient Greece and Rome. In European history the mass of the people were usually a class-in-itself. They were scattered over large areas. They suffered from habits of submission. They lacked education and leaders.

In every epoch the ruling class is more of a class-for-itself. There are fewer people in the ruling class; they travel more; they know one another—they don't need formal unions.[91] And they control the state. "The state is the form in which the individuals of a ruling class assert their common interest."[92]

Because the mass of the people is a class-in-itself, usually there is only a hidden class struggle in society. Occasionally there is a shift toward open class struggle. This "now hidden, now open" struggle runs like a red thread through the history of Europe.[93]

The hidden class struggle is *always* present, for the rulers try to pile ever larger loads of work on the toiling masses.[94] The people are forever gnashing their teeth under the terrible burden,[95] and sometimes their rage goes beyond muttering. The latent class struggle expresses itself "in partial and momentary conflicts, in subversive acts."[96] The slave breaks tools;[97] the serf pollutes the well of the lord. Sometimes there is an act of violence against a master, even a local revolt of many servants. When the slaves on a Roman latifundium rise up and plunder the villa, when the peasants in a feudal dukedom burn down the castle, then the latent class struggle shows itself. The fissure in the social base reveals the lava boiling below. But the revolt is local. There is no motion of the class: most of the slaves are quiet; they remain a class-in-itself. Throughout history the class struggle is usually latent, "concealed."[98]

But sometimes it becomes an open struggle. In every city and every nation there are two populations: the suffering masses and the ruling few, the poor and the rich. Hatred between these groups finally bursts into warfare. Slave insurrections, helot revolts, serf uprisings, peasant wars, poor riots, and workers' rebellions flare up throughout history. Yet for lack of organization the poor are usually not able to sustain these struggles.

In a few historical periods, but especially in modern Western Europe, a lower class has sustained an organized struggle against the privileged class. This is an economic struggle over the social product and a political struggle for state power. The struggling classes are organized; they know what their interests are; and their struggle shows itself in battles of ideas. A fully open class struggle has three forms: economic, political, and ideological.[99] In modern Europe, for instance, the proletariat pits trade unions against employers; both classes support political parties; and ideologists are plentiful.

Marx and Engels sometimes speak of "class antagonisms and class struggles."[100] This may hint at the distinction we are tracing. *Class antagonisms* have existed throughout European history: master and slave, lord and serf lived as oppressor and oppressed, but the slave or the serf belonged to a class-in-itself that lacked organization for a long fight. Though scattered revolts happened often enough, class conflict was usually latent. On the other hand, open *class struggles* occur when there is a fight for political power: communists and republicans in modern France, democrats and oligarchs in ancient Greece.

The Greeks lived in a sea of slaves. For fifth-century Athens, Engels places the number of slaves at 365,000 against 135,000 freemen. But the latent struggle between slaves and freemen was overshadowed by the open struggle between free rich and free poor. The rich grew richer and the poor grew poorer until Athens collapsed.[101]

"The class struggles of the ancient world took the form chiefly of a contest between debtors and creditors."[102] For centuries these struggles raged in all the Greek cities. The conflict between democratic Athens and aristocratic Sparta turned into an international class war that convulsed the whole Greek world. This is how the greatest historian of ancient times describes what happened:

> Practically the whole of the Hellenic world was convulsed, with rival parties in every state–democratic leaders trying to bring in the Athenians, and oligarchs trying to bring in the Spartans. . . . Family relations were a weaker tie than party membership. . . . These parties were not formed to enjoy the benefits of the established laws, but to acquire power by overthrowing the existing regime. . . . Leaders of parties in the cities

had programs which appeared admirable–on one side political equality for the masses, on the other the safe and sound government of the aristocracy. . . . Society had become divided into two ideologically hostile camps, and each side viewed the other with suspicion. As for ending this state of affairs, no guarantee could be given that would be trusted, no oath sworn that people would fear to break; everyone had come to the conclusion that it was hopeless to expect a permanent settlement. . . . So revolutions broke out in city after city, and in places where the revolutions occurred late the knowledge of what happened previously in other places caused still new extravagances of revolutionary zeal, expressed by an elaboration in the methods of seizing power and by unheard-of atrocities in revenge. (Thucydides, *The Peloponnesian War*, chapter 5 of book 3)

More bitter than the war of Athens with Sparta was the war of class with class in all the Greek states. Centuries of these internal struggles exhausted Greece, and it went under in the mutual ruin of the warring classes.[103]

In the opening paragraphs of the *Manifesto* Marx mentions the struggle between freemen and slaves.[104] This latent class struggle flared up occasionally in slave revolts. Today most people remember the Spartacus revolt, a slave war that almost toppled Rome. But there were other slave outbreaks in the ancient world. Massive revolts happened in Sicily. There was the uprising of 40,000 slaves in the mines of Spain, the rebellion of the slaves of Macedonia and Delos, and the great revolt of the miners of Laurium in Greece. Vast uprisings of slaves and poor peasants rolled over the western Roman Empire (the Bagaudae) and North Africa (the Donatists). An Arab writes about the Donatists: "They hate the masters and the rich, and when they meet a master riding in his chariot and surrounded by his slaves, they make him get down, put the slaves in the chariot and oblige the master to run on foot. They boast that they have come to reestablish equality on earth, and they summon the slaves to liberty" (quoted in E. F. Gautier, *Le passé de l'Afrique du nord*, p. 259).

Yet the slave uprising that Marx loves best is the Spartacus revolt (73 B.C. to 71 B.C.). Spartacus led the slaves in a war against Rome. The slave masses of Italy rallied to him, and the revolt became an open class struggle. Marx calls Spartacus "the most splendid fellow in the whole of ancient history."[105]

Not one of the slave revolts was successful.[106] They were spontaneous uprisings of maddened people. Here and there in the ancient world they flared up suddenly, then were snuffed out. They never pushed history forward. In discussing class struggle as the driving force of history, Engels says that one must analyze "those motives which set in motion great masses, whole peoples, and again whole classes of the people in each people; and this not momentarily for the transient flaring up of a straw fire which quickly dies down, but for a lasting action resulting in a great historical transformation."[107]

Marx is thinking of open class struggle when he writes that "in ancient Rome the class struggle took place only within a privileged minority, between the free rich and the free poor, while the great productive mass of the population, the slaves, formed the purely passive pedestal for these combatants."[108] Except for scattered uprisings, the slaves were silent for centuries.

Slaves don't fight their tormentors. They give up. Rome used up slaves like a locomotive burns fuel. Marx and Engels sum up their fate in a sentence: "The very slaves died out again and again, and had constantly to be replaced by new ones."[109] Dragged from foreign lands, jabbering many languages, the slaves had no plan, no party, no leaders. How could they carry on open class struggle?

Faceless masses suffered in the mines, on plantations, in the galleys. The Romans did not consider them people. They were "talking instruments."[110] Their owners could sell, even kill them. They lived without families in barracks, marched to work under the lash, and sank into death.

The class struggle in Rome could only be a fight among freemen, a competition between rich and poor over the surplus product.[111] The free poor had been Italian peasants. These peasants fought in Rome's armies, captured the Mediterranean countries, and policed the Empire. In Italy their farms wasted away from neglect. The rich grabbed these farms to build slave estates, and the peasants moved to Rome. In that city "they never succeeded in becoming more than a lumpenproletariat."[112] They could hardly revolt against the rich: the armies that held down the peoples of the Empire could be used against the people of Rome. A free people easily becomes the prisoner of its imperial armies. This is "what ancient Rome demonstrated on an enormous scale," writes Marx. "The people which oppresses another people forges its own chains."[113] The Roman poor grew corrupt; they called for gladiator fights and free food. Their struggle with the rich paid off in "bread and circuses." Demagogues like Julius Caesar represented them in the class struggle.[114]

Marx sees a big difference between the ancient and modern class struggles. "The Roman proletariat lived at the expense of society, while modern society lives at the expense of the proletariat," he writes. "With so complete a difference between the material, economic conditions of the ancient and the modern class struggles, the political figures produced by them can likewise have no more in common with one another than the Archbishop of Canterbury has with the High Priest Samuel."[115] The Roman proletariat had the demagogue Caesar; the modern proletariat had the revolutionary Blanqui.[116] The Roman proletariat was a parasite on society. It was not a radical class; it never called for revolutionary change. In chapter 2 we saw that the Roman class struggle did not drive history forward but led into a blind alley.[117]

From the ashes of the Roman Empire feudalism slowly emerged, and in the ninth century it took on classic form in France.[118] In the Middle Ages there were many social classes. Spread over the countryside were nobility and serfs; nestling in the towns were guildmasters and journeymen. In the towns there soon arose a rabble of casual laborers.[119]

As in the ancient world, the masses broke out in revolts against the privileged. Society was a volcano, with a cone of privileged orders resting on a peasant base. The lava of peasant anger flowed underground, but sometimes the volcano erupted, and a torrent of hatred buried anything in its path.

"The great risings of the Middle Ages all radiated from the country."[120] These peasant uprisings, like the slave revolts of Rome, had a spontaneous character. Marx and Engels mention the Jacqueries that swept across Western Europe in the fourteenth century.[121] (The nickname of the French peasant was Jacques.) In a Jacquerie the peasants suddenly ran amok, looting and burning the manors of the nobility. The revolt spread across the countryside like wildfire. A band of feudal knights rushed to smother the flames–and hang peasants.

These Jacqueries were merely a step toward open class struggle. They were outbreaks of rage at overwork and hunger; they had no political content. Marx and Engels never tire of repeating that every class struggle is a political struggle.[122] But the peasants could not wage a political struggle. The peasant revolts "remained totally ineffective because of the isolation and consequent crudity of the peasants."[123]

Sometimes a peasant revolt really approached open class struggle. Wat Tyler's Rebellion in England, mentioned by Marx,[124] was not a Jacquerie. The condition of the English peasants had improved, and in 1381 they tried to shake off the remains of the manorial system. Vague communist hopes filled their minds; the equalitarian ideas of Wycliffe were in the air; this peasant revolt seemed an attack on the social order. Perhaps a hundred thousand people marched on London.

King Richard finished off this rebellion.

In 1525 something unheard of happened: there was a *national* peasant revolt in Germany. In two-thirds of Germany the peasants rose against their masters. That revolts broke out everywhere, says Engels, proves that there were people organizing the movement through agents such as Anabaptists. Many of them, like Thomas Münzer, were communists.[125] This social war was turning into an open class struggle, but it met defeat for the usual reasons: the peasants' narrow-mindedness, stubborn provincialism, and timid leaders.[126] Engels sums up the outcome of the war as follows: "The peasants of every province acted only for themselves as a rule refusing aid to the insurgent peasants of the neighboring region, and were consequently annihilated in separate battles one after another by armies which in most cases were hardly one-tenth of the total number of the insurgent masses."[127]

The peasantry was a class-in-itself. The peasants lived in similar conditions, but their mode of production isolated them from one another. Each peasant family was almost self-sufficient on its small farm. A few farms made up a village, and a few villages made up a province. In this way the mass of the peasantry was formed by adding one unit to another, as potatoes in a sack form a sack of potatoes. Thus Marx describes the French peasantry in words that applied to much of Europe.[128]

Often the sack of potatoes fell upon a feudal lord with great force, but the peasant Jacqueries were local spurts, outbursts of anger with no future. The Jacqueries aimed to bring back justice. "The king is the fountain of justice" – the peasants argued that through the ages. They foolishly believed the king a prisoner of his court nobility; they blamed their misery on wicked lords. They fought the nobles for an earlier society. Dying for an illusion, the peasants tried to roll back the wheel of history. Their Jacqueries, says Engels, were reactionary.[129]

The nobility was more of a class-for-itself, was better prepared for class warfare. Marx notes that the organization of the ruling class everywhere had a king at its head.[130] If necessary the king himself could take the field against peasant armies, as in 1328 at Mount Cassel in France.

In the medieval towns there were masters and journeymen in the craft guilds. The journeymen did not revolt against the masters, for they hoped to become masters themselves.[131] But when masters began to allow only their sons into the master class, the journeymen formed associations to carry on a struggle against the masters.

In the towns there was also a rabble of escaped serfs, laborers that worked for wages, the forerunners of the proletariat. From the fourteenth century on, they often rose in revolt.[132] Their revolts against the town order were not effective. The laborers lacked class organization: they were a mass of individuals who had fled into the towns one by one; they were strangers to one another.[133] Here and there they seized power in a town, but were soon starved out by a blockade.

The town struggles were longer and more bitter than the peasant revolts. But the town uprisings had the same local character–they were bound to fail. Only through centuries of development would these town laborers become a class-for-itself, the modern proletariat.

As we approach the modern period, the concept of class struggle takes on a new importance in Marxism. But although in modern Europe the class struggle has a special development, the struggle was significant throughout history. Engels puts it like this: "Marx has proved that the whole of previous history is a history of class struggles, that in all the many and complicated political struggles the only thing at issue has been the social and political rule of social classes, the maintenance of domination by older classes and the overcoming of domination by newly arising classes."[134] This is the thesis that the class struggle is the motive force of European political history, is the source of changes in constitutions and forms of state. Party strife, senatorial debates, demagogic appeals, coups d'état, constitutional reforms, sudden dictatorships, political revolutions are expressions of class struggles. These class struggles expressed in political changes run throughout ancient history: democrats over-throw oligarchs, plebeians gain admission to the senate. But in modern Europe the struggles become more complex. For the first time in European history there begins a rapid advance in productive forces. These forces appear in the sixteenth century and grow steadily; a transformation of the basis of society begins. In the seventeenth and eighteenth centuries the class developing the new forces, the bourgeoisie, carries out revolutions against the old ruling class-es, revolutions that further transform the social structure.[135] Thus the modern class struggle illuminates changes going on in the economic basis of society. Class conflict penetrates every facet of modern society, even the cloudy realms of ideology. Changes in philosophy and religion, says Engels, also express the struggle of classes.[136] Protestantism, for instance, is the ideology of the revolutionary bourgeoisie in its struggle against the forces of feudalism.[137]

In ancient Greece and Rome the class struggle mainly caused political changes; but in modern Europe it drives history forward. The class struggle breaks out in social revolutions that shove history up the staircase of eco-nomic progress, from feudalism to capitalism, and from capitalism to commu-nism. When Marx and Engels call the class struggle "the driving force of his-troy," they are thinking of modern history, of the nobility falling before the bour-geoisie, and the bourgeoisie falling before the proletariat.[138]

Modern society sails toward a goal, but ancient society drifted into a track-less ocean and sank in a whirlpool of struggling classes.[139] As we have seen, there is a world of difference between the old and the modern class struggles.[140]

From the fourteenth to the eighteenth centuries the bourgeoisie grew strong, and Europe became the birthplace of capitalism. Capitalism spread out across the planet and created a world civilization thoroughly fractured by class strug-gles. The spread of capitalism broke up traditional societies and generated new class structures. Marxism's emphasis on class is important for sociology throughout the world today. Class struggles are raging everywhere, and sev-eral breaches in the capitalist system have already occurred. Revolutions have swept over the system in uneven waves of crisis, breakdown, and recovery, but forty percent of the earth's people have broken away from the system. Even in this socialist two-fifths some Marxists see class struggles between bureaucrats and workers. Marc Paillet in his *Marx contra Marx: La société technobureaucratique* and Donald Hodges in *Marxismo y revolución en el siglo XX* give brilliant analyses of this new class struggle.

Misery, unrest, and hostility to capitalism are greatest in the economically backward areas of the planet. There is class struggle in Asia: the transformation of underdeveloped societies sharpens class conflict, and violence occurs as nations shake off foreign domination. There is class struggle in Africa. Some sociologists see only tribal conflicts, but Marxists find emergent class forces. There is class struggle in Latin America: peasant movements, army coups, reform struggles, workers' strikes, guerrilla wars, and foreign interventions.

Western Europe, once the main arena of class struggle, was the laboratory in which people discovered Marxism, a doctrine for the West. And the workers' strikes and struggles in Italy and France show that Marxism still applies to Western Europe. But the expansion of capitalism throughout the world is beginning to de-Westernize Marxism. Marx analyzed societies in Western Europe; today Marxists around the world study Asia, Africa, and Latin America as well.

World capitalism is moving into a time of troubles. The world system, both at its center and its periphery, is out of joint. Across the planet social structures strain and crack; violence breaks out again and again. A useful way to study these social changes is from the standpoint of class.

This makes the continued spread of Marxism inevitable.

VI. Historical Sociology

For Marx there are three groups of factors in historical development: the economic basis of society, the superstructure of juridical and political institutions, and the forms of ideology. The basis shapes the superstructure, and economic and political institutions give rise to ideologies.

ideology
State Institutions
ECONOMIC BASIS OF SOCIETY

Some sociologists claim that Marx sees the economic basis as an independent variable and the political institutions and ideologies as dependent variables, that he thinks the economic structure determines *everything in society*. Marx rejects such strict economic determinism. Though economic change is the most powerful motor of history, it is not the only one: the engine of state, for example, can modify the basis.

Marx sets forth his historical sociology in the famous "Preface of 1859." There he suggests causal relationships between the three variables–basis, state, and ideology–and further analyzes the basis into factors: productive forces and relations of production. The productive forces grow up inside relations of production; changes in the productive forces tend to disrupt the relations of production; the productive forces form the core of the economic basis of society. The forces in this basis feed the engine of historical change, the class struggle over the surplus product, a conflict that causes evolution of society.

We must now look at the central part of the preface, an abstract passage that has puzzled and fascinated modern scholarship.

[1] In the social production of their life, people enter into definite relations that are indispensable and independent of their will, relations of production

which correspond to a definite stage of development of their material productive forces.

[2] The sum total of these relations of production constitutes the economic structure of society, the real basis, on which rises a legal and political superstructure and to which correspond definite forms of social consciousness.

[3] The mode of production of material life conditions the social, political, and intellectual life process in general.

[4] It is not people's consciousness that determines their being, but their social being that determines their consciousness.

[5] At a certain stage of their development, the material productive forces of society come in conflict with the existing relations of production, or–what is but a legal expression for the same thing–with the property relations within which they have been at work hitherto. From forms of development of the productive forces these relations turn into their fetters. Then begins an epoch of social revolution.

[6] With the change of the economic foundation the entire immense superstructure is more or less rapidly transformed.

[7] In considering such transformations a distinction should always be made between the material transformation of the economic conditions of production, which can be determined with the precision of natural science, and the legal, political, religious, esthetic or philosophic–in short, ideological forms in which people become conscious of this conflict and fight it out. Just as our opinion of individuals is not based on what they think of themselves, so can we not judge such a period of transformation by its own consciousness; on the contrary, this consciousness must be explained rather from the contradictions of material life, from the existing conflict between the social productive forces and the relations of production.

[8] No social formation ever perishes before all the productive forces for which there is room in it have developed; and new, higher relations of production never appear before the material conditions of their existence have matured in the womb of the old society itself. Therefore humanity always sets itself only such tasks as it can solve, since, looking at the matter more closely, it will always be found that the task itself arises only when the material conditions for its solution already exist or are at least in the process of formation.

[9] In broad outlines Asiatic, ancient, feudal, and modern bourgeois modes of production can be designated as progressive epochs in the economic formation of society.

[10] The bourgeois relations of production are the last antagonistic form of

the social process of production–antagonistic not in the sense of individual antagonism, but of one arising from the social conditions of life of the individuals; at the same time the productive forces developing in the womb of bourgeois society create the material conditions for the solution of that antagonism. This social formation brings, therefore, the prehistory of human society to a close.¹

Marx uses this theoretical sketch to explain historical change. In principles [5] and [6] of the preface, he says that the productive forces–raw materials, tools, work relations–slowly expand, come into conflict with the relations of production, and explode the economic basis of society in social revolution, a revolution followed by ideological transformation. Feudalism, for example, turns into capitalism: the old society perishes and a new one is born.

Students of Marx claim that he designed this sociology to apply to all societies in history: to Rome's decline and fall, to Mexico's revolutionary transformation, to medieval Spain and contemporary Egypt, to Asia, Africa, and South America. Marx's sociology, so the claim goes, charts the ebb and flow of historical change, dissects old reformations and modern revolutions, studies societies around the planet. Marx's theory explains the Chinese revolution, the fall of ancient Athens, and the evolution of Argentina.

In fact, Marx developed his sociology to explain Western Europe's evolution out of feudalism into capitalism toward communism.

The Aim of the Theory

From beginning to end the preface of 1859 is an explanation of social revolution. In chapter 2 we saw that Marx did not find social revolutions in the Asiatic formation, nor in the ancient world. But revolutions transformed European feudalism into capitalism, and Marx thought that capitalist society was heading for a social cataclysm. Thus the preface explains social revolutions *in Western Europe*.

In a gloss on the preface Marx says that the following concepts may apply to ancient civilization: forces, relations, superstructure, ideology.² But he doesn't mention the crucial concept of social revolution. How could this concept apply to ancient Rome, since social revolutions never happened there? If we apply some of the principles of the preface to non-European civilizations, we may expect results different from the evolutionary schema feudalism–capitalism–communism. In studying Asian history, for example, there is reason to doubt that the traditional societies were feudal. More than half of the Chinese peasants owned the land they tilled, others rented land. They were not serfs; they were not linked to the landlords by ties of personal dependence. The landlords were not warriors, were not a hereditary aristocracy with a king at their head. The mandarins were bureaucrats and scholars.

The preface of 1859–the *whole* preface–introduces a book on political economy. Marx is clear about what he will do in the preface: he will outline the course of his studies in political economy. In 1844 he began these studies in Paris, he says, and continued them in Brussels (1845–1848). There he arrived at a "general result" that he used as a guiding thread for future study. In a single page he sets out this result, the first sketch of a theory of historical development (the ten principles now under discussion).

Marx's theoretical result applies to societies in Western Europe, societies going through revolutions, societies climbing from one economic level to another. The theoretical sketch is a "guiding thread" through the labyrinth of capital's history since the Renaissance. Marx and Engels follow the thread through religious reformations, commercial wars, technological changes, class struggles, and social revolutions. From the Middle Ages onward, capital passed through many forms: usurer's capital, merchant capital, financial capital, and industrial capital. Now capital was heading for "the most tremendous revolution of all time."[3] For what is capital? "Capital is not a thing," says Marx, "but rather a definite social production relation, belonging to a definite historical formation of society."[4] This evolving social formation is centered in Western Europe. We can apply the principles of the preface elsewhere, but only if we use them in a new way.

Let us consider two applications of the principles. The first is the application made by Marx. The second is an application of the principles beyond Europe. These examples will clarify our discussion of the aim of the preface.

Marx and Engels distinguished between "two great and essentially different periods of economic history: the period of manufacture proper based on the division of manual labor, and the period of modern industry based on machinery."[5] These are two epochs in the development of the productive forces. In the period of manufacture the main productive force was the manufactory: a capitalist brought artisans under one roof, supplied raw materials, paid wages, and sold the product. In the period of machine industry the main productive force is the mechanized factory. To these stages–bourgeois manufacture and factory organization–correspond two kinds of production relations: capitalist and communist.

Manufacture made gradual progress from 1500 on.[6] In England a revolution (1640–1689) swept away the feudal political forms, and capitalism surged forward. Capitalist relations of production fit the new manufacture.[7]

The stage was set for another advance in productive forces: the transition from manufacture to machine industry, a transition called the industrial revolution. In England by the eighteenth century the industrial revolution was in full swing. "Steam and the new tool-making machinery were transforming manufacture into modern industry, and thus revolutionizing the whole foundation of bourgeois society. The sluggish march of development of the manufacturing period changed into a veritable storm and stress period of production."[8] The industrial revolution began in 1735.[9] A century later machine industry emerged from its childhood, and the business cycle began in 1825.[10] Before 1825 machine industry was struggling to grow up,[11] and production lagged behind consumption.[12] After 1825 production outran consumption, and economic crises started;[13] the productive forces rebelled against the relations of production; machine industry rebelled against capitalism.[14]

The conflict between forces and relations shows itself in many ways: through mass misery,[15] through class struggle,[16] through industrial pollution,[17] through ecological ruin,[18] and through economic crises.[19] Marx and Engels never tire of repeating that the conflict between forces and relations is bound to vent itself in worsening economic crises.[20] "The commercial crises," they write in the Manifesto, "by their periodical return put to the test, each time more threateningly, the existence of the entire bourgeois society."[21]

The productive forces of the manufactory came into conflict with the feudal relations, and revolution broke out. The productive forces of machine industry are coming into conflict with capitalist relations, and revolution threatens.

Now we turn to our second example, an application of Marx's theoretical principles beyond Europe. Let us think of the American Civil War as a revolution against the planter class of the slave South. The South had always dominated the federal government. In 1856, for example, it controlled both houses of Congress; the president sympathized with the South; so did the Supreme Court. But in 1860 the North's Lincoln captured the presidency. Thus the farmers, laborers, and capitalists of the North began to take the federal government from the planter class; the planters rallied the slave South in war, and the North crushed them. What caused this revolution?

An expansion of productive forces in the capitalist North; the growth of population, transportation, and industry; the development of industrial cities like Cincinnati and Chicago; the rise of powerful business classes—these factors created a struggle against the planter aristocracy. The northern farmers, merchants, and entrepreneurs clashed with the planters over homesteads, tariffs, and internal improvements. The planters resisted tariffs and taxes that would develop industrial capitalism. They prepared to fight the North.

The class struggle was a long contest between two societies, each with its own economy and ideology. The slave society slowed the rising industrial capitalism of the North. In war the North broke the planter class and remodeled the South through Reconstruction.

Marx calls the North's war a revolutionary struggle,[22] and likens it to the bourgeois revolution of 1789 in France.[23] But the American Civil War also differed from the classical bourgeois revolutions. In America the geographical division of the classes changed the character of the struggle between them and the revolution that followed.

We can use the principles in Marx's preface to study this transformation of American civilization in the nineteenth century, but we have to modify them to fit the specific economic evolution. After the change in the economic foundation, states Marx's principle [6], the entire superstructure is transformed. But the political superstructure of the nation was not transformed by the Civil War –it was consolidated! And the change in the economic foundation took place in only one region, the South. This happened because the class division was not horizontal, but vertical.*

What is the meaning of the terms in the preface of 1859: *productive forces, relations of production, mode of production, superstructure,* and *ideology*? In the preface itself Marx never explains these terms. We must now consider them carefully.

The Economic Basis

The Geographical Factor

Marx and Engels say that the productive forces and mode of production of a society are conditioned by its geography. Every society grows up in a land with specific position, contour, climate, and natural resources. Geographical factors condition all historical development.[24]

Marx distinguishes between natural resources and raw materials. Natural

---

*Historians argue endlessly about the causes of the Civil War. The above interpretation can be found in Charles Beard and Mary Beard, *The Rise of American Civilization*; Leo Huberman, *We, The People*; and James Allen, *Reconstruction*. Some will dismiss this as vulgar Marxism, and perhaps it is. The war and Reconstruction have been interpreted as revolution in more sophisticated analyses: William A. Williams, *The Contours of American History*; Louis Hacker, *The Triumph of American Capitalism*; and Barrington Moore, Jr., *Social Origins of Dictatorship and Democracy*. These analyses differ from my simplified one. A famous Marxist student of the Civil War does not see it as a revolution: Eugene Genovese, *The Political Economy of Slavery*. And at the moment American scholarship believes that northern capitalism and southern plantation slavery were not antagonistic, but existed in a profitable relation with each other as economic systems.

resources (like fertile land) are a gift of nature; only labor turns them into raw materials (like land cleared and ploughed).[25] Raw materials are included in the productive forces.

A country with a low level of productive forces may nevertheless be rich in natural resources—coal, oil, and iron in the earth. Oil in the ground is a natural resource, but useless a thousand feet below the surface. Oil in tanks is raw material. Only raw material counts as a productive force, "for every productive force is an acquired force, the product of former activity. The productive forces are, therefore, the result of practical human energy."[26]

Abundant natural resources are a necessary condition for a rise in productive forces, as is a favorable climate.[27] If a country lacks natural resources, nature has assigned it to a backwater of history. "A country whose coal deposits are eroded, placed near a large country rich in coal, is condemned by nature to remain for a long time the farming country for the larger country when the latter is industrialized."[28]

If climate and resources condition the economic development of an area, its contour and position are equally important. Consider the area we know as Western Europe. Why did bourgeois civilization arise there, while Eastern European remained backward and feudal? The secret of the West's development lies in its geographical position and the contour of the land. In 1848 Engels contrasts the historical development of East and West:

> In the second half of the Middle Ages Italy, France, England, Belgium, North and West Germany worked their way out of feudal barbarism one after another: industry developed, trade expanded, the cities arose, and the bourgeoisie became politically important. But a part of Germany remained behind West European development. Bourgeois civilization followed the sea coast and the flow of great rivers, while the inner lands, especially the infertile and impassable mountain chains, remained the seat of barbarism and feudalism. This barbarism concentrated in the South German and South Slavic inner lands. . . . There in the center of Europe, nations of barbarians, speaking many languages, joined together under the scepter of the House of Hapsburg. In Hungary they found a prop of solid barbarism. The Danube, the Alps, the rocky ramparts of Bohemia— these are the basis for the existence of Austrian barbarism and the Austrian monarchy.[29]

Geographical factors condition the mode of production. The absence of rivers and sea-lanes affects relations of exchange. Economic forces interact within the geographical environment of society.

The Productive Forces

The productive forces of an epoch are the raw materials,[30] tools,[31] techniques,[32] work relations,[33] and modes of cooperation[34] people use to produce the things they need. In primitive epochs we find the hoe, the spear, the bone needle, the grinding stone, the hunting party, common tillage, and cooperative labor; in feudal times the mill, the plow, the loom, the axe, the craft tool, the workshop, the strip field, and home industry; under capitalism the steam mill, the power loom, the locomotive, cross breeding, assembly lines, and factory organization.

The productive forces, then, contain three elements: raw materials,[35] tools and techniques,[36] and work relations like modes of cooperation and division of labor.[37]

All raw materials are objects already won from nature: lumber, cotton, oil, iron, ploughed land.[38] And what is a tool? A thing the workers use on the raw materials, a conductor of their activity.[39] People enter into various work relations: first, history shows countless modes of cooperation such as primitives hunting together,[40] slaves building pyramids,[41] apprentices helping artisans,[42] gangs making dikes,[43] people working in factories;[44] second, the division of labor varies from one epoch to another—in the Middle Ages a craftsman made a needle by himself, but later in the period of manufacture a needle passed through many hands before it was finished.[45]

These three elements of the productive forces interact with one another. If a fundamental change occurs in one of these elements, it will spread through the productive forces. And history has seen first one, now another play the revolutionary role.

In the transition from feudalism to capitalism the work relations were the transforming element. We have seen how artisans moved from their workshops into the manufactory and divided up the labor among themselves. Twenty wheelmakers in a shed performed twenty different operations, each doing one thing: one turned, another fitted, a third inserted. Dozens of bakers came under one roof and each carried out a single task, stoking, mixing, kneading, baking. Workers repeated their tasks until they became skilled and rapid. This expansion of the productive power of handicraft techniques resulted from a change in the work relations, from a deepening of the division of labor.[46] Next the alteration in the work relations spread to another element of the productive forces, the tools: specialized labor demanded refined instruments. Consider a tool like the hammer. At the beginning of the manufacturing period there were few kinds of hammers, but by the end of the period there were hundreds of different hammers.[47] Finally the transformations in the productive forces worked toward social revolutions, and feudal relations of production evolved toward capitalist relations.[48]

After several centuries, capitalism had struck root in the Low Countries, France, and England. While it continued to grow and spread, another change in the productive forces began. The great shift occurred in England. This time the tools were the element initiating change.[49] Tools, says Marx, serve as the starting point whenever manufacture is turning into an industry carried on by machinery.[50] The vast array of tools achieved by the manufacturing period called for motors, and they were forthcoming in the industrial revolution. A tool and a motor make up a machine. Machine industry soon transformed the work relations and modes of cooperation; industry herded people into giant factories. "Machinery," writes Marx, "operates only by means of associated labor, or labor in common. So the cooperative character of the labor process is . . . a technical necessity dictated by the instrument of labor itself."[51] Factories made work relations more and more cooperative, more socialized. This change in the work relations, thinks Marx, is driving toward a revolution in the capitalist relations of production. He believes there will "develop on an ever extending scale the cooperative form of the labor process, . . . the transformation of the instruments of labor into instruments only usable in common, the economizing of all means of production by their use as the means of combined, socialized labor. . . . Centralization of the means of production and socialization of labor at last reach a point where they become incompatible with their capitalist shell. This shell is burst open."[52] The capitalist relations of production are exploded by the new productive forces. There is a revolutionary transition toward communist society.

The Relations of Production

These are the property relations.[53] Owning and not owning create these relations of production; capital itself is a relation rooted in ownership. "Capital is not a thing, but rather a definite social production relation," says Marx. "It is the means of production monopolized by a certain section of society, confronting living labor power. . . ."[54] The social group that owns the machines and materials forces the larger group that owns nothing to work in fields and factories. The workers must labor to draw a living wage; the propertyless workers exist in a wage *relation* to the owners. These free workers sell the only thing they have to the owners–living labor power. Wage labor is a relation of production; capital is also a relation of production.[55] Capital means the ownership of the mines and factories by a tiny group facing the majority of nonowners. The owners exist in a capitalist *relation* to the workers. In brief, capital and wage labor are both relations of production arising from the ownership or non-ownership of mines, factories, railways, and stores.

Feudal relations of production can arise only in rural areas where land is the main productive force: the landlord owns it and forces the nonowners to work for him.[56] But these workers are not free; they are bound to the soil like the trees and cows. Under feudalism "conditions of personal dependence are necessary, a lack of personal freedom, no matter to what extent, and being tied to the soil as its accessory, bondage in the true sense of the word."[57] This personal dependence, called *serfdom*, is a feudal relation of production. The serfs can never leave the land; they must work from dawn to dark to produce enough for both themselves and the landlord.

The landlord does not rent or buy the land; he inherits it from his fathers.[58] He belongs to a landowning aristocracy. Either he is a warrior himself, or he has armed men to make the serfs obey him. He does not need economic pressure to keep them at work; he exists in a relation of *lordship* to his serfs.[59] In brief, lordship and serfdom are both relations of production arising from the ownership or nonownership of land.

The Mode of Production

The mode of production of an epoch is the way people grow food, make clothes, build houses, forge weapons, mine ores, work metals, shape pottery, design furniture, build boats, and make tools. It is the way they group and use the productive forces in the labor process. A mode of production is a manner of working or producing, and it includes the relations of production. The mode of production changes as history moves forward.

In primitive society men and women used stone tools and weapons; they cooperated in groups to hunt and grow food.

In the feudal mode of production they worked in scattered workshops and agricultural strips. In the field men sweated to grow food for themselves and the owners of the land; the children tended the landowner's cattle; the women wove clothing. Everyone made things for the manor while the landowner fought off enemies.

In the capitalist mode of production people worked in manufactories with materials supplied by the owner. They worked together, dividing the work so that everyone made part of the product. This division of work created specialized tools. The owners of the manufactory directed the workers and aimed at expanding production for profit.

Then came the industrial revolution. Capitalism knocked down the last feudal forms and captured the entire economy. Though the old social classes still resist, "the progressive evolution of production and exchange brings us to the present capitalist *mode of production*, to the monopolization of the means of production in the hands of the numerically small class,. to the degradation into propertyless proletarians of the other class making up the immense majority" (italics mine).[60] The capitalist owners bring machines, materials, and managerial skills to production; the propertyless workers must supply labor power. Every mode of production includes the relations between the classes involved in producing: the owners and the nonowners.

A drastic change in the productive forces calls for a new mode of production. New forces growing up inside an old mode come into conflict with it. Then a revolution threatens.[61]

The Mode of Exchange

"Production and exchange are two different functions," writes Engels. "Production may occur without exchange, but exchange—being necessarily an exchange of products—cannot occur without production."[62] When economic crises occur, "the mode of production is in rebellion against the mode of exchange."[63]

The mode of exchange of an epoch is the way producers get the things they make to the people who want them. In some epochs they use carts and boats, a village fair, and barter. In other epochs they use ships and trains, the world market, and money. Under completed communism markets and money vanish, for people no longer exchange their products: they follow an economic plan to get things to those who need them. The system of transferring products from producer to user varies from one age to another: natural economy, market economy, planned economy.

In tribal communities without division of labor there is no exchange, because each person produces everything he or she needs. Only societies with people specialized in producing certain things have exchange relations. In societies with divided labor, carpenters exchange the furniture they make for grain and wine. In such societies a low level of production, as under feudalism, means that exchange is limited and crude (local markets and barter). But developed production, as under capitalist manufacture, makes exchange grow in intensity and extent (money and urban markets, ships and world trade).[64]

Exchange relations are shaped by the mode of production.[65]

The Mode of Distribution

"The definite manner of participation in production determines the particular form of distribution," writes Marx.[66] But exchange relations are an intervening variable.[67] The mode of production establishes the mode of exchange, and together they decide the mode of distribution.[68]

The mode of distribution is the way people divide among themselves the things they make; distribution concerns who gets what and how much. Distribution relations change from one epoch to another. In primitive society men and women shared food equally. In feudal distribution the large landowners got more than anyone; the small landowners a good deal; the artisans a living; and the peasants enough to survive. In the capitalist mode of distribution the factory owners get the lion's share. In a communist mode of distribution people get roughly the same.

Distribution relations often hold back the productive forces.[69] Under capitalism, for example, income distribution is unjust; and the low level of wages limits the home market, keeps production from rising, and blocks economic growth.[70] The clash between productive forces and distribution relations leads toward revolutionary crisis.[71]

For Marx and Engels the causal influence flows from the productive forces to the relations of production; these two factors make up the mode of production. The mode of production establishes exchange relations and then distribution relations. But the relations are not passive effects. "Distribution," says Engels, "is not a merely passive result of production and exchange; it in its turn reacts upon both of these."[72] And exchange, too, reacts upon production.[73] "Production, distribution, exchange, and consumption . . . are all members of one entity, different sides of one unit. Production predominates," writes Marx. "A mutual interaction takes place between the various elements. Such is the case with every organic body."[74] The economic basis of society is an organic unity of interacting elements in which the mode of production predominates.

What is the mode of production? In principle [2] of the preface of 1859, Marx says that the relations of production (defined in [5] as the property relations) make up the economic structure of society. Then in [3] he uses the expression "mode of production," apparently as a rough equivalent for this economic structure. He is working out a frame of thought for economic sociology, struggling with new ideas and hammering out concepts for the first time. Precise definitions are missing in his work. There is a tendency to slip into tautology, to say that the mode of production determines the economic structure, and that this structure determines the class relations. But aren't these different ways of saying the same thing?

Let us pursue further the definition of *mode of production*. In any civilization the people who labor in fields, mines, and workshops produce many goods. Some of these go to the laborers to fill their stomachs, put clothes on their backs, and provide fun on occasional holidays. But a lot of things are left over, and Marx calls this the surplus product.[75] The surplus product is the difference between what a society produces and what the productive laborers consume. The surplus is taken over by the ruling class.

In every social formation the surplus assumes a different *form*. In old Asia the surplus was pumped out of the laborers as taxes in kind for a royal bureaucracy; in the slave system it took the form of forced service for the Roman masters; in the feudal period it was a monthly rent of meat, eggs, milk for the lord, and work in his fields; under capitalism it becomes profit, interest, and dividends. In some passages Marx says that one social formation is distinguished from another by the form the surplus takes;[76] but in other passages a social formation is defined by its dominant mode of production.[77] Since the mode of production is the broader defining concept, it probably includes the manner of taking over the surplus product.

We have already seen that the mode of production embraces the productive forces and relations of production or property relations. Now we find that it also takes in the form of extracting the surplus product. For Marx, then, *a mode of production must include (1) a certain level of development of the productive forces, (2) a certain kind of property of the means of production, and (3) a certain form of taking over the surplus product*.

To complete our picture of the economic basis we must include the class relations. In the preface of 1859 Marx does not mention class structure and class antagonisms; he avoids talk of class struggle and imminent political revolution. Why does he skip class in the basic statement of his theory? Research has shown that he was trying to get his book past the Prussian censor: he could not talk about struggling classes in the preface.* But the concept of class is fundamental in his sociology. The economic structure of society defines its class structure.[78]

The class relations are defined in a twofold manner: designation of the social groups related to the means of production as big owners, small owners, and nonowners;[79] and an indication of the power relationships between these groups: which are the rulers and which the ruled, which the exploiters and which the exploited.[80] Changes in class structure revolutionize society. Classes rise to political power under certain material conditions: technical, environmental, economic. The political relationship between the classes shapes a historical epoch. Alterations in the class structure are the crucial social changes.

---

* Arthur Prinz, "Background and Ulterior Motive of Marx's 'Preface' of 1859," *Journal of the History of Ideas*, vol. 30, no. 3 (July–September 1969): 437–450.

As humans emerged from the animal kingdom, the struggle for existence turned into a struggle for enjoyment: the low level of productive forces meant very few luxuries; a minority got them–the ruling class.[81] "All historical antagonisms between exploiting and exploited, ruling and oppressed classes to this very day find their explanation in this same relatively undeveloped productivity of human labor."[82] The undeveloped productive forces *compelled* the ruling class to oppress and fight the masses. To increase its freedom and status "this class never failed, for its own advantage, to impose a greater and greater burden of labor on the working people."[83] Both rulers and ruled were trapped in the class structure and forced to fight one another over the surplus product. Class antagonism beats in the dialectical heart of history.

Productive forces and relations of production, modes of production, exchange, and distribution, the class structure–all these interact with one another in the economic basis. Though the mode of production predominates, Marx sees the economic basis as complex. His critics, however, read into him a concept that is simple. They seize upon three statements and saddle him with a technological theory of history. Here are the passages:

The handmill gives you society with the feudal lord; the steam mill, society with the industrial capitalist.[84]

Technology discloses man's mode of dealing with Nature, the process of production by which he sustains his life, and thereby also lays bare the mode of formation of his social relations, and of the mental conceptions that flow from them.[85]

It is not the articles made, but how they are made, and by what instruments, that enables us to distinguish different economic epochs. Instruments of labor not only supply a standard of the degree of development to which human labor has attained, but they are also indicators of the social conditions under which the labor is carried on.[86]

In these passages Marx carelessly slips toward technological determinism. His critics make these passages the core of his theory. Marx, they say, believes that the powers of production are *nothing but* tools and techniques, that the human is a tool-making animal, and that the technical factor creates history. This, they claim, is Marx's sociological theory. They stress the three passages and overlook several chapters of *Capital*, volumes of Marx's and Engels' *Werke*, and the usual good sense of the founders of historical sociology. There is only one technological determinist interpretation that does not commit these errors, *Marx's Theory of History* by William Shaw.

The Political Superstructure

The concept of the superstructure is set forth in two statements, principle [2] of Marx's preface[87] and this formulation by Engels:

> The economic structure of society always furnishes the real basis, starting from which we can alone work out the ultimate explanation of the whole superstructure of juridical and political institutions as well as of the religious, philosophical, and other ideas of a given historical period.[88]

What is the superstructure of juridical and political institutions? It is the whole complex of state institutions embracing the various areas of government: (1) armies, police, judges, statutes, courts, prisons; (2) kings, presidents, ministries, senates, bureaucracies. Throughout history, maintain Marx and Engels, the state had both social and repressive functions. But the two men stress the state's repressive nature. The following passage from Engels is typical:

> As the state arose from the need to hold class antagonisms in check . . . it is, as a rule, the state of the economically dominant class, a class which through the medium of the state becomes also the politically dominant class. Thus the state of antiquity was above all the state of the slave owners for holding down the slaves, as the feudal state was the organ of the nobility for holding down the peasant serfs, and the modern representative state is an instrument of exploitation of wage labor by capital. By way of exception, however, periods occur in which the warring classes balance each other so nearly that the state power, as ostensible mediator, acquires for the moment a certain degree of independence of both.[89]

But even an independent state guarantees class rule.[90] The state is a class institution.

It mediates in the formation of other class institutions. "Since the state is the form in which the individuals of a ruling class assert their common interests," write Marx and Engels, "it follows that the state mediates in the formation of all common institutions and that the institutions receive a political form."[91] There are state churches: priests with theologies mystify the masses. There are state schools with administrators, faculties, lessons, and drills to teach obedience. The schools provide the education required by the ruling class.[92]

In Marx's theory certain institutional orders are primary, others secondary. The economic institutions, the property relations, and the class structure are basic, while the state, religious, and educational institutions are superstructural. They are controlled by the ruling class. The class uses the state to build and maintain this superstructure.

The ruling class usually controls the state as a tool. But not always. Now and then the state escapes toward semiindependence. This happens in transitional epochs when two classes are struggling for mastery, but neither is strong enough to govern. Absolutism and bonapartism are two forms of the independent state.[93]

The seventeenth and eighteenth centuries were a transitional epoch in which absolute monarchy gained independence from the classes. Neither the rising bourgeoisie nor the weakening aristocracy was strong enough to govern. The king played the two classes against each other and built up his power. By divine right he ruled through the royal bureaucracy and the army, responsible only to God.[94]

From time to time in the nineteenth century bonapartism appeared. Whenever class war exhausted proletariat and bourgeoisie, a bonapartist dictatorship emerged to govern. This happened three times:[95] when the bourgeoisie took refuge from Robespierre and Babeuf in Napoleon's despotism (1799–1814);[96] when the Paris bourgeoisie fled from a revolutionary proletariat into the dictatorship of Louis Bonaparte (1851–1870);[97] and when the German bourgeoisie, frightened by the workers, allowed Bismarck to govern (1871–1890).[98] A bonapartist dictatorship is a military bureaucratic despotism: the leader governs through bureaucracy and army. The model of bonapartism was Louis Napoleon's dictatorship over France in 1851. "In reality," says Marx, "it was the only form of government possible at a time when the bourgeoisie had already lost, and the working class had not yet acquired, the faculty of ruling the nation."[99]

During periods of absolutism and bonapartism the dominant class no longer governed politically, but continued to rule economically. In an epoch of absolute monarchy (seventeenth and eighteenth centuries), the royal bureaucracy governed politically and guaranteed the nobility's economic power. "The nobility–retired politically–got as its share the plundering of the peasantry and of the state treasury and indirect political influence through the court, the army, the church and the higher administrative authorities."[100] Under bonapartism (1851–1870) the French bourgeoisie continued its economic rule: it made prices, set wages, directed investment, formed policy on inflation, decided what goods must come from the factories. The bourgeoisie allowed a bonapartist state to govern for it; this dictatorship adopted bourgeois interests as its own.[101] The bourgeoisie, terrified of the proletariat, saved its purse by forfeiting the crown.[102]

Though the dominant class may not staff the government with its representatives, it rules the economy with an iron hand. But in most historical periods the ruling class directly controls the state and shapes its form. If the state gains independence and a new form, it continues to enforce class rule.

Today most Third World countries are capitalist but have bureaucratic political formations: the army or a single party governs by force. In these countries Marxist scholars have developed the thesis of bonapartism to explain why their governments are not controlled by business groups. Marx's idea has thus produced much theorizing in leftist sociological circles in underdeveloped countries.

The economic basis is the foundation of the political state. What does this mean? If we know the economy of a civilization, can we infer the kind of state built upon it? Does a feudal economy require a king and a capitalist economy a republic? Is there a one-to-one correspondence between the basis and the state?

Not at all. Consider the slave-owning civilizations of the ancient world: there were monarchies, republics, dictatorships, democracies, and despotisms; there were empires and federations, centralized states and home rule; there were theocracies. The same economic basis can manifest itself in various state forms. Marx makes this clear:

> It is always the direct relationship of the owners of the conditions of production to the direct producers . . . that reveals the innermost secret, the hidden basis of the entire social structure, and of the political form of the corresponding state. This does not prevent the same economic basis . . . from showing infinite variations and gradations in the way it manifests itself, because of countless empirical circumstances, natural environment, racial relations, external historical influences, and so forth.[103]

There are various state forms for every basis.

Some forms, however, are more fitting than others. Feudal societies are usually monarchies, capitalist countries often republics. In the centuries-long transition from feudalism to capitalism there is a development from absolute monarchy through constitutional monarchy to republic, say Marx and Engels; in this process there are many stages and transitional forms, but the tendency is clear—monarchy evolves toward republic.[104]

But though the republic is a normal form of bourgeois rule,[105] it is not the only form. The political states of capitalist Europe, writes Marx in 1875, show a "manifold diversity of form."[106] Switzerland, Holland, and France were republics; Belgium and England constitutional monarchies; and Germany a bonapartist despotism.

All these governmental forms make and enforce laws. How does Marx analyze and classify a society's legal relations?

In principle [5] of the preface, he identifies the economic structure of society with the property relations, which are "a *legal* expression for the same thing" (my italics). Law defines the economic basis. But in [2] he speaks of "a *legal* and political superstructure" (my italics). Here he seems to locate law on the second level of his model of society in the political superstructure. Yet in [7] he talks of "the *legal*, political, religious, esthetic or philosophic–in short, ideological forms" (my italics). Law has risen into ideology. Exactly where does law belong in his model of society?

Marx and Engels treat law as ideology, but it spills over into the lower levels of society as well: it outlines the institutions of the superstructure and defines the relationships in the basis. The feudal basis, to give an example, grew up out of German tribalism, and its form hardened through tradition and custom. Only after centuries was this feudal tradition sanctioned by written law.[107] Then in the womb of feudalism the bourgeois basis grew up slowly and burst forth in the French Revolution. The new state laid down laws to define this basis–the *Code Napoléon*. "This *Code Napoléon*," writes Marx, "has not created modern bourgeois society. On the contrary, bourgeois society, which emerged in the eighteenth century and developed further in the nineteenth, merely finds its legal expression in this Code."[108] The Code became a model for bourgeois law throughout the world.[109]

Can we put all this in a general way? The economic roots shoot up through the superstructure and blossom into flowers of legal ideology. Legal systems define the social order. Then jurists hunt for common points in the systems of many peoples, and some points become *natural right*. The yardstick used to measure what is natural right is *justice*, a concept evolved by the philosophy of law.[110]

In brief, the state generates clouds of juridical ideology: these soar into the heaven of justice or filter down into the basis as legal definition.

So far we have treated the state as the main superstructural institution, and this is right for many periods of history. In medieval Europe, however, the state played a subordinate role: from 850 to 1350 the main superstructural institution was the Catholic Church. In a gloss on the preface of 1859 Marx admits this about the Middle Ages: "there Catholicism played the chief part."[111]

But how could the Church be the ruler of medieval society? Wasn't the Church a spiritual institution? And wasn't Christianity mere religion, a matter of prayer and incense?

Christianity had won over the slaves of Rome, spread through the Empire, and become the state religion. The Roman state broke up before invading barbarians; Christianity converted them and moved into the Middle Ages. "In the Middle Ages, in the same measure as feudalism developed, Christianity grew into the religious counterpart to it, with a corresponding feudal hierarchy."[112] Feudalism feudalized the Church. It grew into an economic, military, and political institution, as Engels says:

The great international center of feudalism was the Roman Catholic
Church. It united the whole of feudalized Western Europe, in spite of all
internal wars, into one grand political system, opposed as much to the
schismatic Greeks as to the Mohammedan countries. It surrounded feudal
institutions with the halo of divine consecration. It had organized its own
hierarchy on the feudal model, and lastly, it was itself by far the most
powerful feudal lord, holding, as it did, fully one-third of the soil of
the Catholic world.[113]

Everyone knows that during the Middle Ages the landowning aristocracy was
the ruling class. But they often forget that the Church was the largest landowner. "Long before the time of Charlemagne, the Church had a full third of
all the land in France, and it is certain that during the Middle Ages this proportion held generally for the whole of Catholic Western Europe."[114] In certain
areas the Church owned half of the land. The ruling class, which included
the Church hierarchy, was one of the most powerful and intelligent in history.
"The circumstance that the Catholic Church in the Middle Ages formed its
hierarchy out of the best brains in the land regardless of their estate, birth,
or fortune," writes Marx, "was one of the principal means of consolidating ecclesiastical rule and suppressing the laity. The more a ruling class is able to
assimilate the foremost minds of a ruled class, the more stable and dangerous
becomes its rule."[115]

The Church controlled all education, and theology embraced every form of
ideology: politics, jurisprudence, and philosophy. Theological dogmas were
political axioms, and Bible quotations counted as law in any court. Theologians
kept an eye on the growing body of jurists. Jurisprudence, philosophy, natural
science—every field was judged by whether its content agreed with the doctrines of the Church.[116]

"And this supremacy of theology in the entire realm of intellectual activity
was at the same time an inevitable consequence of the place held by the
Church as all-embracing synthesis and most general sanction of the existing
feudal domination."[117] Priests could read and write. So they dominated both
the monastery of the scholar and the court of the king. The weak royal government was in the hands of the Church, which supplied the king with chancel-
lors, secretaries, notaries, and other lettered personnel. The Church dominated
Europe: its ecclesiastical engines puffed ideological smoke into every corner
of feudal society.

We have seen that every bourgeois attack on feudalism had to begin as an
assault on the Church.[118] "The Catholic Church was, at the time of the Reformation, feudal proprietor of a great part of the English land," writes Marx. "The
property of the Church formed the religious bulwark of the traditional condi-

tions of landed property. With its fall these were no longer tenable."[119] Feudalism and the Church crumbled together. After the series of bourgeois revolutions against feudalism, says Engels, "the state took the place of the Church."[120]

During the Middle Ages a feudal state existed, of course, but there was a king in name only. Armies were loyal to their lords, not to the king. Merely the first noble of the realm, the king was often in conflict with other nobles. Consider one of these nobles, Charles the Bold, who ruled the duchy of Burgundy (d. 1477). He held part of his lands from the emperor and part from the king of France. But this king himself held land from Charles the Bold. In a system of perpetual war between lords, people could not be sure where their loyalties lay, and the central authority became the shadow of a name.[121]

As the first noble of the realm, this authority's main function was repressive: if the inevitable peasant revolts got out of hand he could take the field against them.

In most societies the institutional superstructure is political, but in some periods it appears in other forms. In the Europe of the Middle Ages, in the Massachusetts of the Calvinists, in the Egypt of the pharaohs, the superstructure was religious. "The necessity for predicting the rise and fall of the Nile created Egyptian astronomy, and with it the dominion of the priests, as directors of agriculture."[122]

Today the army directs society in certain developing countries, and a number of superstructures seem military. Whatever the form of superstructure, it rises on an economic basis of class relations. The ruling class supports the superstructure. This class produces ideologies of domination, to which we now turn.

The Social Ideologies

About ideology Marx says little. His studies in economics and sociology are not concerned with it. He planned a system of economic sociology divided into six parts: capital, landed property, wage labor, the state, international trade, the world market.[123] He lived to write only part one: *Capital*.

Marx's writings on capital total four volumes. But the 2,500 pages of *Capital* are only a fraction of the system planned, an exhaustive study of the economic basis and the state.

Ideology does not appear in the system, for Marx doubted that criticism of ideologies could be a science. We must always make a distinction, he says in principle [7], between material changes in economic conditions that can be determined with the precision of natural science and developments in the political and religious ideological forms.[124] The analysis of ideologies is not a science but an art.

Marx and Engels wrote critiques of ideology (*The German Ideology*, *Anti-Dühring*, *The Poverty of Philosophy*), but these are political exposures rather than sociology of knowledge. In their historical sociology the two men focused on the economic basis and its evolution.

Marx made a number of observations about ideology, and in later life Engels sketched an approach to this field. It easily fits into their sociological system, but we must remember the limitations Marx placed on the study of ideologies.

Marx and Engels distinguish between two kinds of ideology–revolutionary ideology and ruling ideology. What is ruling ideology? The ruling class has newspapers, publishers, bookstores, libraries, and universities, "so that, generally speaking, the ideas of those who lack the means of material production are subject to it."[125] The ruling ideology seeps into the lower classes, especially when the class struggle is latent. In every epoch the ruling ideas are the ideas of the ruling class.[126]

The ruling class has to "represent its interest as the common interest of all members of society, that is, expressed in ideal form: it has to give its ideas the form of universality, and to represent them as the only rational, universally valid ones."[127] For example, the bourgeoisie spreads through society the concept of freedom: all people are born and remain free.[128] But what does freedom mean? To the bourgeoisie it means freedom of speech, freedom of religion, freedom to sell one's labor, freedom to set prices for products, freedom to run factories without government regulation of hours and salaries. Is such freedom in the interest of all?

In capitalist society, in feudal society, and in slave society, there are phrases that conceal class interest: *right*, *justice*, *equality*, *freedom*. To uncover the class interest in the word *freedom* Marx gives the following example. In 1845 an American visited England, bringing his slave with him. The American beat his slave regularly, and the English tired of hearing the man's cries; a justice of the peace ordered the American to stop until he left England. "What?" roared the American. "Do you call this a land of freedom, where a man can't beat his own slave?"[129]

"Let us fight for freedom!"–that phrase may be a cry for freedom to exploit others. The bourgeois want freedom for their proletarians, want them free from serfdom, free to sell their labor. And such freedom, believes the bourgeoisie, is in the interest of society; in every epoch the ruling class sees its interest as the general interest. Its ideologists practice self-deception: they are not aware of the motives that drive them to their work, "otherwise there would be an end to all ideology."[130]

The ruling class wants capitalism, but without the monsters it breeds: misery, riots, strikes, poverty, crises, crime.[131] The ideologists tell people that the monsters don't exist. "Perseus," says Marx, "wore a magic cap that the monsters he hunted down might not see him. We draw the magic cap down over eyes and ears as a make-believe that there are no monsters."[132] Ideological magic blinds people to the ills of class rule.

But the monsters torment masses of people, and their suffering worries the ideologists. They write with a "bad conscience." They argue that the social system is improving, that the classes can live in harmony; they try to reconcile irreconcilables.[133]

The bad conscience of the ruling class is the key to its ideology. By contrast, to understand a revolutionary class we must remember its anger. Every revolutionary class develops an ideology against the existing order, a plan to bring the system to an end. Revolutionary plans appear again and again in history. "The existence of revolutionary ideas in a particular period presupposes the existence of a revolutionary class."[134]

Ruling Ideology

The ideologists of the ruling class form a social stratum: they live off ideological work; it is "their chief source of livelihood."[135] In the Middle Ages the Church supported ideologists in every sphere: theology, philosophy, jurisprudence, and political theory.[136] In modern Europe ideologists get their money from the state. Courts support jurists; state universities hire philosophers; state churches keep theologians. These people work hard at their intellectual tasks of thinking and writing about illusions. Jurists of private law, theorists of public law, legal minds of all kinds, philosophers of politics, government theoreticians, political scientists, social philosophers, professors of ethics–these people are paid for "the perfecting of the illusion of the class about itself."[137] They believe they study existing society to understand it, but in fact they are trying to justify it. "This is explained easily from their practical position in life, their job, and the division of labor."[138] Their social position makes them favor existing society, and by defending it they increase their chances for reputation and prestige. But scholars who attack society find themselves outlawed. "We socialists are outlawed not only in political but also in everyday life," Engels writes to a Marxist scholar suffering persecution. "The whole bourgeoisie finds it a pleasure and a duty to starve us. And above all it outlaws scholars . . . , because it sees them as deserters who have left their own class."[139]

What does the word *ideology* mean? For Marx and Engels it is *idea-ology* –a system of ideas. Thus ideology involves theories, doctrines, principles, systems of thought. Ideologists work with concepts, hypotheses, and theories that seem true or false. Myths, images, visions, and feelings are not ideology:

they are not systems of thought. Nor are interests, preferences, and attitudes a field of ideology, for they are neither true nor false–they simply exist. Moral attitudes are built into people by their class and culture.

An ideology is a system of ideas, and these systems develop inside ideological spheres. *Political science*–the first sphere–translates such words as *Staatswissenschaft*[140] and *Politik*.[141] Marx and Engels mark out four spheres: political science, jurisprudence, philosophy, and religion.[142] Twice they add morality to this list.[143] By morality they probably mean moral theories,[144] and they usually include this in the third sphere on the list–philosophy. Sometimes they add art to the list.[145] But the basic spheres are four, and they have existed for thousands of years.

In each sphere systems of thought slowly rise and fall. In the sphere of political science, for example, Montesquieu's constitutionalism was popular in eighteenth-century France until it fell before Rousseau's republicanism.[146] In the sphere of jurisprudence the bourgeois *Code Civil* wiped out feudal law.[147] In philosophy Leibniz was the fashion until Kant replaced him, and people soon left Kant for Hegel.[148] In religion Catholicism sank under the tidal wave of Protestantism.[149] In each sphere ideologists follow one another to the grave.

Each ideological sphere has a tradition reaching back to the Greco-Roman world or to early Christianity, and "in all ideological domains tradition forms a great conservative force."[150] Ideologists writing in the sphere of political science, for instance, have hundreds of constitutions and theories to work with, from Aristotle's *Politics* to Mill's *Representative Government*. Jurists think in a tradition rooted in Roman law. Philosophers study the writings of Thales, Heraclitus, Plato, Aquinas, Descartes, Leibniz, Kant, and Hegel. Religion is an endless debate about the meaning of the Bible, from Augustine to Calvin, from Anselm to Pius IX. Each ideological domain has its classics, its development, its history. "It is above all this appearance of an independent history of state constitutions, of systems of law, of ideological conceptions in every separate domain that dazzles most people."[151] People forget that every constitution, every law, and every philosophy belonged to a historical epoch. They think of ideologists as people outside history, scholars sealed in the library working with thought.

And the ideologists also forget. They forget how they make a living, who their enemies are, and the threats to their way of life. They forget their friends, their class position, and the struggles of their time. They study the writers of the past but ignore the classes, the nations, and the epochs. "These ideologists," warns Engels, "are gullible enough to accept unquestioningly all the illusions that an epoch makes about itself, or that ideologists of some epoch make about that epoch."[152] They are never conscious of anything but thought —and this is a false consciousness. Engels writes,

> Ideology is a process accomplished by the so-called thinker consciously, it is true, but with a false consciousness. The real motive forces impelling him remain unknown to him; otherwise it simply would not be an ideological process. So he imagines false or seeming motive forces. Because it is a process of thought he derives its form as well as its content from pure thought, either his own or that of his predecessors. He works with mere thought material, which he accepts without examination as the product of thought, and does not look further for a more remote source independent of thought.[153]

The real forces driving an ideologist remain unconscious: patriotic feeling, class interest, social guilt. Ideologists see that their class is always trying to pile larger burdens of labor on the toiling masses.[154] The social order seems unfair, and the ideologists want to justify it. Their bad conscience works on them as they write.[155] They want people to accept their lot; they argue that all people get what's coming to them.

In the Middle Ages, for example, theologians argued that serfs would get their reward. These ideologists knew how to quote the Bible: "Blessed are you poor, for yours is the kingdom of God; blessed are you hungry, for you will be filled" (Luke 6:20–21). In a future life–of course! The serfs may be cold and hungry but they are blessed; they suffer for the glory of God. The ideologists glorified the serfdom of the Middle Ages.[156] This glorification did not disappear with the Protestant Reformation. Luther also did it, "extracting from the Bible such a veritable hymn to the God-ordained authorities as no bootlicker of absolute monarchy had ever been able to accomplish. Princedom by the grace of God, resigned obedience, even serfdom, were sanctioned with the aid of the Bible."[157] Lutheran theologians followed him in this.

But they were not cynical: they partly believed in their message and so did their class. In the Middle Ages all people believed in heaven, including the ruling class. A ruling class that no longer believes in the ideas it spreads is limping toward the grave. "In the eighteenth century the French aristocracy said: For us, Voltaire; for the people, the mass, and the tithes."[158] That aristocracy believed in nothing, not even itself. History sent it to the guillotine. This process was a repetition of what had happened in England in the previous century. As the old order decayed, the English aristocracy grew sceptical but preached religion to the people. The aristocracy, or part of it, went under in the great bourgeois revolution.[159]

Ideologists do not manipulate public opinion with the "Big Lie" technique nor sell ideas through hidden persuaders. They are people of learning, proud of their calling: they don't know they work with illusions.

Marx and Engels say in an early work that political illusions remain fairly close to reality, while religious illusions soar into the clouds.[160] In later life Engels develops this idea into a theory of levels.

He arranges the ideological spheres in ascending levels, each further removed from the influence of the economic basis. Political science and jurisprudence hover close to the superstructure of political and juridical institutions, but philosophy and religion soar high into the air.[161] Let us look carefully at these four spheres.

(1) *Political science*. Political parties and government institutions give rise to political principles,[162] state constitutions,[163] and public law.[164] All this material belongs to the field of ideology called political science. It closely reflects the economic basis, the class struggle, and the state institutions.

(2) *Jurisprudence*. This field studies public law and thus overlaps with political science. But jurisprudence is also concerned with private law. It covers sales, debts, torts, obligations, and contracts.[165]

When feudalism dissolved into capitalism, law based on traditional and personal ties changed into law expressing contractual relations. "The bourgeoisie," writes Marx, "has pitilessly torn asunder the motley feudal ties that bound man to his 'natural superiors,' and has left remaining no other nexus between man and man than naked self-interest, than callous 'cash payment.'"[166] Feudalism collapsed, and bourgeois codes of law appeared.[167] In England bourgeois Common Law expressed the new economic conditions badly; in Prussia the *Landrecht* expressed them better; in France the *Code Civil* was the best expression of bourgeois conditions.[168]

"In a modern state, law must not only correspond to the general economic condition and be its expression, but must also be an *internally coherent* expression which does not, owing to inner contradictions, reduce itself to nothing. And in order to achieve this, the faithful reflection of economic conditions suffers increasingly."[169] Law rises into the clouds of ideology. The tangle of laws develops into legal systems and juridical philosophies, into new realms of thought. They become a mystery to the average person. And so a priesthood arises to interpret the law: lawyers, judges, justices, jurists, professors, scholars.[170]

(3) *Philosophy*. High in the ideological ether floats philosophy. "The philosophy of every epoch, since it is a definite sphere in the division of labor, has as its presupposition certain definite thought material handed down to it by its predecessors, from which it takes its start."[171] The economic basis creates nothing new in philosophy; but the basis affects the way past material

develops. The basis mainly affects the lower levels of philosophical thought: moral and political philosophy.[172]

In political philosophy, for example, we can easily see the social influence in the works of Hobbes, Locke, and Rousseau. In his *Leviathan* Hobbes argued for an all-powerful king when monarchism was triumphant throughout Europe. The bourgeoisie grew in influence, and in his second treatise on *Civil Government* Locke argued for curbing the king. In *The Social Contract* Rousseau called for the king's disappearance and a republic while the French prepared their revolution. Each of these philosophers analyzed the *social contract*, an idea as old as the Greeks.[173]

And moral philosophy? This branch of philosophy is more than a description of moral rules such as "Keep your promises" and "Don't hit people." Such rules operate in all institutions, both in the superstructure and in the economic basis. Moral philosophy goes beyond rules that are neither true nor false to "moral theories."[174] Moral philosophy means a theory like Feuerbach's or Kant's, "designed to suit all periods, all peoples and all conditions."[175] Kant's theory appeals to the propertied class, especially because it lays down morality for all classes of society. For Kant the universe is a moral order: if you can't will that everyone should do something, then you should not do it yourself, and so stealing is wrong under all circumstances. *Reason* teaches that stealing is wrong even when you are out of work, your children are starving, and your "betters" are getting fat—such theories delight the propertied classes.

Higher levels of philosophy, like metaphysics, show hardly any economic influence. Metaphysics and religion "have a prehistoric stock, found already in existence by the historical period, of what we should today call bunk," writes Engels. What is this bunk? "Various false conceptions of nature, of man's own being, of spirits, magic forces, and so forth."[176] Dreams, for example, convinced the ancients that the mind could leave the body, and slowly life after death emerged in their religion. The philosophers developed this into a metaphysical theory of the soul.

The Greeks worshipped the heavenly bodies. Aristotle developed this into a theory of the planets: he argued that they consist of perfect substance, travel in circles, and move uniformly. For 2,000 years Aristotle's theory reigned in philosophy, but it was only a step beyond Greek religion. "Philosophy," Marx says, "is nothing else but religion rendered into thought and expounded by thought, therefore equally to be condemned. . . ."[177] And yet philosophy is a step forward.

"Philosophy first builds itself up within the religious form of consciousness, and in so doing on the one hand destroys religion as such, while on the other hand, in its positive content, it still moves only within this religious sphere, idealized and reduced to terms of thought."[178] For Marx religious superstition passes into metaphysics, and this is a step on the road to science. "It would surely be pedantic to try and find economic causes for all this primitive nonsense," says Engels. "The history of science is the history of the gradual clearing away of this nonsense or of its replacement by fresh but always less absurd nonsense."[179]

Marx ridicules "philosophical mystification."[180] Just as masturbation caricatures sexual love, so speculative philosophy parodies the study of the real world.[181] "Where speculation ends—in real life—there real, positive science begins," he writes. "When reality is depicted, philosophy as an independent branch of knowledge loses its medium of existence."[182] Human knowledge is a struggle away from philosophy into science.

Metaphysics soars into the clouds, but there are even higher levels of philosophy, levels that show no trace of economic influence. The economic basis does not affect the study of problems in perception, in logic, in language. Consider the problem of universals. Common names like *redness* or *intelligence* denote universals, while proper names—*Plato* or *the moon* or *this*—denote particulars. Universals can be repeated, particulars only copied or reproduced. Particulars exist in space and time. The problem of universals is this: are they real or only names? This problem was discussed by Plato, by Aristotle, by the medieval schoolmen, by the English empiricists, and by the modern logicians. The problem received different solutions, and sometimes the solution led toward a metaphysical system. Marx and Engels never explain such solutions by economic conditions.

Thus there are many fields of philosophy, some closer to the economic basis than others. Philosophers patch these fields into systems of thought, but not every system counts as ideology. Marx says that ideologies are "forms of social consciousness."[183] An ideology is *social* consciousness, a system of ideas believed by a party or a class or an epoch. A philosopher may publish a system, but to become ideology it must find believers. All ideologists learn to write for their class. The prospect of fame and reputation, the desire for influence and prestige, the love of money and status—these motives work unconsciously as they write.

(4) *Religion.* How did religion first arise? Engels writes, with Marx's approval,

> Religion is nothing but the fantastic reflection in men's minds of those external forces which control their daily life, a reflection in which the terrestrial forces assume the form of supernatural forces. In the beginnings of history it was the forces of nature which were first so reflected, and which in the course of further evolution underwent the most varied personifications among the various peoples. This early process has been traced back

by comparative mythology, at least in the case of the Indo-European peoples, to its origin in the Indian Vedas, and in its further evolution it has been demonstrated in detail among the Indians, Persians, Greeks, Romans, Germans and so far as material is available also among the Celts, Lithuanians, and Slavs.[184]

These national religions arose spontaneously, but the three world religions —Christianity, Buddhism, and Islam—arose artificially, that is, through missionaries or conquest.[185]

Once religion has come into being, the ruling class turns it into an ideology. The ruling class easily used Christianity to justify its rule. The Christian theologians' message, says Marx, was simple: "Submit to the authority, for *all* authority is ordained by God" (Romans 13).[186]

And religion consoles the masses for their suffering. "It is the opium of the people."[187] (In the nineteenth century doctors used opium to relieve pain.) For the laboring masses the promise of heaven relieves the pain of life. "And they will be with God," promises the Bible, "and he will wipe away the tears from their eyes, and there will be no more death, nor pain, nor crying, nor labor, for all that is now past" (Revelation 21:4).

Thus religion becomes an ideology of class domination. But the class structure does not create doctrines out of whole cloth; they arise through theological debate over the scriptures. Consider the question that divided Arminian from Calvinist theologians in the Reformation—is salvation by free will or God's predestination? Calvin took the predestination doctrine from St. Paul, and it spread through the bourgeoisie. Why did Calvinism triumph? Because its ethic of thrift and hard work fit bourgeois practice. And because its predestination doctrine mirrored bourgeois experience: in an age of commercial revolution some bourgeois failed while others succeeded, yet no one knew why. Any entrepreneur could fail, even a clever one; the bourgeois were at the mercy of unknown powers. They could easily believe the doctrine that an unknowable God had predestined a few to salvation.[188]

Of course religion may be more than ruling ideology. From the thirteenth to the seventeenth centuries Christianity provided ideologies for the revolutionary movements that shook Europe.[189] The Christian Bible contains opium, but it also cries out for social justice. Both the Old and New Testaments condemn the wickedness of the rich (Isaiah, Amos, Micah, and Habakkuk; Jesus himself in Matthew 19:24 and Luke 16:19–31).

Religion may be the ideology of a great historical movement. In the seventh century Bedouins poured out of the Arabian peninsula and conquered a vast area from Samarkand to the Pyrenees. The Bedouin conquest pushed Europe into the Dark Ages, broke the power of Byzantium, and made the civilization

of the Arabs. The Bedouins fought under the flag of Islam: Mohammed prom-
ised paradise to anyone falling in a Holy War. The Bedouins believed they
were fighting for the Prophet, but in fact they fought for booty and plunder.[190]

We have examined the four spheres of ideology: political science, jurisprudence, philosophy, and religion. When Marx and Engels list these spheres
they sometimes add art.[191] Is art a sphere of ideology?

We noted that ideologies are systems of ideas, that they counterfeit fields
of knowledge. But what does art have to do with knowledge? Painters, sculp-
tors, architects, poets, and musicians are concerned with the creation of beauty, not with the search for knowledge. Their works may express ideas, but they
are hardly systems of ideology. In his discussions of ideology Engels never
took up art: he wondered what to do with it. Marx, too, found it puzzling. In
a few notes he considered art but came to no conclusion. "It is well known," he
notes, "that certain periods of highest development of art stand in no direct
connection with the general development of society, nor with the material
basis."[192] He is thinking of the explosions of art in Greece and the Renaissance.
He knew that the relation between art and society is no simple matter.

Marx and Engels never worked out a view of art; they left this task for their
followers. Marxists have produced an interesting literature on the subject. To
sample it you can consult works by Christopher Caudwell, Georg Lukács,
Arnold Hauser, and George Thompson.

Revolutionary Ideology

Professional thinkers paid by the state often produce the ruling ideology.
But who creates the ideology of an oppressed class? There is no simple answer to this question, for a lower class may get its ideology anywhere.

Marx makes clear that ideologists of an oppressed class may not be members of that class, may not even be champions of the class. What makes them
ideologists of the class? In their social philosophy they attack theoretical
problems that drive them to certain solutions, the same solutions class interest
drives other people to in practical life. These people read the philosophers'
works and grasp at the solutions they offer for social problems. They make
the philosophy an ideology for their class.[193]

Jean-Charles-Leonard Simonde de Sismondi's works provide an example.
Sismondi was a scholar who wrote on social problems in the early nineteenth
century. The factory system, the stinking cities, the economic crises, the misery
of the proletariat, the ruin of the petty bourgeoisie–all this horrified him. He
preached a return to an earlier society: villages of peasants working their plots,
towns of merchants and artisans, a government of administrators and intellectuals. His works became an ideology of the petty bourgeoisie.[194]

To save itself from extinction the petty bourgeoisie fought against capitalism; it tried to roll back the wheel of history; its utopia lay in the past. From the standpoint of world history this class was reactionary.[195]

Before 1800 a truly revolutionary class was the bourgeoisie, for it was riding the wave of the future. Bourgeois revolutionaries often took their ideologies from bygone epochs: in the bourgeois revolutions the leaders reached back to the ancient world for "the ideals and the art forms, the self-deceptions that they needed in order to conceal from themselves the bourgeois limitations of the content of their struggles and to keep their enthusiasm on the high plane of the great historical tragedy."[196] Cromwell and the English bourgeoisie found in the Hebrew prophets a cry for justice to voice their own; Robespierre and Saint Just found in the ideologies of ancient Rome ideals for revolutionary France.[197] Representatives of a class can take their ideologies from the past, for thinkers often deal with problems that reappear in history. They speak to ages beyond their own.

The early Christian author of the Apocalypse, the last book in the Bible, was such a thinker: again and again his work became the ideology of revolutionary movements in European history. He believes "that the kingdom of God, the capital of which is the New Jerusalem, can only be conquered and opened after arduous struggles with the powers of hell."[198] Those struggles, he prophesies, lie immediately ahead: a series of signs and punishments must soon rain from heaven. "Then follows the great final fight, the saints and the martyrs are avenged by the destruction of the Great Whore Babylon and all her followers, that is, the main mass of mankind; the devil is cast into the bottomless pit and shut up there for a thousand years during which Christ reigns with the martyrs risen from the dead."[199] The thousand-year reign of Christ–the millennium–is just around the corner. That is the message, and it became the ideology of religious sects and peasant revolts in feudal Europe. "The revolutionary opposition to feudalism was alive all down the Middle Ages."[200]

Millennial ideology first arose in the Roman Empire. In the third century the Empire decayed and the masses began to stir: everywhere slaves and poor people looked for a way out of their misery. In the Eastern Empire thousands of preachers and prophets roamed the desert, offering religious escapes from the world.[201] Christianity was one of these religions. "Christianity, as was bound to be the case in the historic conditions, did not want to accomplish the social transformation in this world, but beyond it . . . in the impending 'millennium.'"[202] Christians competed with preachers of other salvation religions. "The entire Orient swarmed with such founders of religions, and between them raged what can be called a Darwinistic struggle for ideological existence."[203] In this struggle Christianity had an advantage: it offered faith in Christ without rites, fasts, ceremonies, and sacrifices. It could save all people.[204] By natural selection in the struggle of ideologies it spread among the slaves, and they carried it through the Empire.[205] Christianity, like every great revolutionary movement, was made by the masses.[206]

Similarly, in nineteenth-century Europe many ideologies competed for the mind of the working class. Bakunin, Owen, Proudhon, Blanqui, Cabet, Lassalle, Dühring, and Blanc preached their socialist ideologies. Engels sees this as another Darwinistic struggle for ideological existence. In this struggle Marxism soon conquered the working-class mind.[207]

The struggle raged fiercely, yet Marxism had an advantage, for it was not an ideology, but a developing science. Insofar as this science represented a class, it could only represent the proletariat. The revolutionary proletariat was the class that held the future in its hands.[208]

Throughout history revolutionaries *believed* in their ideologies; they fought battles for them. In the Middle Ages peasants fought to bring in the Kingdom of God–the prophesied millennium.[209] In the French Revolution the bourgeois fought for the Kingdom of Reason, for Liberty–Equality–Fraternity.[210]

In fact these revolutionaries fought for class interest, but they didn't know it: in their minds they aimed at the interest of society. A class believes it fights for the Kingdom of God or the Kingdom of Reason, not for more food or more self-respect.[211]

The End of Ideology

What about science? Is science part of ideology? Can there be "class science"? Whenever Marx and Engels list the spheres of ideology they omit science.[212] They make it clear that natural science, at least, is a disinterested search for truth. They say that the ruling classes cannot distort mathematics, physics, and chemistry: these disciplines remain above class interest; they are a universal search for knowledge.[213]

What about the "science of society"?[214] Marx and Engels see social science as a road wandering among the fogs of ideology, passing through the labyrinths of Academe, and leading toward the summits of Truth–for those who have not already lost their way. Social scientists usually defend the ruling class, but a few study political and economic problems for their own sake.

Even social thinkers pursuing truth in a disinterested way don't work in a void: their ideas reflect the conditions of the time. In the eighteenth century, for example, Adam Smith tried to analyze society honestly. In that century the government regulated industry, and Smith argued that government regulations hurt the economy–tariffs choked trade. His attack on the old regulations reflected changed economic facts: the industrial revolution and a growing market.[215]

Adam Smith fought mercantilist economics. He attacked government regulation of industry; he urged the government to *let businesses alone*. After his death the industrial revolution turned ugly: child labor, mass hunger, the eighteen-hour day. Reformers begged the government to regulate the working day. But factory owners shouted that government must let businesses alone, and looked back to Adam Smith. His *Wealth of Nations*, written in other circumstances, became their Bible; they turned it into an ideology excusing mass suffering.

In the early nineteenth century the class struggle was undeveloped, and the masses suffered quietly. In quiet periods of history students of the economy study how society really works. The years between 1810 and 1830 were such a period, and its economist was a stockbroker, David Ricardo. In his economic studies Ricardo often gained understanding. He argued that the interests of bourgeois and proletarians clash, that a struggle over the surplus product is inevitable. He could admit this because the proletariat was quiet.[216]

After 1830 the struggle flared up between bourgeoisie and proletariat, and social science turned to the defense of capitalism: economists and sociologists were no longer calm investigators–they were hired fighters.[217] This official science defended capitalism through the nineteenth century. In the sphere of the social sciences, writes Engels in 1886, "the old fearless zeal for theory has now disappeared completely. . . . Inane eclecticism and an anxious concern for career and income, descending to the most vulgar job hunting, occupy its place. The official representatives of these sciences have become the undisguised ideologists of the bourgeoisie and the existing state–but at a time when both stand in open antagonism to the working class."[218] Ideological thinking invades science in times of class struggle.

Academic science may discover truths about society, but its professors are supporters of the social order, and their wishes distort the search for truth. Outside the universities there are Marxist students of society. The social sciences, says Engels, are revolutionized by Marx.[219]

Students working in Marx's manner are not ideologists. The founders of Marxism claim to rise above the class struggle to a vision of world history; they urge a program for studying the chain of social formations.[220] The evolution of the nations, the rise and fall of classes, the development of ideologies –all this flowing sea of history must be charted. Men and women working in the Marxist tradition can do it, because they have "raised themselves to the level of comprehending theoretically the historical movement as a whole."[221]

Marxism is not supposed to be an ideology, but a criticism of ideologies. "So far as such criticism represents a class," says Marx, "it can only represent the class whose vocation in history is the overthrow of the capitalist mode

of production and the final abolition of all classes–the proletariat."²²² The proletariat is the class that uses the Marxist method in social science. Many Marxists, like Georg Lukács in his *History and Class Consciousness*, seem to say
that Marxism is also an ideology. Their views are interesting, but they are not
using the word *ideology* in the way that Marx and Engels use it.

Natural science is not ideology. Social science, as revolutionized by Marxism, is not ideology either. Ideology is false consciousness, while science is
the road to truth. Truth lies "in the process of cognition itself, in the long historical development of science, which mounts from lower to ever higher levels
of knowledge without ever reaching by discovering so-called absolute truth
a point at which it can proceed no further, where it would have nothing more
to do than to fold its hands and gaze with wonder at the absolute truth to
which it had attained."²²³ Engels thinks that truth is whatever scientists working an indefinite length of time agree on

Someday science will replace ideology. In communist society people gain
scientific insight into their relations with one another and with nature. These
relations are no longer concealed behind ideology; their reflex in religion dissolves forever.²²⁴ Philosophy disappears into a world outlook based on the
sciences.²²⁵ Jurisprudence and political theory vanish with private property,
law courts, and national governments.

The Althusserian school of European Marxism holds that ideology will continue under communism. Their arguments deserve the wide attention they
receive, but these thinkers are not using the word *ideology* as Marx and Engels
use it. According to our two revolutionaries, communist society must see an
end of false consciousness. Under communism, science's great leap forward
will make everything preceding fade into insignificance.²²⁶ Science scatters the
shadows of ideology, and humanity marches forward in the full light of truth.

The Social Formation

The term *Gesellschaftsformation* appears three times in the preface of 1859.
Each time the standard English translation renders it differently: social order,
formation of society, social formation.²²⁷ The translator of *Capital*, where the
word often turns up, was even more inventive–he found many English equiva-
lents.²²⁸ Literally the German word means "society-formation."

What is a social formation?

A social formation embraces the civilization of an epoch. It includes the
economic basis, the political superstructure, and the social ideologies. It is
the social whole. It is the totality of social systems and subsystems that make

up the civilization, with the relations between them, especially the economic relations: it is human culture viewed from the standpoint of its economic structure.

What defines a given social formation? What, for example, distinguishes the feudal formation from the capitalist formation? The mode of production "distinguishes the different economic epochs of the structure of society from one another."[229] As economic evolution progresses, formations come into being and pass away. No social formation ever collapses before all the productive forces in it have developed or have at least come into existence, says Marx. In broad outlines Asiatic, ancient, feudal, and capitalist modes of production should be seen as progressive epochs in the economic formation of society [*die ökonomische Gesellschaftsformation*].[230] The future contains a higher formation, in which the earth is owned in common. "From the standpoint of a higher economic social formation," writes Marx, "private ownership of the globe by single individuals will appear quite as absurd as private ownership of one man by another."[231] This final social formation is communism.

Each of the different social formations is defined by *the mode of production dominant in it*. For in each formation there is also "passive survival of antiquated modes of production."[232] Every economic basis contains "remnants of earlier stages of economic development which have actually been transmitted and have survived—often only through tradition or by force of inertia."[233] Economic evolution "takes place only very slowly; the various stages and interests are never completely overcome, but only subordinated to the prevailing interest and trail along beside [it] for centuries afterwards."[234] Societies are historical museums: they contain remnants of economic forms humanity has passed through, "with their inevitable train of social and political anachronisms."[235]

A social formation evolves according to laws discovered by historical sociology. From my standpoint, says Marx, "the evolution of the economic social formation is viewed as a process of natural history."[236] A formation embraces both the past and future: dying modes of production; the dominant, defining mode; and seeds of coming modes. Social formations overlap; the epochs pass into one another. Historical epochs, like geological ages, have no hard and fast lines between them.[237] Marx distinguishes the Asiatic, ancient, feudal, and bourgeois formations only "in broad outlines."[238]

Today many Marxists don't follow his schema exactly, but their periodizations of history must rest on his basic approach: an identification of social formations prevailing in certain regions of space and time.

Interaction and Determinism

We have discussed the levels of society in Marx's theory: economic, political, and ideological. Now we must examine the relations between them. The nature of these relations has aroused controversy among both Marxists and critics of Marx, especially the relation between basis and superstructure.

In the preface of 1859 Marx sets forth the basis-superstructure model. This preface to a work on political economy describes the model used in his studies of capitalism.[239] The model, says Marx, is "briefly formulated."[240] In a page he describes a few of its features that will interest the student of political economy. His description focuses on the economic basis. He analyzes it into two factors, forces and relations. He notes the connection between them: forces condition relations; forces expand and come into conflict with relations; this conflict ends in a revolution of the economic basis. With the change in the basis, the superstructure is transformed.

Marx talks about the economic basis, but about the superstructure itself he says little. He is interested in the economic basis because he is writing a work on economics. The model guided his economic studies for fourteen years.[241]

Marx's followers mistook the preface of 1859 for a complete statement of historical materialism. Because he emphasizes the basis and ignores the superstructure, some of his adherents–like Paul Lafargue–became strict economic determinists. Marx saw their mistake and made his famous statement: "I am not a Marxist."[242] Before he could correct them he fell ill and finally died.

Large numbers of intellectuals soon rallied to Marxism. Some used the Marxist method to shape the facts of history to suit themselves; Engels scolded the young writer Paul Ernst for this.[243] Many Marxists slipped into strict economic determinism. "Marx and I," writes Engels, "are ourselves partly to blame for the fact that the younger people sometimes lay more stress on the economic side than is due to it. We had to emphasize the main principle against our adversaries, who denied it. . . ."[244] The superstructure, explains Engels, while not independent of the basis, yet has some autonomy, a point which "Marx and I always failed to stress enough in our writings."[245]

In five letters (1890–1894)[246] Engels tried to correct the confusions about historical materialism. The basis conditioned the superstructure–that was clear; but what was the role of the superstructure itself? In the 1890s Engels analyzed ideology into levels and examined the superstructure's influence on the basis.

In doing this Engels denied that he was revising Marxism. He claimed that he and Marx had always held the concept of an active superstructure. There was interaction between basis and superstructure; the basis shaped the superstructure, and the superstructure modified the basis; only in the end did the basis triumph. "More than this neither Marx nor I have ever asserted," writes Engels. "The economic situation is the basis, but the various elements of the superstructure . . . also exercise their influence upon the course of the historical struggles and in many cases preponderate in determining their *form*. There is an interaction of all these elements in which, amid all the endless host of accidents . . . the economic movement finally asserts itself as necessary."[247]

Marx was never the economic determinist that his preface made him appear to be. In historical writings of the 1850s he deals with the influence of political struggles on society.[248] In the first volume of *Capital* (1867) he describes the role of political power in speeding up the transition from feudalism to capitalism (chapter 31). In unpublished notes (1857) he observes that ideological forms do not always correspond to the basis, that in some ages art had leaped ahead of economic development, while in others law had lagged behind. And against historical "necessity" he notes the existence of "freedom" and "accident."[249]

Critics have seen Marx as an economic determinist because of the model he used for his theory, the metaphor of basis and superstructure. The metaphor compares society to a physical structure, like a bridge or a building. These structures have a base, usually below the surface, and a superstructure built on this foundation. If the foundation collapses, the superstructure tumbles down, and a new edifice is needed. This metaphor from construction engineering suggests strict economic determinism, for the economic basis seems the crucial factor in a static situation.

The metaphor is not the only one Marx could have used for his theory. He might have compared society to a plant with economic roots, an institutional stem, and flowers of ideology; indeed he flirted with this idea in his notes. Or he could have described society as a ship forced forward by economic engines, but changing speed because of the crew in charge (a political elite). Such a metaphor would indicate the role of political power in history, while the basis-superstructure model implies rigid economic determinism. Marx never insisted on the basis-superstructure metaphor; he himself only used it four or five times in all his work. *The metaphor is not identical with the theory.*[250]

Many interpreters of Marx have confused the model with the theory, an error committed by both critics and followers. But the theory exists independently of any metaphor used to illustrate it. Marx's theory (or theory sketch) shows that certain institutional orders are primary and others secondary, that institutions and classes give rise to ideologies, and that all these factors make up an interrelated whole, a social system. "Political, juridical, philosophical, religious, literary, and artistic development is based on economic development," writes Engels. "But all these react upon one another and upon the economic basis. . . . There is . . . interaction on the basis of economic necessity, which *ultimately* always asserts itself."[251] Marx's theory sketch is a series of literal statements about how society works, and Marxists have the task of filling in the sketch. The sketch, for instance, does not show *how* the economic basis gives rise to ideological forms; but the ways and means by which the forms arise would be clear in a completed theory.[252]

Materialist Theory

We now have Marx's complete framework of concepts: productive forces, relations of production, mode of production, economic basis, political superstructure, social ideology, and social formation. Marxists can use these concepts in the study of societies anywhere. They apply to the Aztecs and the Arabs and the Chinese, to ancient Greece and contemporary Africa, to Soviet Russia, capitalist India, and modern America. Sometimes a concept may not apply to primitive tribal society or hypothetical communist civilization, but in general the concepts provide a frame of thought for studying any segment of world history.

Besides this conceptual framework Marx also sketched the beginnings of a sociological theory: in the preface of 1859 we have a summary of his theoretical propositions. His fundamental proposition, the basis of all social research, is [4]: social being determines consciousness.[253]

"This apparently simple proposition," writes Engels, "that the consciousness of people depends on their being and not *vice versa*, runs directly counter to all idealism, even the most concealed. All traditional and customary outlooks on everything historical are negated by it."[254] Traditional thinkers stressed the role of ideas in history; they took an "idealist" approach to the past. They believed that ideas brought on social changes, that religious and moral conflicts caused historical events. The fall of Rome, the Christian Crusades, the Protestant Reformation, the Thirty Years War, the English Revolution, the triumph of the *philosophes*–everything was caused by ideas.

Marx and Engels reversed this view. They showed that technical, economic, social, and institutional change is basic, while ideas are secondary. "Does it require deep intuition," they ask, "to comprehend that people's ideas, views, and conceptions, in one word, people's consciousness, changes with every change in the conditions of their material existence, in their social relations, and in their social life?"[255] Changes in material interest and social organization bring on crusades, reformations, wars, revolutions, and ideological transformations. A century ago this was a brilliant insight.

For a hundred years Marx's "historical materialism" has worked on the modern mind, and other thinkers have reinforced its impact: Freud, Pareto, Mannheim. Today most social scientists acknowledge the materialist principle. But often they merely pay lip service to it, and sometimes they don't even do that.

Only certain philosophers reject it outright. Up to the time of Karl Marx the historians were working correctly, complains the philosopher Benedetto Croce in his *Essays on Marx and Russia*. "Historiography . . . anterior to that of historical materialism," says Croce, "explained human events in the light of ideas (religious Reformation and Catholic counter-Reformation, criticism and authority, natural laws and traditionalism, Historicism and Jacobinism, and so forth)." This was the right approach, claims Croce, for the creative spirit of history is the strength of ethical ideals, of political parties (p. 79).

Against this Marx argued that we must study human social existence first and ideals second. We must interpret people's phrases, moralities, and religions in the context of their behavior. In history social and economic forces are primary, while ideologies are secondary. This is the materialist principle.

Consider some materialist historical explanations. What explains the spread of Protestantism in the sixteenth and seventeenth centuries? Marx believed that Protestantism was a religion of the bourgeoisie: capitalism was primary, the Reformation secondary.[256] Engels elaborated this insight.[257] Emergent capitalism, the two men thought, produced a commercial class that lived by individualism, thrift, and discipline–values expressed in Calvinism. The bourgeoisie had found in Calvin a brilliant ideologist. By contrast, in *The Protestant Ethic and the Spirit of Capitalism*, Max Weber argues that Calvinism kindled the fires of capitalism. Calvinist ideas of hard work and thrift sparked capitalism into being. !deas, Weber thinks, can make history. His theory contains some truth, for after Protestantism became bourgeois ideology it played a part in capitalism's inevitable expansion. (This insight was already present in Marx.)[258] But Weber claims much more: Calvinism, he seems to say, brought capitalism into being. Weber became an idol of American social science, and many sociologists accept his theory as probably correct.

Why are black people, formerly enslaved from Virginia to Chile, now treated worse in the United States than in Latin America? Why is there less discrimination in Rio de Janeiro? Because of tradition and religion, answer idealist historians. They point to Brazil: there Catholic religion had defined slaves as people, and Portuguese tradition never viewed dark peoples as inferior. But materialist historians find the explanation of Latin "liberalism" in material conditions: the economic and demographic features of colonization in the Americas, the natural and institutional environments of slavery, the plantation systems of the southern United States and Brazil, the formation of classes in these societies. Idealist historians explain prejudice by religion; materialists by the facts of material life.*

Marxist explanations of events focus on social and economic factors. What caused the fall of Rome? Not collapse of the idea of citizenship, but economic decay: an unfavorable balance of trade with Asia, a decline of urban crafts, and a decrease in the supply of slaves. What caused the Crusades? Not the love of God, but material interests: feudal land hunger, the thirst for booty, and a struggle for trade routes. What caused the French Revolution? Not the subversive *philosophes*, but class struggle: the expanding productive forces, the bourgeoisie's drive toward power, and peasant hunger for land. Not ideas, but social and economic changes push history forward. Material conditions change, then ideas rise or fall. Thus as Rome declined, the idea of citizenship collapsed. Feudal knights wanted Moslem land; for the Holy Faith they launched the Crusades to free it from infidels. Aristocrats infuriated that rich businessman Voltaire, and he turned his brilliant pen against the bulwarks of feudal privilege: the Church, the Catholic hierarchy, and Christian theology.

The fundamental principle of Marxism is this: ideology falls into line with material conditions. Changes in material conditions create new social relations, and these reshape human consciousness. Technical, environmental, economic, and class relationships dominate the ideologies of history. The loom of history weaves ideological colors throughout the social fabric. To unravel this fabric we study the changing relation between humanity and the institutional and natural environment, the material world.

---

*For examples of idealist history, see Frank Tannenbaum, *Slave and Citizen*; Gilberto Freyre, *The Masters and the Slaves*; and Stanley Elkins, *Slavery*. For materialist history, see Marvin Harris, *Patterns of Race in the Americas*; Eric Williams, *Capitalism and Slavery*.

Appendix. Marx's Theory of Revolution

The twentieth century has been an age of wars and revolutions. Marx's historical sociology continues to interest large numbers of people because it offers a theory of revolution. Marx himself designed his theory for the study of revolution in nineteenth-century Europe, and we may well ask what relevance his views have for contemporary political workers concerned with social change.

For Marx the industrial proletariat was the historical agency of socialist revolution. During the nineteenth century social conditions drove the European proletariat toward revolution, while in the twentieth century these conditions have largely disappeared, though some of them might reappear. How did Marx and Engels see nineteenth-century conditions?

The proletariat had no vote; trade unions were outlawed; and the police clubbed the working class into a fury. We communists, writes Engels in 1847, "see that the development of the proletariat in nearly all civilized countries has been violently suppressed, and that in this way the opponents of communism have been working toward a revolution with all their strength."[1]

Marx and Engels believed that it takes two classes to make a revolution, and one of these is always the ruling class. The ruling class, by blocking reform, brings on revolution. "Wherever there is a revolutionary convulsion, there must be some social want in the background, which is prevented by outworn institutions from satisfying itself."[2] The outworn institutions of nineteenth-century Europe prevented social reform. From 1815 to 1848 the Holy Alliance ground down the working people of the European Continent: priests and censors, armies and police spies were everywhere. In *The Age of Revolution* the historian Eric Hobsbawm sums up the repressive period as follows: "Never in European history and rarely anywhere else, has revolutionism been so endemic, so general, so likely to spread by spontaneous contagion as well as by deliberate propaganda" (p. 109). Marxism took shape, as we have noted, in the period before 1848.

After 1848 conditions improved in England, but not on the Continent: France writhed under Louis Bonaparte's dictatorship, and Bismarck drove the German socialists underground. Without political rights, without unions, without justice, the proletariat saw only one answer: revolution.

"The working class can be driven toward the flames [of revolution] only by direct state persecution," says Marx.[3] On the Continent this persecution was not lacking. In 1871 the bourgeoisie massacred the Paris proletariat, and in 1878 Bismarck outlawed the German socialist party. Marx and Engels welcomed Bismarck's repression.[4] They saw police beatings as a catalyst of revolution, and hailed the government as an ally. They hoped for more clubbing of the reformist proletariat in England: "These thick-headed John Bulls, whose brainpans seem to have been especially manufactured for the constables' bludgeons, will never get anywhere without a really bloody encounter with the ruling powers."[5]

As the nineteenth century drew to a close, repressive conditions loosened up on the Continent: the proletariat won the vote; unions became lawful; and the policeman's club fell less often. In the twentieth century the integration of the proletariat into capitalist society steadily continued.

In the nineteenth century the proletariat was driven toward revolution by unbearable conditions of life. During the 1840s industrialization was rapid in England, accelerating in France, and beginning in Germany. What did rapid industrialization mean? "The herding together of a homeless population in the worst quarters of the large towns; the loosening of all traditional moral bonds, of patriarchal subordination, of family relations; overwork, especially of women and children, to a frightful extent; complete demoralization of the working class, suddenly flung into altogether new conditions, from the country into the town, from agriculture into modern industry, from stable conditions of existence into insecure ones that changed from day to day."[6] These conditions produced a revolutionary proletariat. Young migrants from rural areas, tossed about in the storm of rapid industrialization, were ready to smash the old society. In the *Manifesto* Marx describes industrialization during the 1840s: "Constant revolutionizing of production, uninterrupted disturbance of all social conditions, everlasting uncertainty and agitation distinguish the bourgeois epoch from all earlier ones."[7] The workers were desperate: "The unceasing improvement of machinery, ever more rapidly developing, makes their liveihood more and more precarious."[8]

England had begun industrialization around 1770, and after 1850 it passed from the stage of rapid development into gradual growth. Then its proletariat became reformist.[9] France and Germany, starting in the 1840s, continued rapid industrialization through the nineteenth century. The proletariats on the Continent remained revolutionary.

After 1850 England's rate of growth slowed down, and its working class began to see capitalism in a new light. About two decades later Marx wrote an interesting description of the English proletariat, which had turned reformist. He did not grasp the full meaning of his description:

> The advance of capitalist production develops a working class which by education, tradition, and habit looks upon the conditions of that mode of production as self-evident laws of Nature. The organization of the capitalist process of production, once fully developed, breaks down all resistance. . . . The dull compulsion of economic regulations completes the subjection of the laborer to the capitalist. Direct force outside economic conditions is of course still used, but only exceptionally. . . . It is otherwise during the historic genesis of capitalist production.[10]

What is the proletariat like, by contrast, during the "historic genesis" of capitalism? This includes industrialization (1770–1850 in England): young people from the country crowd into city slums to work long hours for low pay. This young proletariat lacks "education, tradition, and habit." These workers don't see capitalism as "self-evident." They want to smash it and build a new world. They are revolutionary as they pass through rapid capitalist development. In England this period ended in the middle of the nineteenth century.

"The class struggles here in England," writes Engels in 1892, "were more turbulent during the *period of development* of large-scale industry and died down just in the period of England's undisputed industrial domination of the world."[11] After 1850 the English proletariat lost its revolutionary passion. Revolutionary socialist movements decline where "the transition to large-scale industry is more or less completed . . . [and] the conditions in which the proletariat is placed become stable."[12]

"In Germany," writes Engels in the 1890s, "the development of large-scale industry since 1850 coincides with the rise of the socialist movement. . . . It is the revolutionizing of all traditional relations by industry *as it develops* that also revolutionizes people's minds."[13] In the second half of the nineteenth century, rapid industrialization in Germany produced a revolutionary proletariat. "Our great advantage is that with us the industrial revolution is only in full swing," writes Engels to his German disciples in 1884. He points to England's slow growth: "There the division into town and country, industrial district and agricultural district, is so far concluded that it changes only slowly. The great mass of the people grow up in the conditions in which they later have to live; they are accustomed to them; even the fluctuations and crises have become something they practically take for granted. . . . With us, on the other hand, everything is still in full flow."[14] Slow growth and reformism existed in England during the second half of the nineteenth century; but during the lifetimes of Marx and Engels the other proletariats of Western Europe, passing through rapid industrialization, had a revolutionary outlook–they were rebellious down to the 1890s. In the twentieth century these proletariats also entered the stage of gradual growth, became reformist, and were integrated into capitalist society.

During this period of rapid industrialization in the nineteenth century, fever-ish capital accumulation forced wages down to the level of poverty. "The aver-age price of wage labor is the minimum wage, that is, the quantum of the means of subsistence which is absolutely necessary to keep the laborer in bare existence as a laborer," writes Marx in 1848.[15] He was describing the facts. "The modern laborer . . . instead of rising with the progress of industry, sinks deeper and deeper below the conditions of existence of his own class. He becomes a pauper. . . ."[16] Rapid capital accumulation, starvation wages, and the massing of workers in factories–this was a leveling process. The prole-tariat's conditions of life everywhere became equal. "The various interests and conditions of life within the ranks of the proletariat are more and more equal-ized," writes Marx, "in proportion as machinery obliterates all distinctions of labor and nearly everywhere reduces wages to the same low level."[17] This leveling process produced an international proletariat. Engels says in 1847:

> In England through modern industry, through machines, all oppressed classes are thrown together into a single great class with common in-terests, into the class of the proletariat. . . . But not only in England, in all other lands also [machinery] has had these effects on the workers. In Belgium, in America, in France, in Germany it has made the condition of all workers equal and daily makes it more and more equal; in all these lands the workers now have the same interest. . . . This leveling of the conditions of life, this identification of the Party interests of the workers of all nations is the result of machinery. . . .[18]

Everywhere unskilled workers tended machines, pulled levers on machines, shoveled coal into machines. Machine industry equalized working conditions, gave all workers the same interests, and created an international working class.[19] The socialist ethic of equalitarianism and internationalism arose from the machine process. The European proletariat–desperate, suffering, expand-ing, united–wanted to make a universal revolution and build a new world.

In the twentieth century all this changed. Gradual industrial growth, develop-ing technology, and rising wages split the working class into many strata. The factory proletariat, now a minority of the workers, divided into fractions: skilled operatives, unorganized laborers, industrial unions, craft associations, and labor aristocracies. New technologies produced pyramids of skilled, semi-skilled, and unskilled workers throughout the industrial sector. In the advanced countries the working class expanded far beyond the industrial proletariat: most wage workers became trash collectors, bus drivers, meat cutters, maids, mechanics, clerks, nurses, beauticians, cashiers, salespeople, secretaries, teachers, soldiers, engineers, bureaucrats, scientists, and the like. These working people differ from one another in life style, education, and salary. During the twentieth century differences of income and status have divided the wage-earning class into countless strata, broken up class solidarity, and created different interests and views.

In the nineteenth century the proletariat was in society but not of it. Marx and Engels describe the proletariat as a "class . . . which has to bear all the burdens of society without enjoying its advantages, which, ousted from society, is forced into the most decided antagonism to all other classes. . . ."[20] Society despised the workers as beasts of burden. "The bourgeoisie has more in common with every other nation of the earth than with the workers in whose midst it lives," writes Engels in 1845. "The workers speak other dialects, have other thoughts and ideals, other customs and moral principles, a different religion and other politics than those of the bourgeoisie. Thus they are two radically dissimilar nations."[21] And in 1848 Marx writes in the *Manifesto*: "The proletarian is without property; his relation to his wife and children has no longer anything in common with the bourgeois family relations; modern industrial labor, modern subjection to capital, the same in England as in France, in America as in Germany, has stripped him of every trace of national character. Law, morality, religion, are to him so many bourgeois prejudices, behind which lurk in ambush just as many bourgeois interests. . . . The working men have no country."[22] The proletariat had no stake in the old order and wanted to destroy it.

In the twentieth century the proletariat became an integral part of capitalist society. The working people now have a country; they think of themselves as Germans, French, Americans. Mass consumption, mass education, and mass media have made the workers more like the upper class: the striking differences in family relations, morality, and customs vanished with the nineteenth century. The proletarian no longer sees in the factory owner an enemy from another world. Most workers feel they have a stake in the capitalist order and want to enlarge it. Their integration into capitalism has made them shrink from revolution.

Revolution is a dangerous game, for the insurgent class may meet defeat. "Never play with insurrection unless you are fully prepared to face the consequences of your play," warns Engels.[23] No one can foreknow the outcome of a revolutionary struggle. "It is a matter of course that in every struggle he who takes up the gauntlet risks being beaten."[24] As the proletarian insurrections of 1848 and 1871 showed the French workers, defeat meant prision, exile, and death. And who will risk prison, exile, and death? Only people in despair, people who have nothing to lose. Marx says in 1847: "The loss of the old society is no loss for those who have nothing to lose in the old society, and in all contemporary lands this is the case for the great majority. They have rather everything to gain by the destruction of the old society."[25] And everyone knows Marx's famous slogan of 1848: "The proletarians have nothing to lose but their chains."[26]

Today in the advanced countries the proletarians have something to lose. Higher wages, shorter hours, social security, state medicine, unemployment insurance–the lot of the working class has improved since the nineteenth century. The workers are not satisfied with their slice of the capitalist pie, but they want to enlarge that slice through reforms. They turn away from armed struggle, civil war, and battles of peoples. Many workers wish for a new society, but they refuse to risk prison, exile, and death to gain it. They are no longer desperate.

For all the reasons outlined above, Marx and Engels saw the nineteenth-century proletariat as a revolutionary class. Capitalism, doomed to death by internal conflicts, was approaching its end. "History is the judge–its executioner, the proletarian."[27]

The founders of Marxism underestimated the expansibility of capitalism in Western Europe: they thought it was about to die, yet it had long life ahead of it. But will West European capitalism live forever? Marxists claim that the proletariat could still carry out its historical mission. As social conditions worsen in the closing decades of the twentieth century, says Paul Sweezy in the foreword to his *Modern Capitalism*, the proletariat will become revolutionary again.

In evaluating this idea we must remember Marx's and Engels' conception of the social conditions that make a proletariat revolutionary. History has confirmed their conception of these conditions. In the early twentieth century, for example, the conditions for a revolutionary proletariat existed in Russia: mushrooming cities, huge factories, slum housing, family breakdown, child labor, long hours, low wages, outlawed unions, police beatings, and state censorship. Defeat in war weakened tsarism. The proletariat broke the state and carried out a political revolution (though most historians would say that it soon lost power to an emergent bureaucracy).

By contrast, defeat in war has not brought revolution to developed capitalist countries. Social conditions explain why: better pay, pension plans, health insurance, reformist unions, mass voting. The proletariat lacked the necessary revolutionary passion.

It seems doubtful that the classical conditions making for revolutionary proletariats can easily reappear in developed countries. *No developed country has ever had a revolution from below*. If capitalism is to disappear in these countries, it may occur through a revolution from above carried through by bureaucratic elites with mass support. Bureaucratic socialism may someday come to Western Europe.

The future of revolution from below probably lies in economically backward regions of the world—in Asia, Africa, and Latin America. In the past, such revolutions have happened in repressive societies where illiteracy was high, wages low, unemployment common, misery permanent, and the economy blocked. Revolutions were made by people with their backs to the wall—exhausted, hungry, cold, miserable. These are the conditions in which proletarian revolutions might still occur.

In no country on earth does the industrial proletariat make up the majority of the population. So the proletariat needs allies to carry through a revolution, and in economically backward countries the most likely supporters of revolution are peasants. In Marx's conception of continuing revolution, explained in chapter 3, a proletarian uprising in a peasant country like Germany ignites a mass revolution in England. The international revolution depends on the initial success of proletarian upheaval in peasant countries.

For the proletarian revolution in backward France to succeed, thought Marx, the workers must win over the bulk of the nation, the shopkeepers and peasants. Without them the workers remain isolated.[28] A worker-peasant alliance, he thought, was equally necessary for Germany.[29]

In France a bourgeois-peasant alliance overthrew the aristocracy in 1789, argued Marx, and in the nineteenth century a worker-peasant alliance must overturn the bourgeoisie. As Balzac showed in *Les Paysans*, one source of Marx's and Engels' views on the French countryside,[30] the peasants suffered under bourgeois rule. In 1850 Marx sums up the peasant's plight as follows: "In the course of the nineteenth century the feudal lords were replaced by urban usurers; the feudal obligation that went with the land was replaced by the mortgage; aristocractic landed property was replaced by bourgeois capital. . . . Therefore the peasants find their natural ally and leader in the urban proletariat, whose task is the overthrow of the bourgeois order."[31]

Thus conditions in the countryside persuaded Marx that the peasants would behave in a revolutionary manner. But in fact the peasants had turned conservative. Once they had taken the lands of the aristocracy in 1789, the peasants became suspicious of revolution, especially proletarian revolutions against property. The peasants clung to their property and called for law and order. When the French proletariat revolted against the bourgeoisie in 1848, the peasants withheld support and welcomed the despotism of Louis Bonaparte.

Marx recognizes that the peasants showed a conservative side of their nature: "The Bonaparte dynasty represents not the revolutionary, but the conservative peasant; not the peasant that strikes out beyond the condition of his social existence, the small holding, but rather the peasant who wants to consolidate this holding; not the country folk who linked up with the towns to overthrow the old order through their own energies, but those who in stupified seclusion within this old order want to see themselves and their small holdings saved and favored by the ghost of empire."[32] Yet in spite of the disaster in 1848, Marx believed that bourgeois oppression would bring forth a revolutionary side of the peasant's nature.

In 1871 another proletarian revolution met the hostility and indifference of the French peasant. The bourgeoisie massacred the Paris proletariat. Marx and Engels racked their brains for a way to win peasant support during proletarian revolution.

In the nineteenth century France saw one proletarian revolution after another fail for lack of peasant support. There were uprisings of the urban proletariat in 1830, 1848, and 1871, each more socialist than the last. All of them drowned in the sea of peasant reaction.

In 1894 Engels recognizes that the peasants ruined the proletarian revolution in the nineteenth century: "Since the rise of the working class movement in Western Europe, it has not been particularly difficult for the bourgeoisie to render the socialist workers suspicious and odious in the minds of the peasants as *partageux*, as people who want to 'divide up,' as lazy greedy city dwellers who have an eye on the property of the peasants."[33] Everywhere, says Engels, the peasants were the main reserve of conservatism and reaction.

In the twentieth century a new era opened. Marxist movements encountered revolutionary peasants in Russia and China, peasants that craved land. These peasants backed proletarian revolutions, and Marxists came to power. (In China the revolution was actually carried through by peasants.) Thus Marx's revolutionary strategy of a worker-peasant alliance bore fruit in the East. In the West the peasants had made their revolution in the eighteenth century when they took the land. Then they turned conservative, and the proletariat bled to death under bourgeois-peasant reaction.

We have seen how in the nineteenth century Marx argued that communist revolution could take place in peasant countries where a growing proletariat existed (Belgium, France, Germany); we have noted his strategy of the proletariat leading a worker-peasant alliance. The peasant countries of Eastern Europe, however, had no factory proletariat at that time: there, Marx thought, communism could not triumph.[34]

The alternative view, held by anarchists, saw the proletariats of England and Germany as hopelessly bourgeoisified. Spain, Italy, and Russia were the countries with a communist future. These countries had no factory proletariat. The anarchists looked to peasants, landless laborers, and lumpenproletarians for revolution. Mikhail Bakunin was the theorist of anarchist communism. In Italy, he writes in *Etatisme et anarchie* (1873), there are about 20 million peasants that have nothing at all. . . . Perhaps nowhere is the social revolution closer than in Italy, yes, nowhere, not even in Spain. . . . There is not in Italy, as in many other countries of Europe, a separate stratum of workers in part already privileged through salaries, priding themselves on a certain literary knowledge, and thus impregnated with bourgeois ideas, aspirations, and vanity. The workers who belong to this stratum are distinguished from the bourgeois only by their condition, not by their tendencies. It is above all in Germany and Switzerland that there exist many workers of this type; by contrast in Italty there are very few, so few that they are lost in the mass and have no influence on it. What predominates in Italy is that lumpenproletariat of which Marx and Engels . . . speak so contemptuously and unjustly, for it is there and only there, and not within the bourgeoisified stratum of the working masses, that there lives in totality the spirit and force of the future social revolution. (p. 206)

Marx wondered how corrupt lumpenproletarians and illiterate peasants could create a new world. The lumpenproletarians were the "scum, offal, refuse of all classes,"[35] and the peasants were "the class that represents barbarism within civilization."[36]

In our century this debate about historical agency–which class can make the socialist revolution?–has become less acute for Marxists with the emergence of the Leninist Party. In the underdeveloped countries of the twentieth century, intellectuals have formed communist parties out of elements drawn from various classes, parties ready to lead whatever revolutionary forces exist: factory workers, university students, starving miners, lumpenproletarians, landless laborers, rebellious peasants, declassed intellectuals, migratory farm workers, social bandits, uprooted Indians, poor artisans, underpaid petty bureaucrats, mercenary foot soldiers, rural schoolteachers, oppressed sharecroppers, "the wretched of the earth." Marxist-Leninists have found that under the guidance of a communist party even an illiterate peasantry can bring off a revolution. Then the Party leads the country through industrialization and education into a new social system. These social systems are not capitalist. Will such societies someday achieve the Marxist ideals of freedom, equality, and abundance for all? A few of them have leaderships still committed to these ideals, but tremendous difficulties lie ahead. We must await the verdict of history.

All of the Marxist revolutions of the twentieth century have taken place in economically backward countries. What relevance does Marx's theory of revolution have for advanced countries? Social Democrats claim that Marx turned reformist after the failure of the revolutions of 1848 and that he proposed a theory of peaceful evolution toward socialism for more advanced countries like England. Is there any truth in this widespread view?

We have seen that in the last decade of Marx's life his vision of international revolution remained intact; he died in 1883 believing it. During the 1870s Marx still counted on an economic crisis to trigger the all-European revolution; he still hoped that the democratic revolution would issue in a proletarian uprising. Since the 1840s he had based his work on this vision, and social conditions seemed roughly the same down through the 1870s.

Yet in this decade certain social changes became obvious, and these modified Marx's vision. The theme of a violent European revolution continued to haunt him, but occasionally he touched his theoretical keyboard to play a variation on the theme. What changes in society inspired these variations?

The most important was this: in England part of the working class got the vote. English political parties appealed to that part of the proletariat for support; a new field of mass politics opened up. This fact caused Marx to see the possibility that the English proletariat might someday outvote the bourgeoisie. In his mind this remained a *possibility*, more or less remote, depending on the mood he was in.

But the possibility was there, and on two occasions Marx made statements that seemed to erode his concept of continuing revolution. The Social Democratic claim that Marx turned reformist rests on these statements.

> [1872] We know of the allowances we must make for the institutions, customs and traditions of the various countries; and we do not deny that there are countries such as America, England, and I might add Holland if I knew your institutions better, where the working people may achieve their goal by peaceful means. (Speech to the Hague Congress in 1872)[37]

> [1880] If you say that you do not share the views of my party for England, I can only reply that that party considers an English revolution not *necessary*, but–according to historical precedents–*possible*. (Letter of 8 December 1880 to Henry M. Hyndman)[38]

In these statements Marx was thinking of England; he said that he believed revolution was inevitable on the Continent. To his statement in 1872 that England might avoid violence he adds that "we must also recognize that in most of the continental countries it is force that will have to be the lever of our revolutions."[39]

But what about England? Did Marx believe that England would escape violence? When he faced the (remote) possibility that the proletariat could someday outvote the bourgeoisie he said that England *might* escape violence. But he believed that the chances for avoiding it were small.

For Marx believed that if the proletariat outvoted the bourgeoisie, violence would still happen in England. Marx said that if the English bourgeoisie found itself outvoted it would resort to violence, just as the slave owners of the United States, outvoted in 1860, had resorted to civil war. On 18 July 1871 an interviewer from the *New York World* assured Marx that England would escape revolution through elections and reform. Marx answers him: "I am not so optimistic on that point as you. The English middle class has always shown itself willing enough to accept the verdict of the majority so long as it enjoyed the monopoly of the voting power. But mark me, as soon as it finds itself outvoted on what it considers vital questions we shall see here a new slave owner's war."[40] This was Marx's opinion: if the English proletariat outvoted the bourgeoisie there would probably be civil war. "If," he writes in 1878, "the working class in England or in the United States were to win a majority in Parliament or in Congress, then by legal means it could remove the laws and institutions standing in its way. . . . Nevertheless, the 'peaceful' movement could turn into a 'violent' one through rebellion of those interested in the old state of affairs. If they are put down by violence, it will be 'legal' violence against rebels (as in the American Civil War and the French Revolution)."[41] Marx, says Engels in 1886, finally decided that England was the only country where the social revolution *might* take place by legal means. But Marx "certainly never forgot to add that he hardly expected the English ruling classes to submit to this peaceful and legal revolution without a 'pro-slavery rebellion.'"[42]

Thus Marx clung to his vision of violent revolution through the 1870s. But in certain moods he admitted that the English proletariat *might* someday outvote the bourgeoisie. *If* that happened, there would be civil war. And this perspective was compatible with the concept of international revolution, for a civil war in England, in which the proletariat grasped political power, would spark revolution on the Continent.

Engels outlived Marx by twelve years, and the concept of international revolution flickered in his mind. In 1888 he writes to a Romanian:

Actually we all stand before the same great obstacle, which checks the free development of all peoples and every single people. . . . This obstacle is the old Holy Alliance of the three murderers of Poland [Russia, Austria, Prussia]. Since 1815 Russian Tsarism has directed this Alliance, and in spite of all temporary inner disputes it exists to our day [1888]. In the year 1815 this Alliance against the revolutionary spirit of the French people was founded; in the year 1871 it was strengthened by the theft of Alsace and Lorraine, . . . which made Germany the slave of Tsarism and the Tsar the arbiter of Europe. In 1888 the Alliance is still maintained in order to destroy the revolutionary movements in the three Empires as well as the national struggles and the political and social movements of the workers. Since Russia occupies an almost invulnerable strategic position, Russian Tsarism forms the heart of this Alliance, the greatest reserve of the European Reaction. . . . It may be summed up briefly: a revolution in Russia at the present moment . . . would be the beginning of the revolution in the whole world.[43]

A Russian revolution would trigger a vast explosion on the Continent.

Only at the end of his life did Engels abandon this concept of revolution and go over to the view that the proletariat *in each country* would organize itself through mass politics, grow into a majority, outvote the bourgeoisie, and win the civil war started by the rulers.[44] His new view was the outlook of Social Democratic parties in Western Europe down to 1914. In World War I they began collaboration with the ruling classes.

In Eastern Europe, Lenin and the Bolsheviks clung to the concept of continuing revolution: Russia would throw a lighted torch into the powder keg of Western Europe and set off a chain of proletarian revolutions. The great moment came (the world war), and the Russians gave the signal (1917), but the socialist leaders in Western Europe betrayed the movement. This failure led to the isolation and bureaucratization of the revolution in the East.

Why did the revolution fail in the West? Social Democratic leaders betrayed the movement, sometimes taking part in the suppression of communist uprisings. Communist writers point to these betrayals as the cause of the counter-revolution's triumph. But is this betrayal theory really an explanation?

After the failure of the revolutions of 1848 Engels complains that "when you inquire into the causes of the counterrevolutionary successes, there you are met on every hand with the ready reply that it was Mr. This or Citizen That who 'betrayed' the people. Which reply may be very true or not, according to circumstance, but under no circumstances does it explain anything–not even show how it came to pass that the 'people' allowed themselves to be thus betrayed."[45] The causes for the failure of the revolution, says Engels, "are not to be sought for in the accidental efforts, talents, faults, errors, or treacheries of some of the leaders, but in the general social state and conditions of existence of each of the convulsed nations."[46]

Why did the West European proletariat allow itself to be betrayed during World War I? For an explanation we must examine the general social condition of the convulsed nations. In Western Europe by 1914 most nations had integrated the proletariat into society. Marx and Engels had watched the beginning of the integrative process with misgivings but had not lived to see its result. The West European proletariat–integrated into capitalism through labor centrals, the eight-hour day, representation in parliament, government medicare, monthly retirement checks, and a gradual rise in real wages since 1848–this proletariat had lost its revolutionary passion. By 1918–19, as the old regimes in Germany, Austria, and Hungary tottered and fell, most of the proletariat shrank from the fight for state power. Even its more leftist leaders saw that peasant support was lacking and that the armies of Britain and France were poised to crush socialist revolution. Rosa Luxemburg voted against the revolutionary attempt of her own party, and in Austria the radical Otto Bauer tried to put the brakes on the workers' revolution in Vienna. These facts, rather than the treachery of Social Democrats like Scheidemann and Noske, explain the failure of proletarian revolution in the West.

Notes

I. The New Marxism

1. 23:16. This and the following references are to volume and page of the *Marx-Engels Werke*, 39 vols. (Berlin: Dietz Verlag, 1964–1968). Also included in the *Werke* are two supplementary volumes, referred to as *Ergänzungsband*, 1 and 2. Not included in the *Werke* is Karl Marx's *Grundrisse der Kritik der politischen Ökonomie* (Berlin, Dietz Verlag, 1953). References to this work simply read *Grundrisse* with the page number. References to Marx's *Notes on Indian History: 664–1858*, not included in the *Werke*, are to the English edition published by Foreign Languages Publishing House in Moscow (no date). There is one reference to the English edition of Marx's *Capital* (Moscow: Foreign Language Publishing House, 1961–1962), cited as *Capital* with the volume number.
2. 13:8–9.
3. 3:54.
4. 13:627.
5. 20:587; 3:23; 13:629.
6. 13:629.
7. 3:73.
8. 13:629; 9:221.
9. 20:170.
10. 3:54.
11. 37:491.
12. 22:450.
13. 9:129.
14. 21:403.
15. 3:23.
16. 3:64; 20:170; 9:221; 13:629.
17. 3:64; 20:170; 9:221.
18. 13:629.
19. 20:585–586.
20. 23:92.
21. 23:378–379; 9:132–133.
22. 3:22.
23. 4:462–463.
24. 20:585–586; 21:145.
25. 19:318–319.
26. 19:320.
27. 3:61–62.
28. 4:465.
29. *Grundrisse*:395–396.
30. *Grundrisse*:387.
31. 13:9.
32. 19:111.
33. 19:108–111.
34. 21:304–305.
35. 20:588.
36. 19:401.
37. 21:264.
38. 37:437.
39. Ibid.
40. 37:436.

II. Precapitalist Modes of Production

1. 20:444–448.
2. 21:38–43.
3. 21:31.
4. 21:44–51.
5. 21:31–32.
6. 21:51–57.
7. 21:32–34, 58–59, 135–136; 4:462.
8. 21:58–70.
9. 21:34.
10. 21:37–39.
11. *Grundrisse*:375–376.
12. 21:95–96.
13. 21:97.
14. 23:92; 20:163.
15. 21:135–137; 20:163; 19:318–319; 19:403; 23:378.
16. 4:462.
17. 9:132; 21:97; 23:93.
18. 9:132; 28:268; 18:563, 567; 20:150, 168, 590; *Grundrisse*:377; 26.1:320.
19. 23:28.
20. 9:130.
21. 12:552.
22. 9:132; 28:267.
23. 28:267.
24. *Notes on Indian History*:20.
25. 23:379.
26. *Grundrisse*:377, 390.
27. 9:129.
28. Ibid.
29. Ibid.
30. Ibid.
31. 9:97.
32. 18:563, 567; 20:168; 20:588; 4:365.
33. 20:150–151, 168.
34. 23:92.
35. 9:129.
36. 20:166–167.
37. 9:218.
38. 3:61–62.
39. 9:132.
40. 28:254, 259.
41. 9:221.
42. *Grundrisse*:377, 383; 25:799; 20:163–164.
43. 28:268–269; 12:483–484.
44. 28:252, 254.
45. 23:537 (note 6).
46. *Grundrisse*:371, 377; 23:378.
47. *Notes on Indian History*:23–24.
48. 23:378.
49. 9:223.
50. 23:378–379.
51. 9:131–132; 28:267; *Grundrisse*:377, 386, 392–393; 23:378–379; 18:563; 20:168.
52. *Grundrisse*:393.
53. 23:379.
54. 23:102–103, 372–373; 20:150.
55. 9:133.
56. 30:578.
57. 36:109–110; 21:27.
58. 3:22–24; *Grundrisse*:378–383.
59. *Grundrisse*:383.
60. Ibid., 379, 380.
61. 20:167.
62. 20:585–586; 20:167–168; 21:116, 145.
63. 4:462; 21:116.
64. 20:585–586.
65. *Grundrisse*:378.
66. Ibid., 378, 386.
67. 3:22.
68. *Grundrisse*:380, 395.
69. 25:815.
70. 3:22.
71. *Grundrisse*:378–384.
72. 3:22–23; *Grundrisse*:378–379.
73. *Grundrisse*:382.
74. Ibid., 379, 380, 380–381, 389–390; 23:354n; 25:815.
75. *Grundrisse*:383, 385.
76. Ibid., 378.
77. Ibid., 379; 23:354n; 25:815.
78. *Grundrisse*:394.
79. Ibid., 378, 380, 391, 393.
80. Ibid., 378, 380, 390–391.
81. Ibid., 393, 386.
82. Ibid., 393; 20:167.
83. *Grundrisse*:386.
84. Ibid., 379.
85. 23:755n.
86. 3:23; *Grundrisse*:386.
87. 19:111–112; 3:23–24.
88. 26.2:528–529.

89. *Grundrisse*:387.
90. 23:430–431.
91. 20:167–169.
92. 23:210n.
93. 20:167–168, 585–586; 21:116, 145.
94. 20:585–586.
95. 23:210n.
96. 21:150.
97. 19:302.
98. 19:111.
99. 21:339.
100. 21:145.
101. 21:144.
102. 19:301.
103. 21:145.
104. 21:148.
105. 21:151.
106. 3:171.
107. 3:24.
108. 3:126.
109. 21:148–149.
110. 21:151.
111. 20:164.
112. 23:745.
113. 35:137.
114. 25:799.
115. 25:798.
116. 25:807–808.
117. 23:745.
118. 25:349.
119. 23:184.
120. 3:61.

121. 20:150.
122. 3:24, 64–65; 13:629.
123. 19:320–321.
124. 20:96.
125. 21:146.
126. 21:145.
127. 21:146–147; 19:324.
128. 21:146–147, 139; 19:324.
129. 21:147; 19:324–325.
130. 19:325.
131. 21:148.
132. Ibid.
133. 7:339–340.
134. 21:149.
135. 21:393.
136. 3:73; 39:433.
137. 23:91.
138. 23:773.
139. 25:801–802.
140. 35:137.
141. 3:62–63.
142. 13:616.
143. 23:93.
144. *Grundrisse*:392.
145. *Grundrisse*:393.
146. 3:61–62.
147. *Grundrisse*:387.
148. 3:33; 4:375–376.
149. 3:74.
150. 3:74–75.
151. 3:33.
152. 3:74.

III. Capitalism

1. 23:354n.
2. 13:9; 4:467.
3. 3:25.
4. 3:30; 27:452–453; 4:130; 6:407–408; 13:8–9.
5. 23:356–390.
6. 23:778.
7. 3:54–55; 23:743, 744n, 356; 3:58, 59.
8. 23:777–788.
9. 13:468.
10. 6:107.
11. 21:299–300.
12. 39:483; 6:107.

13. 23:781–782.
14. 27:453.
15. 21:304–305.
16. 22:303.
17. 8:116.
18. 17:336.
19. 22:303.
20. 8:116.
21. 13:9.
22. 27:453.
23. 8:115.
24. 7:210.
25. 1:382.

26. 8:116.
27. 22:300–301.
28. 22:513–514.
29. 7:330.
30. 22:300; 21:304; 18:590; 39:483.
31. 39:99.
32. 22:300; 21:304.
33. 2:568.
34. 19:328.
35. 21:18–19.
36. 21:445.
37. 10:444.
38. 19:329.
39. 7:539.
40. 21:408.
41. 7:539; 21:451; 19:329.
42. 21:408, 450–451.
43. 21:409.
44. 21:432–433.
45. 21:435–436, 449.
46. 7:539; 21:452–461.
47. 23:744n; 3:54–55; 4:496–497.
48. 10:431–485 (*passim*); 12:37–48.
49. 7:210–212; 22:301–302, 305; 21:300, 305.
50. 23:391.
51. 7:344–345; 21:402; 39:483; 21:300–305; 22:299–309.
52. 22:299.
53. 7:343–344; 21:304.
54. 7:344–345.
55. 21:304; 7:344–345; 39:483.
56. 21:304.
57. 7:345.
58. Ibid.; 39:483.
59. Ibid.
60. 7:330–331; 39:483; 37:274.
61. 19:191; 7:342, 348.
62. 22:300; 21:304; 7:411–412; 18:590.
63. 18:590.
64. 21:402.
65. 22:300; 21:402; 38:260; 37:274.
66. 7:343.
67. 39:483.
68. 22:300–301.
69. 19:191.
70. 6:107; 7:210–211.
71. 22:301–302; 21:305.
72. 22:303.
73. 8:561; 22:303–304.
74. 19:193.
75. 19:192.
76. 6:107.
77. 22:307.
78. 12:42; 8:3–108 (*passim*); 7:33; 8:122–123; 7:535, 538–539; 22:306; 1:106; 1:393–394; 21:423–424, 433, 451, 452, 454; 10:633.
79. 22:301.
80. 7:345; 6:107; 4:471.
81. 7:345, 347–351; 22:301; 19:193.
82. 21:304–305.
83. 4:470.
84. 37:155.
85. 13:8–9.
86. 22:512.
87. 4:464n.
88. 8:561.
89. 4:464.
90. 23:781.
91. 23:782.
92. 4:151–152.
93. Ibid.; 20:96–97, 191; 23:183, 184, 742, 745–746, 779–782, 787–788; 25:345–346; 3:56–58; 4:463–464; 19:216; 19:103.
94. 4:466.
95. 23:785.
96. 25:345–346.
97. 3:54–55.
98. 23:781–782.
99. 25:345.
100. 23:392.
101. 19:197.
102. 4:467; 19:211.
103. 21:300.
104. 4:468.
105. 4:580; 16:14; 34:408.
106. 19:228.
107. 18:530.
108. 4:372.
109. 4:467–468; 19:218–219.
110. 19:218–219.
111. 1:515; 6:422–423; 4:322; 4:467–468; 2:504.
112. 21:300.
113. 1:515.
114. 4:467–468.

115. 7:294.
116. 4:462, 364–365.
117. 4:484, 472, 469.
118. 4:462, 468, 363–365.
119. 23:790.
120. 4:469, 484.
121. 4:484.
122. 4:368–369, 141; 22:205; 19:223; 6:422; 20:139–140; 23:790–791; 2:504.
123. 4:469.
124. 1:522; 2:504.
125. 4:463; 22:209; 22:268; 2:504; 23:790–791; 4:364–365.
126. 23:791.
127. 4:472–473.
128. 3:69–70; 4:482; 20:454; 19:223.
129. 4:372–373.
130. 16:414–415.
131. 22:485.
132. 27:502; 7:247–248, 254; 7:89; 21:21; 7:553; 2:130.
133. 3:176.
134. 22:512; 8:561; 19:97; 21:21.
135. 8:115–116.
136. 13:470.
137. 1:391; 4:311; 22:512; 16:414; 38:545.
138. 4:530.
139. 4:367, 374–375, 479; 3:35.
140. 4:493, 372–373, 312–313, 517–518; 7:247–248.
141. 4:374–375; 6:150; 7:79, 481; 38:545; 39:89.
142. 5:333.
143. 4:524; 5:42, 82, 334, 403; 6:397–398; 7:34; 21:22; 38:545–546; 18:584–585.
144. 7:490.
145. 4:373, 481.
146. Ibid.
147. 4:374, 481; 7:481.
148. 4:481.
149. 7:481; 32:669; 16:414–415.
150. 4:367, 374–375; 3:35; 16:414–415; 35:358.
151. 4:392.
152. 4:519.
153. 4:397.
154. 21:21.
155. 6:243.

156. 7:253–254.
157. 7:246–247.
158. 7:247–248, 254.
159. 7:79.
160. 6:150.
161. 6:397–398.
162. 7:79.
163. 22:510–511.
164. 7:97; 27:598; 28:116, 118, 145, 520; 35:268; 9:102.
165. 9:98.
166. 9:100.
167. 30:641.
168. 4:584.
169. 16:14.
170. 18:161.
171. 21:17, 220.
172. 38:545–546.
173. 39:255.
174. 39:89.
175. 22:509f.
176. 23:790–791.
177. 13:639, 7; 29:551, 312.
178. 23:790.
179. 4:466; 9:226; 19:23–24; 22:266; 27:454; 3:35, 45–46, 60; 4:367; 13:639; 25:345–346; 29:360; *Grundrisse*:440; 6:149–150.
180. 4:374.
181. 20:191; 25:345.
182. 21:81.
183. 13:639.
184. 4:466.
185. 25:345.
186. 6:149.
187. Ibid.
188. 16:416.
189. 22:266.
190. 13:9.
191. 3:73.
192. 4:351.
193. 1:404.
194. 16:415.
195. 32:669.
196. 16:415.
197. 3:35.
198. Ibid.
199. 35:358.
200. 4:367.

201. 6:107.
202. 22:512; 8:561; 19:97; 21:21.
203. 37:318.
204. 6:7–8.
205. 2:568.
206. 2:569.
207. 5:81.
208. 2:613.
209. 4:375.
210. 21:221–222.
211. 4:494; 2:582.
212. 12:3.
213. 22:272–273.
214. 29:358; 29:360; 30:301;´30:342;
    32:207; 16:415; 34:320; 34:378; 36:58;
    37:320–321; 39:248; 25:146.
215. 30:342.
216. 9:101.
217. 23:28; 25:252, 259–267, 277, 500–
    501; 20:265–266; 19:218–219, 225;
    21:300; 34:171; 36:376; 36:386.
218. 4:467–468; 23:790–791; 1:522;
    6:422–423.
219. 18:585.
220. 35:357; 36:58; 36:280; 22:276–277.
221. 12:3.
222. 13:392; 27:137.

223. 29:153, 211–212, 225, 304.
224. 29:225.
225. 29:212.
226. 30:641.
227. 30:324.
228. 31:342–343.
229. 23:28.
230. 35:161.
231. 37:416.
232. 18:567.
233. 34:296.
234. 34:403.
235. 35:276.
236. 4:576.
237. 18:674.
238. 28:580.
239. 29:358.
240. 29:360.
241. 3:35.
242. 3:34–35, 312.
243. 4:374.
244. 22:311.
245. 4:573–582.
246. 4:461.
247. 3:176.
248. 32:596–597.
249. 4:495.

IV. Communism

1. 4:580; 4:490; 19:194.
2. 17:557.
3. 4:490–491.
4. 3:29n; 3:50; 4:373–374, 376–377;
   4:481; 18:243, 279–280; 23:528;
   20:271–273, 275–278; 19:330; 35:445.
5. 3:50; 23:373; 21:161; 20:271–272.
6. 23:528; 20:271–272, 276; 18:279–280.
7. 23:528n; 3:50.
8. 20:277.
9. 18:279–280; 20:276.
10. 20:276.
11. 4:373–374.
12. 2:545.
13. 2:546.
14. 18:425.
15. 3:29n.
16. Ibid.

17. Ibid.
18. 20:273.
19. 18:301.
20. 2:521–535.
21. 4:491–492; 19:191.
22. 19:194.
23. 23:373; 3:50; 20:271–272.
24. 3:33.
25. 23:443–444.
26. 23:510–511; 20:274–275.
27. 23:512.
28. Grundrisse:592.
29. 23:444.
30. 23:445.
31. 4:375–376.
32. 19:194.
33. Grundrisse:505, 599.
34. Grundrisse:505.

35. 25:828.
36. 4:375–376.
37. 34:129.
38. 20:275.
39. 20:276.
40. Ibid.
41. 20:288; 24:316–317.
42. 19:28.
43. 20:167.
44. 4:482; 19:223–224; 21:165–167; 21:170–171; 36:11.
45. 19:28.
46. 4:482.
47. 18:308.
48. 19:195.
49. 17:340.
50. 19:224.
51. 18:343.
52. 18:635.
53. 20:169.
54. 19:104.
55. 4:482.
56. 23:93; 25:859; 20:288.
57. 18:222; 19:18–19; 23:552.
58. 20:122.
59. 19:19.
60. 19:21; 3:528.
61. 23:514.
62. 3:164.
63. 21:75.
64. 27:452.
65. 23:514; 21:64–70.
66. 3:164.
67. 21:72–73.
68. 21:83.
69. 21:73; 2:208.
70. 21:75.
71. 3:164.
72. 1:149.
73. 2:356; 4:478; 19:197; 21:73–74; 23:514.
74. 4:478.
75. 21:77.
76. 4:377.
77. 4:373.
78. 19:198.
79. 4:373.
80. 20:300.
81. 23:507–508.
82. 19:32; 16:553.
83. 4:377.
84. 20:296; 21:77, 158; 36:341.
85. 2:546.
86. 23:514; 20:296; 21:77, 158.
87. 21:77.
88. *Ergänzungsband* 1:534–535; 4:377; 4:478–479.
89. 21:10.
90. 27:462.
91. 21:73.
92. 21:78–84.
93. 21:83.
94. 19:28.
95. 4:481.
96. 4:372.
97. 17:343.
98. 7:89; 17:625; 19:28; 28:508; 7:553.
99. 18:529.
100. 4:481.
101. 7:89.
102. 22:235.
103. 17:545–546.
104. 35:160.
105. 17:339–340.
106. 18:636.
107. 17:339.
108. 36:11.
109. 17:546.
110. 4:373; 4:481.
111. 4:481.
112. 4:373; 4:481.
113. Ibid.
114. 4:373.
115. 4:481.
116. 4:373.
117. 4:374.
118. 24:358; 19:20.
119. 19:21.
120. 4:481.
121. 4:375.
122. 19:21; 3:528.
123. 4:374.
124. 18:61.
125. 8:204.
126. 18:630.
127. 18:633.
128. 7:252; 22:503–504.
129. 36:426.

130. 22:499.
131. 19:330.
132. 18:633.
133. 4:374–375.
134. 37:447.
135. 21:267.
136. 34:129.
137. 23:537.
138. 18:620.
139. 34:129.
140. 2:542–543; 17:339.
141. 4:182.
142. 8:506–509.
143. 2:542.
144. 25:828.
145. *Grundrisse*:593.
146. 25:828.
147. 20:264.
148. 23:455, 596; 25:95–96.
149. 6:400.
150. *Grundrisse*:505.
151. 18:306.
152. 25:93, 95–96.
153. 20:274.
154. *Grundrisse*:599–600.

155. 2:521.
156. Ibid.
157. 38:189.
158. 20:186.
159. 3:379.
160. 20:312.
161. 3:502.
162. 18:221.
163. 4:486.
164. 3:534.
165. 1:378.
166. 4:160.
167. 19:103–104; 20:168–169; 3:417; 18:220–221.
168. 17:343.
169. 3:229.
170. 2:138, 140.
171. 20:171; 1:338–339; 37:321; 3:70; 5:64; 8:412.
172. 3:70.
173. 25:784.
174. *Ergänzungsband* 1:547.
175. 2:543.
176. 20:324.

V. Classes

1. 4:462n; 4:363–365.
2. 25:892–893.
3. 22:307–308; 8:339.
4. 22:307.
5. 4:462n; 4:363–365.
6. 25:798–799; 23:599.
7. 23:249–250.
8. 19:103–104; 20:168–169; 3:417; 4:371–372; 18:220–221.
9. 21:299; 25:892–893.
10. 4:462–471.
11. 21:299.
12. 4:482.
13. 4:364–365.
14. 4:469.
15. 4:470–471.
16. 8:160–161.
17. 23:746; 7:374; 22:301–302.
18. 23:749; 22:301–302.
19. 7:210–211; 6:107; 7:374.

20. 29:358.
21. 8:336–337; 8:139–140.
22. 20:152.
23. 8:139.
24. 4:47; 6:244.
25. 25:807–808.
26. 4:462; 25:822.
27. 25:342.
28. 25:335–349.
29. 7:12, 79; 25:527, 560.
30. 8:399; 7:12, 79; 7:211; 7:247.
31. 3:57.
32. 4:484.
33. 4:469, 472, 484.
34. 8:11–12; 7:536; 22:488, 489.
35. 23:354n; 25:815; 8:9–10; 21:21.
36. 23:761–762.
37. 7:338; 23:673.
38. 7:26.
39. 2:89.

40. 16:10.
41. 7:445; 2:647; 37:320; 37:288.
42. 22:510; 3:53; 4:47, 49.
43. 4:463.
44. 17:637.
45. 7:79.
46. 17:336–337.
47. 37:295–296; 39:391; 8:139–140.
48. 3:46–47.
49. 4:472.
50. 2:38.
51. 8:139.
52. 38:245.
53. 37:295.
54. 35:232; 37:231.
55. 8:138–139; 38:245.
56. 8:141.
57. 7:12–13.
58. 4:349.
59. 8:141–142.
60. 8:142.
61. 7:335; 32:410.
62. 34:406.
63. 4:471–472.
64. 8:182.
65. 8:182–185.
66. 28:580.
67. 7:400–401.
68. 2:581; 4:44; 3:178.
69. 4:182.
70. 4:181.
71. 21:299; 19:102.
72. 28:504; 39:207.
73. 20:241.
74. 21:299.
75. 28:507.
76. 28:507–508.
77. 19:102.
78. 20:25.
79. 4:577; 4:581; 4:462; 8:562; 22:298; 19:103; 21:28; 21:70.
80. 4:462–463.
81. 9:130.
82. 8:562.
83. 6:397.
84. 3:33.
85. 22:299–304; 21:304–305.
86. 7:343.
87. 4:180–181; 8:198.

88. 3:53–54; 3:62, 4:181; 28:381–385.
89. 4:470–471.
90. 4:143, 181.
91. 19:256.
92. 3:62.
93. 4:462.
94. 20:169.
95. 7:340.
96. 4:141.
97. 23:210–211n.
98. 21:298–299.
99. 7:541.
100. 21:28.
101. 21:116.
102. 23:149–150.
103. 4:462.
104. Ibid.
105. 30:160.
106. 21:150.
107. 21:298.
108. 8:560.
109. 3:23.
110. 23:210–211n.
111. 8:560.
112. 3:23.
113. 16:417.
114. 8:560.
115. Ibid.
116. 7:89; 8:121; 30:617.
117. 21:144–145; *Grundrisse*:368.
118. 21:146–149.
119. 3:25.
120. 3:52.
121. 3:185.
122. 19:258; 4:471; 21:300, 302; 33:332–333; 3:34; 21:492–493; 32:675.
123. 3:52.
124. 3:185.
125. 7:383, 401–402.
126. 7:390.
127. 7:412.
128. 8:198.
129. 4:313.
130. 3:25.
131. 3:52.
132. 3:185.
133. 3:51.
134. 19:102.
135. 21:299–300.

136. 8:562.
137. 21:303–305.
138. 19:102–103; 21:298–299; 34:407.

139. 4:462.
140. 8:560.

VI. Historical Sociology

1. 13:8–9.
2. 23:96n.
3. 13:470.
4. 25:822.
5. 23:38.
6. 25:345; 20:191.
7. 27:453.
8. 19:197.
9. 23:392.
10. 23:20.
11. 19:193.
12. 27:455.
13. 19:218–219; 27:455.
14. 4:467–468.
15. 21:300.
16. 19:214.
17. 20:275–276.
18. 20:455.
19. 4:467–468.
20. 4:369; 4:369–370; 4:467–468; 6:422–
    423; 7:98; 23:28; 25:252, 259–260,
    277, 500–501; 19:218–219, 221–222,
    225, 227–228; 19:104; 31:466–467;
    34:171; 36:386; 26.2:528.
21. 4:467–468.
22. 30:300.
23. 30:307.
24. 3:21; 39:205; 23:535–537; 25:270;
    4:504–505.
25. 23:193–196.
26. 27:452.
27. 23:535, 536–537; 25:270.
28. 16:466.
29. 4:504–505.
30. 23:193–196.
31. Ibid.; 20:250.
32. 39:205.
33. 21:299.
34. 3:30; 23:407.
35. 23:193–196.
36. Ibid.; 392n; 20:250; 39:205.
37. 3:30; 26.2:529; 23:386, 407, 790–791.

38. 23:193–196.
39. 23:194.
40. 23:353.
41. 23:353–354.
42. 23:341.
43. 23:348.
44. 23:350–351.
45. 23:357.
46. 23:356–359.
47. 23:361.
48. 21:299–300.
49. 23:391.
50. 23:393.
51. 23:407.
52. 23:790–791.
53. 13:9.
54. 25:822.
55. 25:886–887.
56. 25:792.
57. 25:799.
58. 25:807–808.
59. 25:798.
60. 20:151–152.
61. 20:249–250, 258.
62. 20:136.
63. 20:257–258.
64. 13:630.
65. 4:105.
66. 13:627.
67. 13:630.
68. 20:137.
69. 20:138.
70. 19:217–218.
71. 25:891.
72. 20:138.
73. 20:136.
74. 13:630–631.
75. 25:884.
76. 23:231.
77. 13:9.
78. 8:562; 19:210; 39:205; 20:25, 137–
    138, 248.

79. 4:462; 8:9; 21:21; 25:892.
80. 39:205; 20:137–138.
81. 34:171.
82. 20:169.
83. Ibid.
84. 4:130.
85. 23:393n.
86. 23:194–195.
87. 13:8.
88. 20:25.
89. 21:166–167.
90. 8:154; 7:539; 31:208.
91. 3:62.
92. 4:478.
93. 21:166–167; 36:54; 8:29; 3:344–345; 4:31; 17:337–338; 18:258.
94. 21:166–167; 36:54; 37:154; 8:29; 4:464; 4:31, 346; 3:46, 344–345.
95. 21:167.
96. 19:192.
97. 8:154; 17:337–338.
98. 18:258; 7:539.
99. 17:338.
100. 37:154.
101. 31:208.
102. 8:154.
103. 25:799–800.
104. 38:481; 4:342; 4:464; 36:54; 19:29; 21:167.
105. 7:344.
106. 19:28.
107. 25:801–802.
108. 6:245.
109. 37:491.
110. 18:276–277.
111. 23:96n.
112. 21:304.
113. 22:299.
114. 19:324.
115. 25:614.
116. 21:304; 7:343; 21:491–492.
117. 7:343.
118. 21:304; 7:343; 22:299.
119. 23:749, 749–750.
120. 21:492.
121. 21:396.
122. 23:537.
123. 13:639; 13:7; 29:551; 29:312.
124. 13:9.
125. 3:46.
126. Ibid.; 4:480.
127. 3:47.
128. Ibid.
129. 3:191.
130. 21:303.
131. 4:488.
132. 23:15.
133. 23:21.
134. 3:47.
135. 3:46.
136. 21:304.
137. 3:46.
138. 3:50.
139. 36:596.
140. 39:97.
141. 4:480.
142. 37:490–495; 21:302–303; 21:494; 21:303–304; 39:97; 37:463; 4:480; 13:9; 39:206; 20:82; 3:26.
143. 3:26; 4:480.
144. 20:87.
145. 13:9; 20:82; 37:437; 39:206.
146. 39:97.
147. 22:304; 21:301–302.
148. 39:97.
149. Ibid.
150. 21:305.
151. 39:97.
152. 7:342.
153. 39:97.
154. 20:169.
155. 23:21; *Grundrisse*:364.
156. 4:200.
157. 7:351.
158. 11:323.
159. 22:302–303.
160. 3:39.
161. 21:302–303; 37:490–495; 37:463; 39:97.
162. 37:490.
163. 37:463; 39:97.
164. 21:300, 301.
165. 21:301–302.
166. 4:464.
167. 22:303–304.
168. 21:301–302.
169. 37:491.
170. 18:276–277.

171. 37:493.
172. Ibid.
173. 37:492–493.
174. 20:87.
175. 21:289.
176. 37:492.
177. *Ergänzungsband* 1:569.
178. 26.1:22.
179. 37:492.
180. 3:460.
181. 3:218.
182. 3:27.
183. 13:9.
184. 20:294.
185. 21:284–285.
186. 1:102.
187. 1:378.
188. 22:300.
189. 21:285.
190. Ibid.; 22:450n.
191. 13:9; 20:82; 37:437; 39:206.
192. 13:640.
193. 8:141–142.
194. 4:484–485.
195. 4:472.
196. 8:116.
197. Ibid.; 2:128–129.
198. 22:464–465.
199. 22:466.
200. 7:344.
201. 19:305.
202. 22:449–450.
203. 19:305.
204. 22:459.
205. 19:305.
206. 21:10.
207. 22:460.
208. 23:22.
209. 7:353–354.
210. 19:190.
211. 3:34, 47–48; 8:141–142.
212. 37:490–495; 21:302–303; 21:494; 21:303–304; 39:97; 37:463; 4:480; 13:9; 39:206; 20:82; 3:26.
213. 18:400.
214. 21:280.
215. 39:97.

216. 23:20.
217. 23:21.
218. 21:306.
219. 13:470.
220. 37:436–437.
221. 4:472.
222. 23:22.
223. 21:267.
224. 23:93–94.
225. 20:129; 21:270.
226. 20:324.
227. 13:9.
228. *Capital*, I:16, 95, 184, 194, 231, 250, 624, 778; *Capital*, III:784, 822; 37:437.
229. 24:42.
230. 13:9.
231. 25:784.
232. 23:15.
233. 39:205.
234. 3:72.
235. 23:15.
236. 23:16.
237. 23:391.
238. 13:9.
239. 13:8.
240. Ibid.
241. Ibid.
242. 37:436; 35:388.
243. 37:411.
244. 37:465.
245. 39:96.
246. 37:435; 37:462; 37:488; 39:96; 39:205.
247. 37:463.
248. 7:12f; 8:111f; 37:493.
249. 13:640.
250. *Grundrisse*:439; 3:36; 8:139; 13:8; 17:336.
251. 39:206.
252. 39:96, 98.
253. 13:9.
254. 13:470.
255. 4:480.
256. 23:93.
257. 22:300; 21:304–305.
258. 23:292n.

Appendix. Marx's Theory of Revolution

1. 4:372.
2. 8:5.
3. 33:64.
4. 34:382; 34:515; 22:548.
5. 31:243.
6. 19:197.
7. 4:465.
8. 4:470.
9. 29:358; 29:360; 30:301; 30:342; 32:207;
   16:415; 34:320; 34:378; 37:320–321;
   39:248; 25:146.
10. 23:765.
11. 38:563.
12. 36:230.
13. 38:563.
14. 36:251.
15. 4:476.
16. 4:473.
17. 4:470.
18. 4:417–418.
19. 3:60.
20. 3:69.
21. 2:351.
22. 4:472, 479.

23. 8:95.
24. 8:77.
25. 4:416–417.
26. 4:493.
27. 12:4.
28. 7:21.
29. 29:47.
30. 37:43–44, 132; 25:49.
31. 8:201–202.
32. 8:199.
33. 22:485.
34. 18:633.
35. 8:161.
36. 7:44.
37. 18:160.
38. 34:482.
39. 18:160.
40. 17:643.
41. 34:498–499.
42. 23:40.
43. 37:4–6.
44. 22:509–527.
45. 8.6.
46. Ibid.

Bibliography

In the first part of the bibliography (A) are listed works *not* by Marx and Engels cited in this book. In the second part (B) are listed works by Marx and Engels in English that I have used to translate the references to their German *Werke*. Throughout this book the numbered references are to the *Marx-Engels Werke*, 39 volumes, Berlin, Dietz Verlag, 1964–1968.

A. General Works Cited in the Text

Afanasyev, V. *Marxist Philosophy: A Popular Outline*. Moscow: Foreign Languages Publishing House, n.d.

Allen, James S. *Reconstruction: The Battle for Democracy 1865–1876*. New York: International Publishers, 1963.

Althusser, Louis. "Sobre el concepto de ideología." In *Polémica sobre marxismo y humanismo*, translated by Marta Harnecker, pp. 176–186. Mexico City: Siglo XXI, 1968.

Aristotle. *The Politics*. Baltimore: Penguin Books, 1962.

Bakunin, Mikhail. *Etatisme et anarchie*. Translated by Marcel Body. Leiden: E. J. Brill, 1967.

Balzac, Honoré de. *Les Paysans*. Paris: Editions Gallimard, 1975.

Beard, Charles and Mary Beard. *The Rise of American Civilization*. New York: Macmillan, 1936.

Bernier, François. *Voyages de François Bernier*. Amsterdam: n.p., 1700.

Bernstein, Eduard, *My Years of Exile*. London: Leonard Parsons, 1921.

Caudwell, Christopher. *Illusion and Reality: A Study of the Sources of Poetry*. London: Lawrence and Wisehart, 1950.

Chesnokov, D. I. *Historical Materialism*. Moscow: Progress Publishers, 1969.

Chilcote, Ronald and Joel Edelstein (eds.). *Latin America: The Struggle with Dependency and Beyond*. New York: John Wiley and Sons, 1974.

Childe, V. Gordon. *Man Makes Himself*. New York: New American Library of World Literature, 1951.

Cole, George. *What Marx Really Meant*. New York: Alfred A. Knopf, 1934.

Croce, Benedetto. *Essays on Marx and Russia*. Translated by Angelo de Genaro. New York: Frederick Ungar, 1966.

Daniel, Glyn E. *The Idea of Prehistory*. Cleveland: World Publishing Company, 1963.

Elkins, Stanley. *Slavery: A Problem in American Institutional and Intellectual Life*. Chicago: University of Chicago Press, 1959.

Fourier, Charles. *Le nouveau monde industriel et sociétaire*. Paris: Librairie Sociétaire, 1848.

Frank, Andre Gundar. *Latin America: Underdevelopment or Revolution*. New York: Monthly Review Press, 1969.

Freyre, Gilberto. *The Masters and the Slaves: A Study in the Development of Brazilian Civilization*. Translated by Samuel Putnam. New York: Alfred A. Knopf, 1946.

Fromm, Erich. *The Anatomy of Human Destructiveness*. New York: Holt, Rinehart and Winston, 1973.

Gautier, E. F. *Le passé de l'Afrique du nord*. Paris: Payot, 1952.

Genovese, Eugene. *The Political Economy of Slavery*. New York: Random House, 1966.

Godelier, Maurice. *Sur les sociétés précapitalistes*. Paris: Editions Sociales, 1970.

González-Casanova, Pablo. *La democracia en México*. 4th ed. Mexico City: Ediciones Era, 1971.

Gough, Kathleen. "Sexual Politics." *Monthly Review*, vol. 22, no. 9 (February 1971): 47–56.

Hacker, Louis Morton. *The Triumph of American Capitalism*. New York: Columbia University Press, 1946.

Harris, Marvin. *Patterns of Race in the Americas*. New York: Walker, 1964.

Hauser, Arnold. *The Social History of Art*. 4 vols. Translated by Stanley Godman. New York: Alfred A. Knopf, 1951.

Hegel, Georg Wilhelm Friedrich. *Vorlesungen über die Philosophie der Geschichte*. Stuttgart: Philipp Reclam Jun., 1961.

Hobbes, Thomas. *Leviathan: or the Matter, Form, and Power of a Commonwealth Ecclesiastical and Civil*. In *The English Philosophers from Bacon to Mill*, edited by Edwin A. Burtt. New York: Random House, 1939.

Hobsbawm, Eric. *The Age of Revolution: 1789–1848*. London: Weidenfeld and Nicolson, 1962.

Hodges, Donald. *Marxismo y revolución en el siglo XX*. Mexico City: El Caballito, 1978.

Howitt, Alfred William. *The Native Tribes of South-East Australia*. London: Macmillan, 1904.

Huberman, Leo. *We, The People: The Drama of America*. New York: Monthly Review Press, 1960.

Jones, Richard. *An Essay in the Distribution of Wealth and on the Sources of Taxation*. New York: Kelly and Millman, 1956.

———. *Literary Remains: Lectures and Tracts on Political Economy*. New York: A. M. Kelly, 1964.

Kosambi, Damodar. *Ancient India*. New York: Pantheon Books, 1965.

Kuusinen, Otto. *Fundamentals of Marxism-Leninism*. Moscow: Foreign Languages Publishing House, 1961.

Laclau, Ernesto. "Feudalism and Capitalism in America." *New Left Review*, no. 67 (May–June 1971): 19–55.

Lafargue, Paul. "El método histórico." In *El materialismo histórico según los grandes marxistas*, translated by Foreign Language Publishing House of Moscow, pp. 47–90. Mexico City: Ediciones Roca, 1973.

———. "Reminiscences of Marx." In *Reminiscences of Marx and Engels*, edited by the Institute of Marxism-Leninism of the Central Committee of the Communist

Party of the Soviet Union, pp. 71–86. Moscow: Foreign Languages Publishing House, n.d.

Lenin, V. I. *The Historical Destiny of the Doctrine of Karl Marx*. In *Collected Works of V. I. Lenin*, vol. 18. Moscow: Foreign Languages Publishing House, 1963.

———. *Imperialism, The Highest Stage of Capitalism*. In *Collected Works of V. I. Lenin*, vol. 22. Moscow: Foreign Languages Publishing House, 1964.

———. *The State*. In *Collected Works of V. I. Lenin*, vol. 29. Moscow: Foreign Languages Publishing House, 1965.

———. "Summing-up Speech on the Report of the C. C. of the R. C. P. (B.), March 9." In *Collected Works of V. I. Lenin*, vol. 32. Moscow: Foreign Languages Publishing House, 1965.

———. *What the "Friends of the People" Are and How They Fight the Social Democrats*. In *Collected Works of V. I. Lenin*, vol. 1. Moscow: Foreign Languages Publishing House, 1963.

Lichtheim, George. *Marxism: An Historical and Critical Study*. New York: Praeger, 1961.

———. *From Marx to Hegel*. New York: Herder and Herder, 1971.

Locke, John. *An Essay Concerning the True Original, Extent and End of Civil Government*. In *The English Philosophers from Bacon to Mill*, edited by Edwin A. Burtt. New York: Random House, 1939.

Löwy, A. G. *Die Weltgeschichte ist das Weltgericht*. Vienna: Europa Verlag, 1969.

Lukács, Georg. *The Historical Novel*. Translated by Hannah and Stanley Mitchell. Boston: Beacon Press, 1963.

———. *History and Class Consciousness*. Translated by Rodney Livingstone. Cambridge: MIT Press, 1971.

Machiavelli, Niccolo. *The Prince*. New York: Random House, 1939.

Madison, James, Alexander Hamilton, and John Jay. *The Federalist*. New York: Heritage Press, 1945.

Mandel, Ernest. *Marxist Economic Theory*. New York: Monthly Review Press, 1968.

———. "Die Marxsche Theorie der ursprünglichen Akkumulation und die Industrialisierung der Dritten Welt." In *Folgen einer Theorie: Essays über "Das Kapital" von Karl Marx*, pp. 71–93. Frankfurt: Suhrkamp, 1967.

Mao Tse-Tung. *The Chinese Revolution and the Chinese Communist Party*. In *Selected Works of Mao Tse-Tung*, vol. 3. London: Lawrence and Wisehart, 1954.

Maurer, Georg L. *Geschichte der Frohnhöfe, der Bauernhöfe und der Hofverfassung in Deutschland*. 4 vols. Erlangen: n.p., 1862–1863.

Mikhailovsky, Nikolai K. "Karl Marks pered sudom g. Zhukovsky." *Otechestvennye Zapiski*, no. 10 (October 1877): 326–327.

Mill, James. *The History of British India*. 3rd ed. London: Baldwin, Cradock, and Joy, 1826.

Mill, John Stuart. *Principles of Political Economy*. London: J. W. Parker, 1848.

Montesquieu, Charles Louis de Secondat. *De l'esprit des lois*. Paris: Editions Garnier Frères, 1962.

Moore, Barrington, Jr. *Social Origins of Dictatorship and Democracy: Lord and Peasant in the Making of the Modern World*. Boston: Beacon Press, 1966.

Moreland, William Harrison. *India at the Death of Akbar*. Delhi: Atma Ram, 1962.

Morgan, Lewis Henry. *Ancient Society*. Edited by Eleanor Burke Leacock. New York: World Publishing Company, 1963.

Owen, Robert. *Report to the Committee for the Relief of the Manufacturing Poor*. In

The Life and Ideas of Robert Owen, edited by A. L. Morton, pp. 170–172. Berlin: Seven Seas Publishers, 1969.

Paillet, Marc. *Marx contra Marx: La société technobureaucratique*. Paris: Denoël, 1971.

Plato. *The Republic*. In *The Dialogues of Plato*, translated by B. Jowett. New York: Random House, 1937.

Plekhanov, George. *Socialism and the Political Struggle*. In *Selected Philosophical Works of G. Plekhanov*, vol. 1. Moscow: Foreign Languages Publishing House, n.d.

Popper, Karl. *The Open Society and Its Enemies*. 2 vols. 4th ed. London: Routledge and Kegan Paul, 1962.

Prinz, Arthur. "Background and Ulterior Motive of Marx's 'Preface' of 1859." *Journal of the History of Ideas*, vol. 30, no. 3 (July–September 1969): 437–450.

Reich, Wilhelm. *The Invasion of Compulsory Sex-Morality*. New York: Farrar, Straus, and Giroux, 1971.

Ricardo, David. *Principles of Political Economy and Taxation*. London: J. M. Dent, 1936.

Rousseau, Jean Jacques. *The Social Contract*. Translated by Charles Frankel. New York: Hafner Publishing Company, 1948.

Russell, Bertrand. *Freedom versus Organization: 1814–1914*. New York: W. W. Norton, 1934.

Shaw, William. *Marx's Theory of History*. Stanford: Stanford University Press, 1978.

Smith, Adam. *Wealth of Nations*. New York: Random House, 1937.

Stalin, J. V. *History of the Communist Party of the Soviet Union (Bolsheviks)*. Toronto: Francis White, 1939.

Strouve, Vassili. "El concepto modo de producción asiático: legitimidad y límites." In *El modo de producción asiático*, edited by Jean Chesneaux and translated by Roger Bartra, pp. 145–157. Mexico City: Editorial Grijalbo, 1969.

Sweezy, Paul. *Modern Capitalism and Other Essays*. New York: Monthly Review Press, 1972.

———. *The Present as History*. 2nd ed. New York: Monthly Review Press, 1953.

Tannenbaum, Frank. *Slave and Citizen: The Negro in the Americas*. New York: Alfred A. Knopf, 1947.

Thapar, Romila. "Interpretations of Ancient Indian History." *History and Theory*, vol. 7, no. 3 (1968): 318–335.

Thomson, George. *Marxism and Poetry*. New York: International Publishers, 1946.

Thucydides. *The Peloponnesian War*. Translated by Rex Warner. Baltimore: Penguin Books, 1954.

Tylor, Edward Burnett. *Primitive Culture: Researches into the Development of Mythology, Philosophy, Religion, Language, Art and Custom*. London: n.p., 1871.

Wallerstein, Immanuel. *The Modern World-System: Capitalist Agriculture and the Origins of the European World-Economy in the Sixteenth Century*. New York: Academic Press, 1974.

Washburn, Sherwood L. "Tools and Human Evolution." *Scientific American*, vol. 203, no. 3 (September 1960): 63–75.

Weber, Max. *General Economic History*. Translated by Frank H. Knight. New York: Collier Books, 1961.

———. *From Max Weber: Essays in Sociology*. Translated and edited by Hans Gerth and C. Wright Mills. New York: Oxford University Press, 1974.

———. *The Protestant Ethic and the Spirit of Capitalism*. Translated by Talcott Parsons. London: George Allen and Unwin, 1930.

Williams, Eric. *Capitalism and Slavery*. Chapel Hill: University of North Carolina Press, 1945.
Williams, William Appleman. *The Contours of American History*. Chicago: Quadrangle Books, 1966.
Woddis, Jack. *New Theories of Revolution*. New York: International Publishers, 1972.
Zubritsky, Yuri. *A Short History of Precapitalist Society*. Moscow: Progress Publishers,

B. Works by Karl Marx and Friedrich Engels

1. Joint Works and Collections

Karl Marx and Friedrich Engels. *Basic Writings on Politics and Philosophy*. Edited by Lewis S. Feuer. Garden City, N.Y.: Doubleday Anchor, 1950.
———. *On Britain*. Moscow: Foreign Languages Publishing House, 1962.
———. *The Civil War in the United States*. 3rd ed. New York: International Publishers, 1961.
———. *Collected Works*. 9 vols. New York: International Publishers, 1975–1978.
———. *On Colonialism*. Moscow: Foreign Languages Publishing House, n.d.
———. *The First Indian War of Independence: 1857–1859*. Moscow: Foreign Languages Publishing House, n.d.
———. *The German Ideology*. Moscow: Foreign Languages Publishing House, 1964.
———. *The Holy Family*. Moscow: Foreign Languages Publishing House, 1956.
———. *Ireland and the Irish Question*. Moscow: Progress Publishers, 1971.
———. *Letters to Americans: 1848–1895*. New York: International Publishers, 1953.
———. *Literature and Art: Selections from Their Writings*. New York: International Publishers, 1947.
———. *On the Population Bomb*. Edited by Ronald Meek. Berkeley: Ramparts Press, 1971.
———. *On Religion*. Moscow: Foreign Languages Publishing House, 1957.
———. *Revolution in Spain: 1854–1873*. Moscow: Foreign Languages Publishing House, n.d.
———. *The Revolution of 1848–1849: Articles from the "Neue Rheinische Zeitung."* New York: International Publishers, 1972.
———. *Selected Correspondence*. Moscow: Foreign Languages Publishing House, n.d.
———. *Selected Works in Two Volumes*. Moscow: Foreign Languages Publishing House, 1962.
———. *Writings on the Paris Commune*. Edited by Hal Draper. New York: Monthly Review Press, 1971.

2. Individual Works and Collections

Karl Marx. *Capital*. 3 vols. Translated from the third German edition by Samuel Moore and edited by Friedrich Engels. Moscow: Foreign Languages Publishing House, 1961–1962.
———. *The Cologne Communist Trial*. New York: International Publishers, 1971.
———. *A Contribution to the Critique of Political Economy*. Translated by N. I. Stone. Chicago: Charles H. Kerr, 1904.
———. *The Economic and Philosophic Manuscripts of 1844*. Translated by Martin Milligan and edited by Dirk Struik. New York: International Publishers, 1964.

————. *The Grundrisse*. Edited and translated by David McClellan. New York: Harper and Row, 1971.

————. *Letters to Dr. Kugelmann*. New York: International Publishers, 1934.

————. *Notes on Indian History: 664–1858*. Moscow: Foreign Languages Publishing House, n.d.

————. *The Poverty of Philosophy*. New York: International Publishers, 1963.

————. *Precapitalist Economic Formations*. Translated by Jack Cohen and edited by Eric Hobsbawm. New York: International Publishers, 1964.

————. *Theories of Surplus-Value*. 2 parts. Translated by Emile Burns and edited by S. Ryazanskaya. Moscow: Progress Publishers, 1969.

————. *Writings of the Young Marx on Philosophy and Society*. Edited and translated by Lloyd Easton and Kurt Guddat. Garden City: N.Y.: Doubleday Anchor, 1967.

Friedrich Engels. *Anti-Dühring: Herr Eugen Dühring's Revolution in Science*. 3rd ed. Moscow: Foreign Languages Publishing House, 1962.

————. *The Condition of the English Working Class in 1844*. Translated by Florence Wischnewetsky. London: Allen and Unwin, 1952.

————. *Correspondence: Paul and Laura Lafargue*. 3 vols. Edited by Emile Bottigelli. Moscow: Foreign Languages Publishing House, 1959.

————. *Dialectics of Nature*. Translated by Clemens Dutt. Moscow: Foreign Languages Publishing House, 1954.

————. *Germany: Revolution and Counterrevolution*. Edited by Eleanor Marx. New York: International Publishers, 1969.

————. *The Origin of the Family, Private Property, and the State*. Introduction and notes by Eleanor B. Leacock. New York: International Publishers, 1972.

————. *The Peasant War in Germany*. Moscow: Foreign Languages Publishing House, 1956.

————. *The Role of Force in History: A Study of Bismarck's Policy of Blood and Iron*. Translated by Jack Cohen and edited by Ernst Wangermann. New York: International Publishers, 1968.

————. *Selected Writings*. Edited by W. O. Henderson. Baltimore: Penguin Books, 1967.